IS GASCOIGNE GOING TO HAVE A CRACK?

IS GASCOIGNE GOING TO HAVE A CRACK?

SPURS IN THE 90s

MAGIC, MAYHEM AND MEDIOCRITY

GARETH DACE

FOREWORD BY
JULIE WELCH

pitch

First published by Pitch Publishing, 2024

Pitch Publishing
9 Donnington Park,
85 Birdham Road,
Chichester,
West Sussex,
PO20 7AJ
www.pitchpublishing.co.uk
info@pitchpublishing.co.uk

A CIP catalogue record is available for this book from the British Library.

ISBN 978 1 80150 702 8

Typesetting and origination by Pitch Publishing

Printed and bound in India by Replika Press Pvt. Ltd.

CONTENTS

Foreword by Julie Welch 7

Introduction 9

Preface: Spurs In The 80s 14

1989/90 – Local And National Pride 23

1990/91 – When The Year Ends In One 40

1991/92 – Managing The Eleven 65

1992/93 – Hope Springs Eternal. 84

1993/94 – Ossie's Nightmare. 105

1994/95 – Walking In A Klinsmann Wonderland . . . 126

1995/96 – Is It Going A Bit Pony?. 158

1996/97 – Frustration! 184

1997/98 – Gross Misjudgement 210

1998/99 – Spurs Are On Their Way To Wimbledon . . 235

1999/2000 – A Thursday In Chisinau 265

Postscript (October 2023) 287

Acknowledgements. 290

Bibliography 292

Appendices 294

FOREWORD

by Julie Welch, author of *The Biography of Tottenham Hotspur*

FOR SPURS fans of a certain age like me, the 1990s has always been a decade to be swept under the rug – or at the very least remembered with a shudder. I'm someone who started supporting the club in the days of Blanchflower, Mackay, Jones and White, when Tottenham Hotspur was king – the first club to do the double, and the first English club to win a European trophy. I went through my teens thrilling to the goalscoring feats of our G-Men, Greaves and Gilzean. I was lucky enough to start my football reporting career in the heyday of Perryman, when he led Spurs out of the slump of the mid-1970s back to 1980s glory, with a little help from Hoddle, Villa and Ardiles, not to mention Archibald and Crooks. The 1990s were always going to have to go some to match everything that had come before.

It wasn't as though the decade started badly, but the joy of winning the FA Cup in 1991 was tainted by Spurs being in danger of going bust, and the sale of one of our greatest ever players, Gazza, to Lazio, to stave off the creditors. The decade ended not just with Arsenal and Chelsea being better than us, but West Ham too. Oh, sure, we finished up with a trophy but I could barely bring myself to celebrate because it was won under the management of George Graham. In short, how could Spurs in the 1990s hope to have a place in my heart? I memory-holed almost all of it as nothing but a succession of tedious and sometimes unintentionally comic seasons of mid-table mediocrity, underperforming players and relegation scares.

How wrong I was. This fantastically interesting and forensically researched book does a marvellous job of recreating the drama, suspense, heartache, excitement and sheer fun of being a Spurs fan back then, with a supporting chorus of informed voices that reflect on not just what went wrong but what went right. This was a decade when we witnessed events, bad and good, that have gone down in Tottenham folklore. There was the Venables and Sugar soap opera, two powerful men going head-to-head in court, fans burning their season tickets outside White Hart Lane in protest at the sacking of 'Bambi'. There was the nation's stunned disbelief and rival clubs' envy when Sugar signed Klinsmann, the greatest striker in Europe and the most reviled footballer in England. He promptly charmed the pants off everybody with that dive after scoring on his debut at Hillsborough. There was the 'Famous Five', Ossie's doomed attempt to recreate Brazil 1970, and the pathos of his sacking after a very bad night at Meadow Lane. But that season we also had the privilege of seeing Sheringham and Klinsmann form the best strike partnership in the league, and even after that had ended far too soon, we carried on seeing Teddy and Anderton at their peak. Later, when – let's face it – Spurs really were rubbish, we'd go and watch them just to see Ginola. And we saw Klinsmann return in January 1998 to save us from the drop with his four goals in that 6-2 thriller against Wimbledon at Selhurst Park.

As the definitive guide to an era when Spurs soared, nearly crashed and burned, but emerged triumphant – or at least intact – this immensely enjoyable and readable book is a rich history of a decade you'd forgotten was so much fun and an essential addition to your Tottenham Hotspur bookshelves.

INTRODUCTION

IS GASCOIGNE GOING TO HAVE A CRACK? SPURS IN THE 90s – A DECADE OF MAGIC, MAYHEM AND MEDIOCRITY

IT WAS the best of times' it was the worst of times. Charles Dickens may have written *A Tale of Two Cities* before Tottenham Hotspur Football Club (or 'Spurs' to use the more affectionate and less formal name) were conceived by a group of local schoolboys in the early 1880s but if ever there was a sentence to describe the club in the 1990s, this neatly summarises a decade of joy and heartache.

If you are reading this, there is a good chance that you lived through some of, if not all, the 90s as a Spurs supporter. This book will remind you of some of the characters, matches and highs and lows that defined the decade.

For the rest of you, perhaps you have found Spurs more recently and you are intrigued about the frequent references to 'Spurs in the 90s' on message boards, social media and podcasts. I suppose you may even be a supporter of another club and just have a fascination for football and/or the 90s. Either way I hope that reading this book will bring to life some of those experiences we went through that very much set the context for Spurs in the 21st century.

The decade is often referenced as the benchmark for a mediocre and traumatic era in which to have followed Spurs but, while these adjectives are valid, the 90s also produced two trophy successes and saw some of the finest players in the club's history don the lilywhite shirt. For Spurs, the 90s provided a bigger mix of magic, mayhem and mediocrity than any other period of the club's history.

When modern-day fans complain because 'we have only drawn away to Southampton and now sit five points off a Champions League place', those of us who were around in the 90s will wryly smile and reflect that this is still infinitely better than losing 6-1 away at second-tier Bolton, being deducted 12 points before a ball of the 94/95 season had even been kicked or going to bed in 1991 not knowing whether our club would even exist in the morning.

Yet there were also the moments of unbridled joy and optimism. While this book will commentate on the undoubted fall in prominence that the club suffered throughout the decade, it is not intended to simply amplify a negative narrative but also to act as a reminder of the outstanding moments and optimism on the horizon even if they invariably culminated in a false dawn.

In the wider football context, the 90s was a remarkable decade that saw the way that the game was played, consumed and thought about seismically change in a more dramatic fashion than any other decade since the professional game was established in the Victorian era. By the mid-80s English football was on its deathbed – following the tragic Bradford City fire that killed 56 spectators in May 1985 *The Sunday Times* described football as 'a slum sport played in slum stadiums increasingly watched by slum people, who deter decent folk from turning up'. Worse was to follow with the Heysel Stadium disaster in 1985 and then the Hillsborough tragedy in 1989.

The genesis of its revival can be timestamped to the 1990 World Cup in which England heroically reached the semi-finals before being knocked out on penalties by West Germany. The star of the England team was Spurs' midfielder Paul Gascoigne (known affectionately as Gazza) who became one of the most famous personalities in the country; his fame and initial adulation transcended Spurs and football. Gascoigne's tears following defeat in Turin introduced a new audience to football and in doing so opened commercial opportunities.

This fast-tracked decisive talks between the game's governing bodies and leading clubs to establish the Premier League in 1992 and while nothing on the pitch appeared too different initially, by the end of the decade top-level football was evolving into a far more slick and polished product that created a virtuous cycle of followers, commercial opportunities and ultimately revenue that allowed the English game to open its doors to a host of foreign players and coaches who would revolutionise the way football was played.

The newfound riches were not exclusive to England as the creation and expansion of the UEFA Champions League provided a new platform for clubs to build their brands, not just on the continent but across the world. By the year 2000, football, business and popular culture were all intertwined in a manner unimaginable as the 90s began. How each individual club responded to the rapidly-changing landscape would have a more profound impact than in any decade previously. In this book you will see how Spurs adapted to the macro climate around them and all too often failed to grasp the opportunities that they themselves had created.

The decade began with Spurs in seventh place in the First Division and drawing 0-0 at Coventry City on New Year's Day 1990. On 29 December 1999 – the final game of the decade – Spurs drew 1-1 away at Aston Villa to leave them in sixth. Two unremarkable draws may give you the impression that very little had changed in ten years. But this could not be further from the truth, for the 90s is full of baffling inconsistencies and quirks. In those 3,652 days, Spurs changed ownership, nearly went out of business, won a trophy at either end of the decade and suffered three relegation scares in between. They embarked on their longest run without conceding a goal but also suffered the worst run of successive defeats in the club's history.

There were more trivial and comical occurrences like missing three penalties within 80 minutes of football, scoring four goals in a Premier League-record four minutes and 44 seconds and being the team to prevent Manchester United from winning an unprecedented Quadruple in 1999. Spurs initially embraced the new foreign markets that saw a flock of overseas players come to play in England but despite discovering 'gold' when Jurgen Klinsmann's arrival in 1994 stunned the football world, they then had their fingers burned and allowed Arsenal and Chelsea, Spurs' two biggest local rivals, to take their mantle and benefit from the superior technical and tactical ability that existed on the continent.

As you will discover, no two seasons were the same and it became virtually impossible to predict what the next 12 months would look like; each campaign produced its own unique narrative, though there are several recurring themes throughout. Conveniently for narrative purposes the decade can be defined by the two cup successes at either end (90/91 and 98/99) and right in the middle came the incredible 94/95 season, which may not have provided the coveted trophy but produced so much excitement. These three seasons tend to be the most memorable ones but as you will see the seasons in between also play their part in the development and trajectory of the club and deserve to be brought under the microscope.

I will share with you my own personal recollections so that you can see how the decade developed through my eyes. I was only eight when the 90s began and had been following Spurs for little more than a year, albeit obsessively enough that I had the equivalent of several decades of knowledge on my shoulders.

I have used poetic licence as to when one season ends and the next begins. As you will read, there was often as much drama during the off-season, particularly at the start of the decade, as there was during the regular season. For example, I have included the detail of Alan Sugar's takeover at the beginning of the 91/92 chapter rather than add it to the end of the FA Cup-winning success of 90/91. There are occasions where you will read a description of a particular match in some detail and other times where I will present a narrative encompassing several months to get you from A to B as naturally and as fluently as possible.

For each season I have provided a 'Spurs XI' for the campaign. The science I have applied to generate this is to have looked through the squad list for each season and identified which players, in each position, made the most league starts. Despite having seven different head coaches (or coaching teams) the formation was almost exclusively 4-4-2 or a close version of that, so I therefore present most in this shape. It may be that the XI I present never actually lined up together.

Some 30 years on I can look back with fondness for the 90s as, over the passing of time, the emotions that were once very raw have subsided. English football itself has evolved but the 90s were a significant catalyst. How the game was governed, how it was played, who played it and how it was consumed changed more during this decade than any other in the game's history dating back to the Victorian era.

Some changes are no doubt for the better – on the pitch the enhanced technical and physical capabilities of the players adopting more progressive tactics – but equally there were aspects of the game that are sorely missed, particularly the lovable naivety and irreverence that have been lost owing to the professionalism and the slick corporate machine that has taken over in the 21st century.

Welcome back to the 1990s!

PREFACE

SPURS IN THE 80s

FOLLOWING THE turbulent period of the mid-70s that culminated in Spurs being relegated to the Second Division for one season, the 80s are largely remembered as a golden decade for the club. Manager Keith Burkinshaw put together an exciting and winning team built around the creative genius of Glenn Hoddle and Ossie Ardiles. Back-to-back FA Cup success in 81 and 82 were followed up with European honours when Spurs won the UEFA Cup in 1984.

That 1984 UEFA Cup success was Keith Burkinshaw's final game in charge, having announced in advance that he would leave the club at the end of the season. His decision was made due to significant differences with the club's new ownership. After the club had been owned by the Wale and Richardson families for decades, the urbane Irving Scholar, a lifelong Spurs obsessive who had made millions in real estate, led a consortium that bought a majority stake in the club in partnership with Paul Bobroff.

Scholar was an innovator and launched Tottenham Hotspur on the London Stock Exchange in 1983, making it the first football club to become a public limited company – meaning that supporters and/or serious investors could buy shares in the club thus opening new and innovative methods of revenue.

Tottenham Hotspur plc became the parent company with Tottenham Hotspur Football & Athletic Club becoming its main subsidiary. Each had its own board of directors and constitution – Scholar became responsible for the running of the football and athletic club but did not sit on the main plc. Bobroff was a member of both. As part of the plc's diversification strategy, designed to create multiple sources of revenue, a number of businesses were acquired under the plc umbrella, including, among others, a ticket agency, a women's clothing business and the Danish kit manufacturer Hummel, who made Spurs' kits from 1985.

On the field Spurs continued to maintain their position as a leading power in English football. Though no further silverware would follow the 1984 UEFA Cup win, Spurs mounted title challenges in 1985 and 1987 – on both occasions falling short to the dominant Merseyside pair of Liverpool and Everton. That 1987 team, managed by David Pleat, adopted a highly unusual deviation from the standard 4-4-2, deploying just one striker in Clive Allen. This was far from a defensive tactic as Allen scored 49 goals throughout the season, ably assisted by Hoddle, Waddle and Ardiles in a fluent and dynamic midfield.

Going into March of 1987 Spurs had the chance to win all three major domestic honours. Alas, the genesis of the dreaded concept 'Spursy' could be dated back to the fact they ended the season empty-handed, most spectacularly losing the FA Cup Final in heartbreaking style 3-2 to underdogs Coventry.

It was the end of the cycle for a great Spurs team that was quickly broken up. As expected, Hoddle left to play for Monaco in France, leaving a huge creative void to fill. Unexpectedly Richard Gough, a rock in the spurs defence, returned to Scotland for family reasons. Only a few weeks into the following season David Pleat departed the club too for non-footballing reasons. Scholar pushed the boat out to bring Terry Venables back to the club he had supported as a boy and played for in the 1967 FA Cup Final.

Venables by his own admission had never lived up to his potential at White Hart Lane as a player but as a coach, initially at Crystal Palace and then Queens Park Rangers, he rose to prominence as a master tactician and charismatic man-manager capable of getting the best out of his players. Having impressed in England, he drew the attention of Barcelona who gave him the opportunity to manage one of the biggest clubs in world football. He achieved instant success, leading Barcelona to their first league title in 11 years in his first season. The following year they reached the European Cup Final, though were beaten on penalties by Steaua Bucharest.

Despite Barcelona only missing out on another league title in 1987 by a solitary point to Real Madrid, Venables's days were numbered after a poor start to the next season and he was sacked in September a few weeks before the vacancy at Spurs materialised. He had intended to spend a year out of football to travel with his family but was wooed by Scholar, who had flown over to Florida to meet with him. By the end of November and with Spurs treading water in mid-table, Terry Venables became Spurs' new manager.

The 87/88 season was a difficult one. The team was still in transition and during the season three other prominent members of the previous season's team – veteran goalkeeper Ray Clemence (retired), Ossie Ardiles and Steve Hodge – all moved on, though in Gary Mabbutt, Paul Allen, Chris Hughton and Gary Stevens the squad still possessed great professionals and a legacy of a successful prior era. Venables was able to bring in Terry Fenwick, who he had worked with previously at QPR, and striker Paul Walsh, who was surplus to requirements at Liverpool. The season descended into a flirtation with relegation with Spurs finishing 13th and humiliated by Port Vale in the FA Cup fourth round. Only the maverick skills of Chris Waddle offered much to be positive about as attendances nosedived. At the end of the season Clive Allen followed Hoddle to play in France.

Scholar continued to back Venables in the transfer market. Having purchased Fenwick, Walsh and Bobby Mimms during the season, Venables had a further £3.5m made available in the summer to sign Paul Stewart from Manchester City and Paul Gascoigne from Newcastle. Gascoigne was already considered to be one of the most precocious young talents in Britain and Scholar and Venables worked wonders to tempt the 21-year-old to Spurs ahead of Liverpool and Manchester United. Venables inherited a highly revered youth set-up led by Keith Blunt and Keith Walden.

Spurs were perennial winners of the regional Under-18 youth league and produced over 40 young players who would go on to make their first-team debuts during the 90s. Among the older members of this group, David Howells, Vinny Samways and Guy Butters had already established themselves in Venables's first-team squad by 1989 and the likes of Ian Walker, Sol Campbell, Stuart Nethercott and Stephen Carr would go on to serve a number of future Spurs managers in the decade that followed.

The 88/89 season started ignominiously with Spurs sitting bottom in November, though Gascoigne instantly endeared himself to the home crowd by scoring on his home debut against Arsenal in September. Once Gascoigne and Waddle clicked and Stewart started to score goals, performances and results improved. Spurs ended the season in sixth position – a significant improvement on the previous campaign's flirtation with relegation – though early cup exits were a huge disappointment. Venables continued to improve his first-team. Goalkeeper Bobby Mimms, signed only the season before as a successor to Ray Clemence, endured a terrible time and was replaced by 6ft 4in Norwegian Erik Thorstvedt for £500,000.

The 80s symbolised everything that Spurs was supposed to be about – managers who shared the supporters' desires to play attractive attacking football, signing and nurturing exciting players, innovation on and off the field and challenging for the highest honours and trophies at home and in Europe. Spurs sat at the top table of English football as a member of the unofficial 'Big Five' along with Arsenal, Liverpool, Everton and Manchester United, whose owners were able to exert collective influence on those governing English football – namely the Football League and the Football Association. Rumours persisted about the prospect of a breakaway league that would allow the Big Five to drive greater commercial gain. England's ban from European competitions, issued in 1985 following a string of incidents culminating in the Heysel Stadium disaster, was due to come to an end in 1990. This would allow English clubs to rub shoulders with the continental elite again and there was every expectation that Spurs would return to their place as a European heavyweight.

While the team required investment, so did the stadium. The West Stand had been completely knocked down and rebuilt as a futuristic-looking two-tiered stand in 1982. The finances required had stretched the club's existing board considerably and been the catalyst for Scholar to ultimately mount a takeover of the club.

The club had discussed for some time the need to redevelop the East Stand – perhaps the most iconic side of White Hart Lane, most famous for The Shelf – the terrace that ran along the width of the touchline at a good height providing a fantastic vantage point. The stand had been designed and built in the 1930s with now substandard facilities but following the tragedy at Bradford City in 1985 in which their wooden stand burned down during a match, killing 56 supporters, it was clear that for safety reasons work was needed urgently.

Scholar and the board had to find a solution that would ensure the stand was safe, provided suitable facilities and was also affordable, not affecting the ability to purchase players. The only solution was to build within the existing structure, replace the roof and replace the back of The Shelf with a row of 36 executive boxes. This was not well received by supporters who activated to form a group called Left on the Shelf with the acronym LOTS. They believed the club were now more interested in attracting corporate guests through hospitality packages than the 'ordinary' fan.

Through a number of PR exercises, which included Scholar and Venables engaging with LOTS for an organised meeting, tensions thawed – but it would not be the end of fan activism at Spurs. The future revenue of the boxes offset the cost of the building work but it would have a knock-on effect on Spurs' finances, a situation that was continuing to brew in the background.

HOW I SAW IT:

On reflection my life falls into two phases. The first begins at birth on 5 January 1981 at Chase Farm Hospital, Enfield

– about five miles from White Hart Lane. For just over seven and a half years I lived a comfortable life, blissfully ignorant of the joys and pain of following a football team. The second phase of my life began precisely on 10 September 1988 when I attended my first ever Spurs match at White Hart Lane. It was a north London derby against Arsenal and I was there because Dad, a grassroots-level referee, had been selected to be fourth official for the game (this is essentially a spare match official should the referee or linesman become injured and unable to continue). He was a member of North Middlesex Referees Society, a local body that was asked to provide a fourth official for most Spurs and Arsenal home games.

It was by no means inevitable that Dad would become a Spurs fan. He was brought up in Highbury and his father and uncle regularly took him to watch Arsenal during the 50s. When he left school and started working at Barclays Bank circa 1960, he hadn't really developed a strong allegiance to either side of north London and it was still common for residents to go and watch whichever team was at home.

Spurs in the 60s were the best team around, winning the first ever league and cup double of the 20th century with a swashbuckling team that is still eulogised today. Dad was temporarily hooked, and with a disposable income, some helpful contacts at the FA who could supply cup final tickets, and a sense of adventure that drew him to travelling to watch Spurs play in Europe (he was in Rotterdam to see the 1963 European Cup Winners' Cup Final success against Atletico Madrid), Spurs became his team for the most successful and decorated period in the club's history.

Dad was a regular visitor to White Hart Lane throughout the 60s but took up refereeing shortly after he married my mum in 1970. From then on weekends were dedicated to officiating in the Amateur Football Alliance and from there he was able to make some very useful contacts within refereeing that provided an opportunity to be involved on the periphery of the professional game via some reserve and youth-team football.

Mum's interest in football didn't extend beyond washing Dad's kit, but on her side, the Lewins, I had several football connections. One of my older cousins is Gary Lewin who became Arsenal's physiotherapist in 1986 and would later join the England set-up. My other cousin, Colin, joined Gary at Arsenal in 1995 and subsequently took over as head physio. I only really saw them at Christmas and occasional Lewin family parties, but I was always fascinated by the insights they were able to provide and both were very good to me in offering me treatment, often at Highbury or at the London Colney training ground, for the plethora of injuries I had as a kid.

My younger sister, Samantha, had little interest in football. Most likely because I'd often drag her into the garden to act as a goalkeeper as I smashed Mitre size 5 footballs at her from close range. She has loyally told people ever since that she supports Spurs but when I told her I was going to write this book she advised that she could do the same in two words: 'They Lost.'

I recall being amused that Spurs had two players – Hoddle and Waddle – who had names that rhymed and was told by my (Arsenal-supporting) grandad that they also had a player called 'Twaddle' – which I believed and told people at school! One May Saturday afternoon in 1987 Dad explained to me that Spurs were playing in the FA Cup Final and that I might want to watch it. I occasionally kicked a ball around in the garden but had little interest in watching football on TV so played in the garden instead. Dad told me later that Spurs had lost and gave a chronology of the goals that had been scored. I don't recall feeling any emotion but the fact I still remember it might be a sign of being hardwired to expecting Spurs to lose more often than they win.

Despite being something of a retired Spurs fan – I don't suppose he had been to White Hart Lane to watch a match as a spectator in 20 years – Dad was keen for me to choose Spurs and one of my earliest football memories was him coming home from having refereed an under-15 game at the Spurs training ground with a white Hummel shirt he had found lying around in a changing room. It came down as far as my knees but I had an instant fascination for it.

As football became a more common pursuit on the school field, I became more intrigued throughout summer 1988. Dad refereed a Tottenham Hotspur staff match on the pitch at an empty White Hart Lane. I went along too and remember being quite overwhelmed by the size of the stadium and height of the stands, particularly the East Stand on the far side which was almost ghostly in semi-darkness. It proved to be the one and only time I was there in the presence of the famous Shelf in its full glory before executive boxes were added.

After the match Dad took me into the old club shop – then a small and chaotic building on the corner of the High Road and Park Lane; it wasn't quite Toys 'R' Us but was still enchanting to a seven-year-old, with shelves full of merchandise and large images of Chris Waddle and Gary Mabbutt. I was bought the home navy shorts and white socks to accompany my still very oversized youth-team shirt.

My other hook was the Panini sticker album released in summer 1988. I don't think I got anywhere near even quarter-filling it but I was drawn to the 20 First Division clubs' fact files and it was burned into my seven-year-old brain that Spurs had finished the previous season in 13th place, that Terry Venables was the manager and that Spurs' nickname was 'The Lilywhites'.

I didn't have to wait long to attend my first proper game at White Hart Lane. As I mentioned before, Dad had been appointed to be the fourth official for the north London derby against Arsenal and I was taken along with a friend's father to sit in the first row of the West Lower. By the time I next attended a live game – an end-of-season home win against Everton poignantly a week after the Hillsborough tragedy – Spurs consumed me. My Year 3 teacher described me at parents evening as 'mentally always on a distant football pitch somewhere'. My bedroom was adorned with posters of Gascoigne, Waddle and Walsh, and the away yellow kit I received for my birthday was virtually glued onto me.

I became the fount of Spurs knowledge from a young age and was well known in class and in school as the Spurs obsessive. I believed my level of obsession was normal – surely every other eight-year-old was glued to Teletext on a Saturday afternoon and could memorise Mitchell Thomas's previous clubs? In 1989 there were only sporadic live matches on TV – usually on a Sunday afternoon – but these normally provided the basis for playground chat on Monday morning.

Growing up in Cuffley, right at the bottom of Hertfordshire, which borders north London, meant that school was a very even split between Spurs and Arsenal. The conclusion to the season was a chastening one for me when Arsenal won the league with the final kick of the season at Anfield. Mum said that I looked as though I'd seen a ghost immediately after. I'd realised that the fortunes of Spurs and Arsenal were inexplicably linked and the concept of 'Good and Bad' was well and truly established in my mind. I think I accepted that Arsenal were a better team than Spurs at that point – objectively they won the league and had beaten Spurs twice during the season – so it was tough. I think this helped manifest an inferiority complex that has never been far from the surface in all walks of life for me since.

1989/90 – LOCAL AND NATIONAL PRIDE

THORSTVEDT
THOMAS SEDGLEY MABBUTT VAN DEN HAUWE
P.ALLEN GASCOIGNE HOWELLS SAMWAYS
LINEKER STEWART

HOW I SAW IT:

This was my first full season following Spurs, and football. I loved the pre-season period and was delighted to be shown the back page of the newspaper one morning to see a smiling Gary Lineker in full Spurs kit on the pitch at White Hart Lane having joined us from Barcelona. However, one of the tabloids horrified me a few weeks later when it led with the headline 'WADDLE SOLD TO FROGS' to announce Chris Waddle's sale to Marseille. At that point Waddle was my favourite player ahead of even Gascoigne and I was initially in denial, telling other kids at the summer holiday football camp I attended that it was not true.

Having had my appetite whetted the previous season I could dream of nothing else but going to watch a game at White Hart Lane. My first visit to see Lineker came in a midweek cup game against Southend. Dad and I sat at the front of the upper tier of the South Stand but we really struggled to beat the fourth division team 1-0.

Dad was fourth official quite regularly at Barnet, then in the Vauxhall Conference, and I regularly went with him to watch the games. Barnet became my second team but my focus was always on the Spurs score. I'd have to rely on the PA's half-time score updates, though it always felt as if Spurs were losing at half-time and this always seemed to generate an amused cheer from the Underhill crowd.

For the first time in my Spurs-supporting life, we beat Arsenal that October. It was a midweek fixture but I was on a family holiday in Florida at the time. There was no way of finding out the score until we got home nearly a week later. As soon as we landed at Luton Airport we phoned my grandad who told me that Spurs had won 2-1. Perhaps I needed to be 3,000 miles away from north London for every derby?

Not for the last time in my life Spurs ruined my birthday. Falling in the first week of January, my birthday invariably coincided with the FA Cup third round. We were drawn at home to Southampton and I was taken by Dad and sat towards the back of the East Stand. I spent £5.50 of my birthday money on a pair of replica home socks though never completed the kit. We were 2-0 down by half-time and never looked like getting back into it until Howells scored a good goal with ten minutes remaining. Dad insisted on leaving early to avoid the traffic and when we heard a huge roar as we walked along White Hart Lane, we both assumed the ferocity of it must have been for an equaliser. I can only liken the abject misery of learning, through BBC Radio's full classified check, that in fact it was Southampton's fans we had heard, to the modern-day disappointment at having a goal chalked off by VAR.

Better days lay ahead. At the start of February, we were at White Hart Lane to witness a Lineker hat-trick in a 4-0 win over Norwich, though my memories are equally vivid of finding that people were in our seats, this time in the West Lower. It seemed that the ticket office had duplicated the seats and so I spent most of the first half anxious that we would be thrown out despite having legitimate tickets.

When not at White Hart Lane, or Barnet, I consumed games at home via Teletext or increasingly by listening to Capital Gold Sport. Dad had once shown me how to access BBC Radio 2 on our old dial-up AM radio. By chance and having tuned through several foreign radio stations I stumbled across the very excited tones that I would discover belonged to Jonathan Pearce, now of *Match of the Day*, in his very early years as a commentator.

Finishing above Arsenal at the end of the season was a big deal. I heard the final game of the season pan out on Capital Gold, fully anticipating that they would score a late goal to win at Norwich and leapfrog us at the last. Spurs were 'The Pride of north London' and by default I was 'Pride of Class 3'.

SEASON COMMENTARY

Spurs ended the previous season with great momentum winning nine of the final 15 games, which culminated in a sixth-place finish having sat bottom before Christmas. While all on the pitch appeared rosy, there were clouds circling the club's financial situation and the relationship between key members of the plc and Football Club boards.

During the 1989 off-season, optimism among the fans spiked when Spurs completed the signing of Gary Lineker from Barcelona. The England striker, who had won the World Cup Golden Boot in 1986, had played for Venables in Barcelona but following the appointment of Johan Cruyff as manager in 1987 had been played out of position as a wide forward. He became surplus to requirements at the Nou Camp and was keen to move back to England. Venables, utilising his contacts at his former club, brokered a deal while also persuading Lineker to rejoin him in north London.

Gary Lineker may not have been new to English football, but his return after three years in Barcelona gave Spurs fans the chance to witness first-hand one of the game's most natural goalscorers of a generation. It was evidence that Spurs still sat at the top table of English football and could attract the world's best talent.

Lineker officially joined Spurs on 1 July for a fee of £1.5m that also included the permanent transfer of Nayim, also from Barcelona, who had impressed during a loan period in the second half of the 88/89 season. Even by 1989 standards £1.5m for Lineker alone would have been a bargain – he guaranteed goals and was already familiar with Gascoigne and Waddle whom he played alongside for England.

However, the deal was not met with the same level of joy in the boardroom as it was among supporters and Venables. In Scholar's 1993 book *Behind Closed Doors,* he revealed that having discussed the potential deal in a board meeting, the plc chairman Paul Bobroff had sanctioned the deal confirming that the money was available as long as money could be generated from subsequent player sales. However, according to Scholar, as soon as Venables left the room to conclude the deal, Bobroff advised that the money was not available in the club's accounts and the only way to meet the initial down payment of £600,000 would be for Scholar to personally underwrite it. Scholar describes the incident as the first time he became aware of the looming financial situation, which he claims was the fault of the plc board and not him, being solely responsible for the running of the football club.

Most supporters would still have been oblivious to the turmoil brewing in the boardroom. The prospect of a front three of Gascoigne, Waddle and Lineker was mouthwatering. Venables could call on an embarrassment of riches in attack with Stewart and Walsh also available as senior strikers. Stewart had endured a difficult start to his Spurs career, having missed a penalty on his home debut, but would go on to score a respectable 14 goals in his first season at White Hart Lane.

However, unbeknown to supporters and even Lineker, who himself had joined the club expecting to be supplied by Gascoigne and Waddle, the dream would be dashed when a deal to sell Waddle to Marseille was completed for a British transfer fee of £4.25m.

Scholar had been contacted by a French intermediary acting on behalf of Marseille owner Bernard Tapie. The call from Paris came just ten minutes before Lineker was unveiled as a Spurs player at White Hart Lane. Scholar claims that he never wanted to sell but that Venables could see the business sense in selling a 28-year-old if the club received an offer in excess of their valuation of £2m. They agreed to entertain talks, and were stunned when the French club were not put off by what they felt was a ridiculous price of £5m that would also include Paul Walsh.

Walsh was subsequently dropped from the negotiation, but a deal was agreed for £4.25m, with Waddle keen to make the move to the south of France. The move was confirmed before the end of July.

Daniel Wynne, who first attended games at White Hart Lane as a four-year-old in the 70s, was as disappointed by the sale of Waddle as any other player to have left the club before or since:

> Hoddle and then Clive Allen leaving meant that the great 1987 team had been broken up – from an attacking perspective Waddle was all that was left and he'd really stepped up to the mark in what was otherwise a very average team for a couple of seasons. He had all the attributes of an iconic Spurs player – creativity, flair – he was a mercurial talent and we had him at the peak of his career. He clearly formed a great bond with Gazza on and off the pitch so when we found out that Lineker was coming too – they all played together for England – there was a feeling of real excitement; the three of them would be unstoppable. But alas this was Tottenham Hotspur and during this period nothing good ever seemed to last very long. In this case it was literally a week. To say I was gutted was an understatement.
>
> These were of course the days before social media so conspiracy theories, especially during the off-season period, weren't spread anywhere near as quickly but there was always a feeling that the news of his sale was deliberately kept back until after we'd announced Lineker's arrival.

Believing that the large fee for Waddle had significantly alleviated the club's debt, Scholar immediately invested money back into the team. Steve Sedgley joined from Coventry for just over £1m. The 21-year-old had grown up in Enfield but began his professional career at Coventry where he made his debut as an 18-year-old in 1986. He established himself in the

Sky Blues' team during the season and was unfortunate only to be an unused sub in the 1987 FA Cup Final against Spurs.

Also moving to White Hart Lane was full-back Pat Van Den Hauwe from Everton. The Welsh international, who had enjoyed success and gained notoriety as a fiercely competitive defender in Everton's great teams of the mid-80s, had won two league titles and the European Cup Winners' Cup and brought with him experience and a toughness that Spurs had lacked. However, the deal to bring Van Den Hauwe to Spurs for under £1m only caused further tension in the boardroom with Bobroff and Scholar clearly reading the financial situation differently. Scholar had approved the deal without the knowledge of Bobroff, who was adamant that the money should have been allocated to offset the plc's overdraft.

The incomings, specifically that of Lineker, helped identify Spurs as a team on the up. On the eve of the season Spurs were listed at 8/1 to win the league championship – joint third favourites alongside Manchester United and behind only Arsenal and Liverpool. However, this optimism didn't encompass the wider fanbase as a crowd of just over 17,000 turned up for the opening game of the season at home to Luton Town on 19 August, though this was in part down to the closure of the lower tier of the East Stand as building work continued.

Lineker, wearing the number 10 shirt, started alongside Paul Stewart in attack and Sedgley came on as a second-half substitute. Goals by Stewart and a second-half winner by Paul Allen gave Spurs all three points on opening day for the first time in three years although the victory was not convincing. Spurs' flaws were exposed when Luton equalised within seconds of the second half starting.

Despite the opening-day win, Spurs and Lineker suffered an indifferent start. There were no wins, or goals for Lineker, for the next three games, which included a draw at newly promoted Manchester City and defeats at Everton and Aston Villa.

Next up was a home derby against Chelsea who themselves had just won promotion back to the top flight. Far from the behemoth that they would become in the 21st century, Chelsea had endured a mixed bag of fortunes during the 80s, spending half the decade as a second-tier team. Having been relegated in 1988 they came back up at the first opportunity with a then-record tally of 99 points and were even considered by some commentators as an outside bet for the title. The rivalry between the two clubs' sets of supporters was fuelled by anti-Semitic racism aimed at Spurs over nearly two decades. On the field the rivalry was largely one-sided with Spurs the more successful of the two clubs. Spurs had got the better of Chelsea, losing just one of their past 12 meetings dating back to the mid-70s. Only once in the last ten years had Chelsea finished above Spurs in the league.

Buoyed by their return to the top flight and decent start to the season, the Chelsea team travelling to White Hart Lane in September 1989 included two former Spurs heroes – Micky Hazard and Graham Roberts, who had both been part of the 1984 UEFA Cup-winning team. It proved to be a brutal afternoon for Spurs. Hazard, in particular, impressed in midfield and was involved in Chelsea's second goal. Spurs had briefly looked competitive when Walsh set up Gascoigne to reduce the deficit to 2-1 but two late Chelsea goals sealed an emphatic victory – their largest over Spurs since the mid-60s. Chelsea would go on to become Spurs' bogey team for the next decade. The defeat also dropped Spurs into 19th position – talk of a title challenge had dissipated within a month of the season starting.

The defeat proved to be the nadir of the season. The following week Lineker scored his first competitive goal for the club in a 2-2 draw at Norwich although it was frustrating that Spurs had led 2-0 at half-time and not held on for the win. The goal kickstarted Lineker's Spurs career as the following week, back at White Hart Lane, he completed a hat-trick to give Spurs a 3-2 win over QPR – their first victory since the opening day.

Moving into October Spurs were given an almighty scare by fourth-tier Southend in the League Cup second round. Having narrowly won 1-0 at White Hart Lane the return fixture at Roots Hall saw Spurs go two goals behind in 40 minutes. Quick-fire goals by Paul Allen and Nayim either side of half-time brought Spurs level but by that time Paul Stewart had been sent off. With a man advantage Southend retook the lead midway through the second half. It took the game into extra time but Spurs held their nerve to sneak through on away goals.

The near miss at Southend was incongruous with the fine league form Spurs enjoyed throughout October. Comfortable wins at Charlton and at home to Sheffield Wednesday provided six points and three more goals for Lineker but more significantly they sandwiched a midweek victory over Arsenal at White Hart Lane. It stopped a run of six straight losses in the north London derby with goals from Samways and Walsh, both in the first half.

Full of confidence, Spurs then achieved their most remarkable victory of the season, recording a 3-0 win away at Old Trafford in the League Cup third round. This was a Manchester United team languishing towards the bottom of Division One with Alex Ferguson still under huge pressure but such a comprehensive result coming a week after the north London derby win was a huge statement of intent. Spurs played with confidence and swagger at Old Trafford even without Gascoigne available. A first-half goal by Lineker gave Spurs the lead. Samways coolly slotted in a second immediately after half-time and then Nayim capped an incredible night with a crisp volley late on to seal an emphatic win.

David Howells was part of the Spurs team that won so convincingly at Old Trafford and recalls:

> This wasn't quite the great Manchester United team that would go on to dominate for much of the 90s but going to Old Trafford always felt like a real test of our credentials. We were confident in ourselves having beaten Arsenal the week before, so much so that even Gazza being out with injury didn't dampen our enthusiasm. 'Links' was on a hot streak going into the game and when he opened the scoring it seemed to flatten the home crowd and that just galvanised

> us further. Vinny got a second just after half-time – it was a neat move down on our right – and then Nayim's late goal was the icing on the cake. I don't suppose many teams recorded emphatic victories like that at Old Trafford and it proved to us again that we could beat any team on our day.

Winning at Anfield four days later in the league would have been an even bigger statement but Spurs found John Barnes in irresistible form and Liverpool performed with machine-like efficiency to record a 1-0 victory with Thorstvedt, Spurs' best performer, keeping the score down.

Having started the season so out of sorts, the October results helped to consolidate Spurs' position in the top half of the table. But a run that saw two wins, two draws and two defeats from the next six matches exposed the inconsistencies that existed. A win at Crystal Palace in mid-November lifted Spurs briefly into the top six. This theme continued through the winter months. December saw another three-game winning streak in the league, with the second of those coming again at Old Trafford. Lineker scored a very rare goal from outside the penalty area in a 1-0 win. It meant that Spurs had won twice within seven weeks at a ground where they would go on to wait another 24 years until the next victory.

The final game of the 80s on 30 December was a highly entertaining home match against Nottingham Forest. Lineker scored the first and last goals of the game but Forest scored three times in between to register a 3-2 win. It was a fitting end to the decade for Spurs with the match symbolising in microcosm the club's aspiration to entertain but ultimately falling agonisingly short.

The turn of the decade didn't provide immediate joy at White Hart Lane. By the end of January Spurs had been knocked out of both cup competitions. Southampton came to White Hart Lane in the FA Cup third round and found Spurs on an off-day. Having fallen two goals behind, Spurs were always chasing the game. David Howells pulled one back with 11 minutes remaining but on the break the visitors added a decisive third. It meant that Spurs had not got beyond the fourth round in three years since reaching the 1987 final.

After beating Manchester United, Spurs had to rely on a replay at White Hart Lane to get past Tranmere of Division Three in the next round but moving into the quarter-final stage there was genuine optimism that Spurs could go all the way in England's secondary domestic cup competition especially with Liverpool, Arsenal and Aston Villa already knocked out. Spurs were given the hardest draw possible – away to Nottingham Forest – who had not only beaten Spurs at the end of December but were also the trophy holders, having won the competition in 1989.

The tie took place in late January and, much like the recent league match, proved to be an entertaining game. Forest settled quicker and found themselves two goals ahead before Lineker pulled one back on the hour mark. Steve Sedgley then scored his first goal for the club with a powerful shot from the edge of the area to bring the game level at the end of 90 minutes, resulting in a replay at White Hart Lane.

The replay, drawing a large crowd of 32,357, was just as thrilling as the league game had been 25 days earlier. Sadly, it produced exactly the same outcome with Spurs scoring the opening goal and last of the five but conceding three in between. There was no doubt that the best two teams left in the competition had played each other and Spurs would have fancied their chances of getting past Coventry in a two-legged semi-final and then Division Two Oldham Athletic in the final.

Being knocked out of both cup competitions denied Terry Venables's team the opportunity to compete for silverware in 1990 but perhaps more significantly deprived the club of much-needed income. Scholar revealed that during that spring period the overdraft facility was increased to £6.5m.

Going into February Spurs were in tenth, 16 points behind leaders Liverpool. The following season (90/91) would be the first since 1985 that English teams would be allowed to compete in European competition but this would be a phased approach with only the league runners-up admitted into the

UEFA Cup. The FA Cup winners would be entered into the Cup Winners' Cup.

Spurs hammered Norwich 4-0 with Lineker scoring a hat-trick. The following week Spurs were able to avenge the early-season home defeat by Chelsea by winning 2-1 at Stamford Bridge through a very late Lineker goal. The back-to-back wins pushed Spurs up into fifth, ten points behind Aston Villa who were second.

Any chances of catching Villa were extinguished when they came to White Hart Lane at the end of February and won 2-0, which started a run of three defeats from the next four matches.

This run included a disappointing 1-0 reversal at home to Crystal Palace but it was a memorable occasion for the Polston family. Brothers John and Andy, who had both come through the youth set-up, played, becoming Spurs' first siblings to appear in the same game since 1912. It would prove to be Andy's only appearance in the first-team, though older brother John played 28 times before moving to Norwich the following season. In this fixture, another youngster, Mark Robson, made his last of nine Spurs appearances.

Defeat at QPR on 17 March meant Spurs had dropped back down to ninth and the season appeared to be meandering. Nobody leaving Loftus Road that day would have seen what was coming.

For the first time since 1967 Spurs embarked on a six-game league-winning streak starting with a statement victory at home to Liverpool under the floodlights at White Hart Lane and live on ITV. It proved to be a good night for Spurs and for Paul Stewart who came off the bench to score the only goal of the game with a powerful header eight minutes from time.

It had been a difficult season for Stewart who had become marginalised in attack despite playing alongside Lineker. His most recent goal had come in the home game with Everton back in December and he then endured nine games without a goal before developing an injury in January keeping him out the team for eight weeks. His goal against Liverpool kickstarted the team's late-spring resurgence. Stewart scored in his next three games with the highlight a thumping volley at home to Coventry on Easter Saturday that won ITV's Goal of the Month competition. During that game Spurs had fallen two goals behind but recovered to win 3-2.

Apart from a brief injury that kept him out of the team throughout January, Gascoigne had been an ever-present in the team all season though he hadn't scored for Spurs since November. As he found full fitness and form he was able to push his case to be included for England in the forthcoming World Cup tournament in Italy.

Knowing now what happened in Italy that summer it is bizarre to imagine there was any doubt that Bobby Robson would pick Gascoigne in his 22-man squad. Gascoigne had not started in any of England's five matches that season, only featuring as a sub on two occasions, and was behind established midfielders such as captain Bryan Robson and Liverpool's Steve McMahon, while David Platt had enjoyed a breakout season for Aston Villa.

Gascoigne's upturn in form for Spurs in spring culminated in an all-action display which provided a goal and an assist in a home win against Manchester United at White Hart Lane, perhaps spurred on by knowing that Bobby Robson was there in attendance and that England captain Bryan Robson (no relation) was his direct competitor in Manchester United's midfield. Gascoigne ran the show with a goal and an assist for Lineker (who in turn was the provider for Gascoigne) to cap a 2-1 victory – the third Spurs enjoyed over Manchester United in the same season.

It was enough to convince Robson to give Gascoigne a start in the subsequent midweek international friendly against Czechoslovakia at Wembley – the final game before Robson would name his World Cup squad. It was only Gascoigne's second start for the senior team but he showed no signs of nerves, transferring his club form to his country. Gascoigne set up two and scored from a trademark mazy dribble and powerful finish. The camera panned to a delighted Robson on the bench who must at this point have identified the role Gascoigne could play that summer.

The fact that Gascoigne and Lineker were to become a recognised partnership for both club and country generated positive attention to the club. Lineker's goalscoring exploits for his country and angelic persona on the field (he had the distinction of never receiving a caution throughout his career) meant that he was always held in high regard by supporters of all teams. Gascoigne was a player that all schoolboys wanted to emulate in the playground. For Spurs to have both at the same time resulted in a huge number of impressionable observers choosing to support Spurs.

Tyrone Foster, known as 'T' on the popular Spurs podcast *The Fighting Cock,* was in his early teens and although already fully invested as a Spurs fan remembers the adulation towards Gascoigne and Lineker.

> From a young age I recognised how Spurs were a team made up of individuals, often quite brilliant ones. Arsenal were functional; Liverpool were the best team and had great players but it was Spurs who still had that tag as the real entertainers in the First Division. I always felt around this time, especially going into the World Cup though, that the national team was the biggest talking point in the media so having Gascoigne and Lineker who transcended both made Spurs a really big draw and it brought a lot of pride to us.

Going into the final fortnight of the season Spurs were up into third place, the highest they had been since Venables took over. With only two games remaining there was now a very real opportunity to finish third, above Arsenal.

The two rivals had exchanged places as highest-placed north London club through the early to mid-80s, though, Spurs' two FA Cups and UEFA Cup victory gave them the upper hand and bragging rights. Starting with the 1987 League Cup semi-final victory, however, the balance in north London had tipped well and truly in Arsenal's favour. League Champions in 1989, Arsenal had won six north London derbies on the spin until the game at White Hart Lane in October but then won the return game back at Highbury in January.

To finish above Arsenal, as reigning league Champions, in 1990 provided a meaningful, even if intangible, success and was evidence of the direction that Terry Venables was taking the team in. To secure this Spurs needed to win both remaining games or hope that Arsenal would drop points in any of their remaining three matches.

Off the back of six straight wins Spurs travelled to Wimbledon on a gorgeous late-April day. Wimbledon had already beaten Spurs at White Hart Lane and relished the opportunity to cause an upset. An early goal by John Fashanu proved insurmountable as Spurs were finally beaten. Meanwhile Arsenal beat Millwall at Highbury to move within a point and with a game in hand. That spare fixture followed in midweek when Southampton made their first of two visits to north London in four days. Trailing to an early second-half goal Arsenal scored twice late on to win 2-1 and go ahead of Spurs with just one game to play for each.

Spurs therefore required Arsenal to drop points at Norwich knowing that they also needed to beat Southampton at home. There was a buoyant mood at White Hart Lane and the home team calmed any nerves by scoring twice in the first half without reply, through Stewart and Allen. Though Southampton would score a very late consolation, all attention was on events at Carrow Road. Arsenal trailed 2-1 at half-time but equalised with 15 minutes remaining. But couldn't find their customary late winner. Within minutes a delirious White Hart Lane crowd could revel in the joy of finishing the season in third place as north London's top club for the first time since 1987.

Looking ahead, it was difficult to conclude whether Spurs were about to mount a credible challenge to Liverpool or whether they would be able to maintain their position ahead of Arsenal. On their day Spurs had proved they were a match for both of those sides and the run at the end of the season, albeit when under no real pressure, had provided a glimpse of better things to come. There was a largely established pattern of play and a starting XI which naturally focused around the partnership of Gascoigne and Lineker – the latter finishing the season as the First Division's top goalscorer. There was cautious optimism that this was a team going places and that the 90s could deliver even more than the 80s had.

Away from the first-team, Spurs' youth team, managed by Keith Walden, provided optimism for the future by winning the much-revered FA Youth Cup for the first time since 1974. Spurs were, by some distance, the most successful youth team in the south of England and had won the South East Counties League for the fifth successive season. Keith Walden and Pat Holland coached the team but were well supported by a highly networked group of scouts who scoured London and the south-east for the best young players. In an interview with the Spurs blogsite superhotspur.com in March 2022 Keith Walden recounts that his youth team was so good that they would regularly play against and beat the first-team during training sessions – so regularly that Terry Venables had to request that the younger year group come and take their place.

By modern-day standards the facilities available to Walden and his coaching team were primitive; the first-team's rented training ground in Mill Hill was basic and doubled up as the base for the reserve team and senior youth teams. The 1990 FA Youth Cup, a replica version of the FA Cup that involves straight knockout rounds for under-18 teams from the professional and semi-professional leagues with an insistence that games be played at the main stadium, pitted Spurs against their Middlesbrough counterparts in a two-legged final in May. Up at Ayresome Park Spurs recorded a 2-1 win with goals from winger Scott Houghton and forward Anthony Potts. In the return leg at White Hart Lane Ollie Morah scored Spurs' goal in a 1-1 draw that resulted in a 3-2 aggregate victory that saw captain Ian Hendon lift the trophy.

It was a glimpse of what might lie ahead, though any seasoned observers of youth-team football will attest to the fact that even at 18 years old there was no guarantee of a future career at the highest level. Potts was the team's leading scorer with 30 goals that season. He was one of the most highly rated talents in the country but succumbed to a number of devastating injuries in the years that followed and which resulted in his release by the club in 1993 before a brief stint at non-league Dagenham and Redbridge. Potts retired at 25 and becomes a tragic reminder of the number of highly touted youth-team players who for one reason or another aren't able to fulfil their potential.

Of the 1990 FA Youth Cup team, goalkeeper Ian Walker enjoyed the most successful career in the Spurs team – he would make his debut the following season. Defender Stuart Nethercott went on to make 62 first-team appearances while Scott Houghton and David Tuttle had brief spells in the first-team. There was plenty more to be hopeful about within Spurs' youth set-up though, with a number of other highly promising players progressing through the ranks who would have greater impacts on the first-team.

There seemed so much to be positive about – a third-place finish, the team, headlined by Lineker and Gascoigne, appearing to be on an upward trajectory and the youth-team success providing cause for further optimism for the future of the team.

However, still unbeknown to supporters, the optimism on the pitch became even more incongruous with the mood in the boardroom with the debt continuing to rack up to jaw-dropping proportions and strain on relationships between members of the plc and football club board. As the summer progressed, Scholar took a lead on securing new investment into the club that was urgently needed just to ensure that the final payment to Barcelona for Gary Lineker could be met in August.

Theo Delaney, co-host of *The Spurs Show* podcast, had been following Spurs since the early 70s and so had seen many successes but also the false dawns. Having got his first White Hart Lane season ticket in 1988, Theo describes the doubts he had about whether Spurs were on the verge of glory despite the brilliance of Gascoigne.

> It was really only Spurs fans, who watched him every week, who knew how good Gazza was before

> he exploded onto the international scene at the World Cup. The combination of him and Lineker was incredible to watch and we could all see that we were potentially onto something circa 1990 but the frustration, as has so often been the case though, was that there were a lot of average players around them so we really needed some further investment into the rest of the squad. The club's perilous financial situation was still unknown so in hindsight of course this was not going to be the start of something sustainable.

With the domestic season finished, all attention turned to the summer's World Cup tournament taking place in Italy. Spurs fans had the opportunity to follow their team by proxy as Lineker scored four times and Gascoigne established himself as one of the best midfielders in the world.

1990/91 – WHEN THE YEAR ENDS IN ONE

THORSTVEDT
THOMAS SEDGLEY MABBUTT VAN DEN HAUWE
P.ALLEN GASCOIGNE HOWELLS NAYIM
STEWART
LINEKER

HOW I SAW IT:

There's a theory that the world is never a better place than when you're ten years old and this is absolutely true in my case. Living in affluent middle-class Hertfordshire meant 90/91 provided me a world full of wonder that was encapsulated by watching Spurs win the FA Cup and then going on holiday to Disney World within the space of three weeks in May.

My first real experience of watching an international tournament – the 1990 World Cup – and seeing England progress to the semi-final only further embedded my adulation of Paul Gascoigne, Gary Lineker, football and the world in general. I took Gazza's rise to national treasure as a personal accreditation as, for over a year in advance, I'd styled myself on him. I gelled my hair back, specialised (in my back garden) in curling free kicks and, if I'm honest, cried in public a little too often.

I was barely able to get to any games that season. Dad, being an amateur referee, was always at his own games on Saturday, so I had to rely on Capital Gold Radio or occasionally the even more primitive Teletext service to follow live scores. I can remember the anticipation of the opening game against Manchester City and listened in delight with Jonathan Pearce shrieking in wonder at Gascoigne and Lineker's homecoming performance that generated a 3-1 victory. The autumn of 1990 was a great time to be alive – Spurs were invariably winning; Gazza was scoring and somehow managing to enhance his persona off the pitch by releasing a single 'Fog on the Tyne' with Geordie band Lindisfarne (the first record I was ever bought of course!) and appearing on *Wogan*.

Expectations were sky-high until the first week of November when we were the live ITV Sunday game for the visit of Liverpool. Unbeaten in ten and having won against the same opponent towards the end of the previous season, I fully anticipated another victory on the march to a first league title in 30 years. Watching on from home, my heart sank as Liverpool did a job on us – McMahon nullified Gascoigne and Rush and Beardsley were clinical on the break. Such a huge disappointment, especially as it was on live terrestrial TV and I knew that we, and I, would be the butt of the jokes in the playground the next morning (there were several Liverpool fans at my school who would become Manchester United supporters within a few years).

Spurs ruined my Christmas with defeats at Coventry on Boxing Day and then a few days later at Southampton. I listened to both games on the radio. At least I had my *Gazza – the real me* VHS (look it up on YouTube – it depicts Gazza at his absolute peak ahead of the storm that was to engulf him and tarnish his legacy) received on Christmas Day for comfort.

FA Cup third-round day fell on my tenth birthday. Though I would love to have found out that I was going to be taken to Blackpool to watch Spurs, I had the consolation of finding out that Dad had pulled in some favours and that I would be appearing as Barnet FC's mascot for their third-round FA cup tie against Portsmouth. Not only had they reached the third round for the first time in years but they were also riding high and might finally get promoted to the Football League. As a result, the game was one of *Match of the Day*'s featured ties and I was visible on national television that evening leading the team out at Underhill. I therefore had to rely on the half-time announcements from Underhill to learn that we were goalless at Blackpool and then had the agonising wait to be back in the car to tune into *Sports Report* at 5pm to learn that Paul Stewart had scored the only goal of the game in a narrow 1-0 victory.

The only league games I went to that season were home and away against Wimbledon. We won 4-2 at home in November but got hammered 5-1 at Plough Lane – an experience made all the more upsetting by finding that my 40p pocket money wasn't enough to buy a bag of crisps from the half-time vendor.

Spring 1991 was a strange time for me as I began to take a real interest in QPR. Their training ground was at the sports club in Ealing where Dad was General Secretary. This meant that when I went to work with him I would regularly meet some of their players and we'd frequently be given complimentary tickets – I went to Loftus Road more than White Hart Lane. Additionally two of my best friends – Matt and Richard Koenig who lived in Cuffley too – were QPR season ticket holders so I also got taken with them and their father Pete. At some point over Easter Dad bought me a QPR home kit and there are several pictures of me wearing it though I still considered myself to be a Spurs fan.

One of the games I went to with the Koenigs was a midweek match against Aston Villa in which QPR won with a dramatic late comeback. As a ten-year-old my reaction to their winning goal was one of genuine and authentic visceral delight. For the first time Spurs now had genuine competition for my support but the match four days later was the perfect tonic and cemented any doubts that I may have had.

I still consider Sunday, 14 April 1991 as one of the greatest days of my life; it is without doubt the best of my Spurs-supporting life as we beat Arsenal 3-1 to reach the FA Cup final. Since I'd first started watching football in 1988, I had lived through six north London derbies and the only one we had won took place while I was in America so didn't get to enjoy gloating rights the next day at school. I'd endured the heartbreak of watching England lose on penalties to West Germany in the previous summer's World Cup semi-final but the game against Arsenal had even more on the line for me personally. I knew that we were the underdogs and was constantly reminded that Arsenal were top of the league and embarking on their second league title in three seasons.

Even by ten years old I preferred to watch Spurs games on TV by myself so stayed up in my bedroom. I really don't recall much about the build-up to the match but I would have been delighted and relieved to learn that Gazza was starting the match. The opening ten minutes of the game were an absolute dream – I was already hardened to the fact that Arsenal usually won and would score late goals so I was probably suffering mixed emotions of elation that we had scored twice but with the realisation that 80 agonising minutes lay ahead.

As the game panned out I think it was my first experience of realising that sometimes you can just tell that it's going to be your day. Arsenal seemed to miss some good chances chasing the game at 2-1 and I also knew that Seaman really should have saved Lineker's goal that proved to be the decisive one. With the game having kicked off at midday I was able to bask in the glory of the result for the rest of the day. I recall it being a particularly glorious warm spring day and I spent the rest of it with some local boys in the year above me at school who were also Spurs fans and equally at peace with the world.

It had never occurred to me that I'd actually be going to Wembley for the final but as we sat down for Sunday roast sometime in early May I was alerted to something under my table mat. Two FA Cup Final tickets! Through his refereeing connections Dad had been able to successfully apply for tickets and here they were sharing table space with horseradish sauce and roast potatoes. I felt like Charlie Bucket finding the final golden ticket and, given half a chance, would have taken them to school the following morning for 'show and tell'.

FA Cup Final day was still a magical event in 1991 – probably the most high-profile game in the domestic calendar. I vaguely recall the long walk from where Dad parked, past Brent Town Hall to the stadium, with air horns blasting and the sea of white and red shirts on either side of Wembley Way. We were sat up high behind one of the corners. I recall a very unfortunate Nottingham Forest fan sat in the row in front of us and him instinctively standing up when Pearce scored. I wasn't fully aware of the magnitude of Gazza's injury nor that this was his final game in a Spurs shirt, even as he was stretchered off.

I can still picture now staring directly down the line of the ball as Paul Stewart's shot came towards me and into the corner to equalise. The winning goal was down the far end and it appeared that it was Gary Mabbutt who had scored. It was only when I got home that I discovered it was actually an own goal. When Gary Mabbutt lifted the trophy I had found utopia and assumed that this was something I'd experience as a Spurs fan regularly, probably even next year as we'd won the FA Cup in 81 and 82.

Upon arriving home I found that Mum had written up some posters stating 'Spurs are the Champions' and placed them on the front door and windows. I spent the next hour on the phone re-telling my memories of the game to my other Spurs friends – Jarv, Matt and Gamey. For some reason the thing that was most etched in my memory was how Sedgley and Howells seemed to have interchanged positions regularly throughout.

As a ten-year-old I really had no comprehension of the dire financial situation Spurs were in and knew nothing of Robert Maxwell or how legitimate he might be as Spurs chairman. Perhaps this is symbolic of the world in general at that age that I was able to focus my concerns purely on what happened on the field. Therefore 90/91 was one of the happiest periods of my life.

SEASON COMMENTARY

Spurs went into the season with the tailwind of a strong end to the 89/90 campaign which saw them finish in third place ahead of Arsenal. The club's perilous financial situation undoubtedly contributed towards an underwhelming summer with only young left-back Justin Edinburgh from Southend of Division Three and 20-year-old Scottish striker John Hendry from Dundee joining the club.

However, Terry Venables had found a formula that encompassed a balanced system spearheaded by Gascoigne and Lineker. The pair had been the stars of England's memorable

World Cup 1990 campaign in Italy that summer – Lineker for his four goals and Gascoigne for his dynamic midfield displays and ultimately the tears in Turin after he received a yellow card that would have kept him out of the final had England got past West Germany in the semi-final.

For his opening home programme notes Venables expressed how pleased he was that the team were able to mix the creativity and flair of the two superstars with grit, determination, and a will to win, though he emphasised how important was that both of them now focused on their club commitments. Venables also referenced the significance of the year ending in a 'one' (Spurs had won a trophy in 1901, 1921, 1951, 1961, 1971 and 1981) and the role that luck would also need to play.

Lineker, at this point in his career, was more reclusive and stayed away from media attention. Gascoigne by contrast was being elevated to one of the most recognisable celebrities in the country and his fame soon transcended popular culture. His representatives had been quick to jump on his newfound fame and by the end of the year he would appear on *Wogan*, the UK's most high-profile talk show, turn on the Christmas lights on Oxford Street in London, and even reach number two in the UK singles chart with his rendition of 'Fog on the Tyne' with Lindisfarne to reaffirm his Geordie roots. 'Gazzamania' was gripping the nation.

In the past two seasons Spurs had started slowly – dropping into the relegation zone before the end of October in each. There was a determination to change this and the players returned to pre-season early (except for Gascoigne and Lineker who were given extended breaks after their World Cup exploits). The first-team travelled to Ireland and Scandinavia as part of their pre-season preparations and then returned to White Hart Lane a week before the start of the season to play West Ham United in a benefit match for Ray Clemence, who was now part of Venables's first-team coaching set-up.

The bookies once again fancied Spurs to do well in the league, installing them as 10/1 challengers for the title, though their odds to lift the FA Cup were shorter, especially as this was a season ending in the fabled 'one'.

Manchester City visited White Hart Lane on the opening day but the visitors were mere extras to the main attraction of Gascoigne and Lineker. It took just two minutes for the England striker to open his account for the season, latching onto a long ball and drilling past the City goalkeeper from close range. The visitors threatened to ruin the script when they equalised just four minutes later but this only set the scene for Gascoigne to steal the show.

Lineker put Spurs back ahead before Gascoigne himself collected the ball on the left, drove at the City defence before creating an angle to drive a left-footed shot inside the far post to leave White Hart Lane raucous.

This opening-day victory kickstarted a ten-game unbeaten league run which saw Spurs keeping pace with Liverpool and Arsenal at the top of the first division and building a hope that a title challenge might be on the cards. Gascoigne was in imperious form, scoring ten goals in the opening 13 games, which included a hat-trick against England team-mate Peter Shilton when Spurs beat Derby 3-0 at White Hart Lane.

A 2-0 win away to newly promoted Leeds United meant Spurs had kept four consecutive clean sheets in a row. It would take a late Crystal Palace equaliser at White Hart Lane to finally breach the Spurs defence in the next league game – a total of 524 minutes passed between the goals conceded to Manchester City on opening day and this one on 22 September.

Paul Hawksbee, a Spurs fan having grown up in nearby Stoke Newington and Edmonton, is best known now for his work as presenter of talkSPORT's daytime show *Hawksbee and Jacobs*. Paul remembers the fervour surrounding the team in the early part of the season:

> I remember that opening-day victory over City; it was a beautiful August Saturday that very much seemed to reflect the sense of optimism around the club and English football in general immediately off the back of Italia '90. So much so that when Gazza and Lineker came out onto the pitch they got as loud an ovation from the travelling City fans as they did from the

> home fans. Gazza seemed to carry his invincibility from the summer into his club form and the hat-trick against Peter Shilton – who'd been his international team-mate during the world cup – was magnificent.
>
> Despite that and the start we made to the season I still saw us predominantly as a cup team.

Gascoigne also scored four goals against Hartlepool in a league cup tie but the rest of the team also made valuable contributions. Given a rare start due to an injury Lineker sustained playing for England in the midweek beforehand, Paul Walsh scored a hat-trick in a 4-0 victory over Sheffield United at White Hart Lane.

The following week David Howells enjoyed one of his best moments in a Spurs shirt with a talismanic performance against Nottingham Forest at The City Ground.

With Forest a goal ahead at half-time (the first goal Tottenham had conceded in five away games that season), Spurs' unbeaten start to the season seemed in real jeopardy. Having been with the club since his schoolboy years, Howells had made his full debut in 1986, initially as a striker. Over time, and under Venables's guidance, Howells became something of a utility player, able to operate in defence, midfield or attack. Come 1990 he slotted into central midfield performing a support role alongside Gascoigne.

Midway through the second half Howells fired in a left-footed shot from the edge of the area to deservedly draw Spurs level. With the game stretched and both teams looking for a winner Howells was called into action at the other end. Thorstvedt misjudged a clearance presenting Gary Crosby a chance from 25 yards out; his shot was on target but Howells had reacted quickest, positioning himself on the line to block a certain goal. Spurs were able to scramble the ball clear and eventually worked the ball up the field to force a corner. Howells, now in the opposing six-yard box, got the decisive touch with his head to find the far corner to win the game 2-1.

It would be the only time in his 12-year Spurs career that Howells scored twice in the same game yet it almost felt like a hat-trick with the goal-line clearance thrown in too.

Between March and November Spurs had recorded 46 points from 20 games, which was league championship form, but bigger challenges lay ahead when reigning champions Liverpool spoiled the party at White Hart Lane with a typically highly efficient performance to win 3-1 and seemingly knock the wind out of Spurs.

This defeat proved to be a real turning point – Spurs would go on to win just another five of their remaining 28 league matches!

Throughout the remainder of 1990 Spurs became frustratingly inconsistent, winning three and losing four in the next ten. Home form was decent with three wins from the next four and a rallying comeback against Sunderland to rescue a 3-3 draw, but away from White Hart Lane Spurs were shaky, failing to win any of the next five away games in the calendar year. Having conceded just once in the opening five away games of the season they leaked goals. Eleven were conceded in the next five, which included an agonising 3-2 defeat at Stamford Bridge in early December in which Lineker uncharacteristically missed from the spot.

In a 'sliding doors' moment Spurs held on with nine men to beat ten-man Luton at White Hart Lane just before Christmas. Both Pat Van Den Hauwe and Nayim were sent off during the first half – the first time in the club's history that Spurs had received two red cards in the same game – forcing Terry Venables to adjust to the situation. Stewart excelled, playing deeper in midfield, and scored both goals to turn around an early deficit. His Spurs career would now see him play most effectively as a midfielder rather than as a striker.

At Christmas Spurs were still third behind Arsenal and Liverpool but had been pulled back into the chasing pack. Any faint hope of resurrecting a title challenge were extinguished over Christmas with defeats at Coventry (0-2) and Southampton (0-3) followed by a last-minute home defeat at the hands of Manchester United on New Year's Day. This was an ominous sign of how 1991 would pan out for Gascoigne, who received a red card for swearing at the referee, which resulted in a three-game ban.

Spurs' league form continued to drop like a stone in 1991. Between victory over Luton until Easter, Spurs recorded just one victory in 11 games, and that was against bottom-placed Derby. The biggest loss came at Wimbledon – Spurs' final visit to Plough Lane as Wimbledon would ground-share at Selhurst Park from the following season – a crushing 5-1 defeat in February,, which was the heaviest loss they had suffered since 1985.

That Spurs' form had nosedived was perhaps explained when it was later revealed that Terry Venables had personally been trying to source external funding to alleviate the club's crippling debts, which continued to accumulate, and this meant that his time on the training ground was limited. In hindsight it is telling that Venables did not feature in the official squad group photo taken at the start of the season. The great start to the league season proved to act as a buffer against any relegation concerns rather than acting as a springboard for a sustained title challenge. It meant that as 1991 began, full focus could be given to the cup competitions.

The League Cup had provided a kind path through the early rounds in autumn with wins over Hartlepool (Gascoigne scoring four), Bradford and Sheffield United, which saw Spurs into a quarter-final, but Chelsea, who were fast establishing themselves as Spurs' bogey team, ran out 3-0 winners in a replay at White Hart Lane following a 0-0 draw at Stamford Bridge.

Spurs were bidding to win the FA Cup for a record eighth occasion and fortune seemed to be on their side when they were presented with four ties against lower-league opposition from rounds three to six. The third-round tie at Blackpool on 5 January had the potential for an upset with the game played in high winds off the North Sea. Players and supporters who travelled to Bloomfield Road will recall the infamous occurrence of Erik Thorstvedt taking a goal kick which barely made the edge of his area before hitting a gust of wind and changing direction in mid-air, fortunately sailing out for a corner. The game was decided by a scruffy Paul Stewart goal midway through the second half. Spurs rode their luck during the game with Blackpool having two goals chalked off for innocuous-looking fouls.

Gascoigne played a decisive role in the next four rounds; his two goals at home to second-tier Oxford in the fourth round contributed to a 4-2 victory at White Hart Lane. The second was a goal of pure genius, with Gascoigne slaloming between defenders before netting at the Paxton Road end.

In the fifth round Spurs were again drawn against lower-league opposition, this time on the south coast at second-tier Portsmouth. As had been the case at Blackpool, conditions proved a leveller on a very heavy pitch at Fratton Park and the surface played its part in unsettling Spurs before a ball was kicked when Terry Fenwick, named in the starting XI, broke his leg in the warm-up.

David Howells recalls how Paul Gascoigne inadvertently intervened before the game to seal Justin Edinburgh's fate as a Spurs cup winner:

> Gazza was such a nightmare that no one wanted to share a room with him the night before the game as he'd keep them up all night. Justin [Edinburgh] wasn't due to be in our match-day squad for the Portsmouth game, so he was assigned to be Gazza's room-mate. Of course, he got up to his usual antics and dragged Justin down to the squash courts until well after midnight and he was red-eyed having barely slept the following morning. When Terry Fenwick got injured in the warm-up Justin had to take his place in the starting XI with Pat moving over to right-back. We won and Justin kept his place all the way through to the final.

Spurs were pedestrian and fell a goal behind during the first half. Not for the first, nor last, time, Gascoigne was the saviour, taking the game by the scruff of the neck and scoring twice; the winner with just six minutes remaining, to avoid a replay.

With Spurs somewhat stumbling through the competition, the stars seemed to be aligning when both Liverpool and Manchester United (the two previous winners) were knocked out in the fifth round. Arsenal were the only other team in the top half of Division One still in the competition as the quarter-final draw was made. Spurs were awarded another fortuitous-looking tie with a home game against Notts County.

The high-flying Second Division side, who would go on to achieve promotion at the end of the season, stunned White Hart Lane when they took a deserved half-time lead. Step forward again Paul Gascoigne. From his corner the ball was worked to Nayim whose shot deflected off the instep of Craig Short's left foot and found the net for an equaliser midway through the second half. Gascoigne then sealed the turnaround, slotting home from just inside the area for what would be his last ever goal at White Hart Lane.

The following day Gascoigne underwent a scheduled double hernia operation but by the time he went under the knife it had been revealed that Spurs would play against Arsenal in the FA Cup semi-final. Gascoigne would have just five weeks to recover from his operation in order to play. Under the medical supervision of club's consultant physio John Sheridan, Gascoigne defied human science by returning to play with a game to spare. He played 60 minutes in a midweek league game at Norwich just four days before the huge semi-final showdown. It was also a fitness test for David Howells who came through the whole game, having missed the last ten weeks.

Spurs lost 2-1 at Carrow Road but rested several first-team regulars – Thorstvedt, Mabbutt, Stewart, Samways, Lineker and Allen were all given the night off. There were debuts for Ian Walker, Ian Hendon (both had been part of the FA Youth Cup-winning team from 1990) and Peter Garland and rare outings for David Tuttle, John Hendry and John Moncur.

However, it was still unknown how capable Gascoigne would be in a game of such high intensity and importance. Sheridan, who had first joined the club in 1986 when he followed David Pleat from Luton, explains in his 2021 autobiography *The Limping Physio* just how determined Gascoigne was to return for the semi-final. Sheridan revealed the relief of Terry

Venables in learning that his star player would be available for a game that could go some way to determining Spurs' very existence.

While supporters' attentions were drawn to the upcoming match, it was matters in the boardroom that became more significant. Throughout the season several reports, starting on the financial pages but spreading to the back pages, gave clues as to the perilous state of Spurs' financial affairs. By the end of January, the club had announced a loss of £2.6m in the financial year. Relationships, particularly between Bobroff and Scholar, became terminally fractured. The Midland Bank, who had taken over the club's accounts, had extended deadlines to significantly reduce the overdraft facility but were charging up to £50,000 per month throughout spring 1991. The club's accounts had effectively been transferred to the bank's 'Intensive Care Unit'.

Venables continued to lead several talks about possible consortium takeovers that would see him become part of a rescue package, though none of the initial proposals came to fruition. One proposal would have seen White Hart Lane sold and leased back to the club.

The most obvious source of revenue was the sale of the prized asset Paul Gascoigne. His market value was speculated to be circa £10m, or at least in excess of the-then current world-record transfer fee. That stood at the £8m for which Roberto Baggio had been transferred from Fiorentina to Juventus for the previous summer. Italian football was king in Europe at this time and seemed the most likely destination for Gascoigne. Scholar was adamant that he would not be sold and suggests, in his book, that negotiations with the Italian club Lazio that began in February were initially more performative to appease Midland Bank. Scholar hoped that an alternative solution would be found that would allow Spurs to keep Gascoigne but by the beginning of April, with no alternative funding solution found, a deal was agreed between the two clubs that would see Gascoigne move to Italy at the end of the season for £6.7m – a fee perhaps reflecting Spurs' need to sell rather than his market value.

Scholar spoke with Gascoigne's advisers to find out what it would take to keep him at Spurs but was disappointed to hear it would be a signing-on fee of £2m before salary that clearly was not financially viable without a significant investment. The deal with Lazio would not be rubber-stamped until the end of the season though, providing some wiggle room.

Alan Fisher, who writes the excellent blog *Tottenham onmymind,* recalls the continued speculation and hyperbolic reporting in the media at the time:

> You couldn't avoid the club's financial problems, it was all over the papers, but if I'm honest, my focus was on the pitch and the cup run. It was the same for my Spurs-supporting mates. Talk about money and we just rolled our eyes, Spurs fans moaning about the board was hardly out of the ordinary. I thought there would be limits on transfers, a shame as we had built a decent team and two or three good players coming in would have made a big difference, completed Venables's team-building if you like. I didn't have any sense of just how bad it was and certainly not that the club could go under. Looking back, maybe I was just naive, but you have to remember, things were different in those days. Now, we're part fans, part accountants. In the same breath as we argue about team selection, everyone talks of transfer targets, budgets, TV money, money from the new stadium. Back then, 'Get your cheque book out Mr Chairman,' – well, something less complimentary, but if you said Spurs could go bankrupt, you'd be laughed at. I read about Gazza and others being sold, but I thought, how could they do that, sell our best players? We're in the final, we could challenge for the league next season. Little did we know.

Terry Venables managed to shield the squad from the speculation about the club's financial situation as David Howells remembers:

> Terry [Venables] kept us well protected to be fair; we were always paid on time and I don't recall there ever being any concern or worry about the club's situation. We were aware of the stories about Gazza leaving but he never said anything about it to us but as time went on it seemed increasingly obvious he was going to be on his way.

For both on-field and off-field reasons, the FA Cup semi-final scheduled for midday on Sunday, 14 April was monumental. To add to the magnitude of the occasion, the FA decided to play the game at Wembley Stadium for the first time in the competition's history. The national stadium, heralded as the iconic home of football, was the only logical choice of venue for two London teams with huge fanbases (the last occurrence of an all-London semi-final had been in 1978 when Arsenal played Orient at Stamford Bridge), though playing at Wembley broke with tradition and, to many non-Spurs or Arsenal fans, ruined the mystique of the competition.

By mid-April Arsenal had all but secured the League Championship title. They sat five points clear of Liverpool, having only lost once all season. They looked on course to secure a second double in their history and were heavily backed by pundits and the bookies to beat Spurs at Wembley. By contrast Spurs had won just two of their 12 league games in 1991 and had no assurances that Gascoigne would be able to play to anywhere near his physical capability following his injury lay-off.

Perhaps it was their own state of hubris but nothing could have prepared Arsenal for what hit them in the opening stages of the game.

Terry Venables made a few tweaks to his usual tactics, which he referenced in his 2014 autobiography *Born to Manage*. The plan was to invite Arsenal's full-backs Lee Dixon and Nigel Winterburn into more advanced positions thus creating more space for Lineker to run into the channels and provide more space for Spurs' three central midfielders Gascoigne, Stewart and Samways. The manager recalls that Gascoigne was even more frenzied than usual pre-match, screaming to his team-mates that Spurs just had to win.

After just five minutes Spurs were awarded a free kick from a central position 35 yards from goal after a foul on Paul Stewart. Nominally Arsenal set up a three-man wall and the BBC Commentator Barry Davies's immortal words described the sheer audacity of Gascoigne's intention:

'Is Gascoigne going to have a crack? He is you know.'

Gascoigne had a reputation for scoring free kicks. Since joining Spurs in 1988 he had scored seven of them but there is no doubt that the one at Wembley was the best and the most important. Using a unique combination of power and bend he found the very top corner to beat David Seaman's dive. Davies's commentary continued as the ball went into the top-right corner and Gascoigne charges towards the Spurs dug-out mobbed by his team-mates:

> Oh, I say. Brilliant. That is Schoolboys' Own stuff. Oh, I bet even he can't believe it. Is there anything left from this man to surprise us? That was one of the finest free kicks that this stadium has ever seen. Seaman got his hands, couldn't hold, Spurs have the lead, Paul Gascoigne the scorer.

Arsenal, who had been so efficient all season, were stunned and Spurs were able to score a second five minutes later. Gascoigne combined with Paul Allen for two successive give and gos on the right of the penalty area and the cross was prodded home by Lineker – a type of goal as much his trademark as Gascoigne's free kick had been for him. Arsenal rallied and pulled a goal back just before half-time through Alan Smith's header, setting up a nervy second half. If ever there was a feeling that Spurs' name was 'on the cup', it came to fruition as they held their nerve. Merson hit the post and Kevin Campbell had a good chance saved by Thorstvedt.

With 15 minutes remaining Mabbutt set up a counterattack within his own half that released Lineker. The England striker was more famed for his predatory instincts inside the area but this time was effective outside of it. Once again Barry Davies's commentary became iconic, referencing Vinny Samways's off-the-ball run that created space for Lineker to drive into a shooting position. If Seaman couldn't be faulted for Gascoigne's free kick, he couldn't escape criticism for letting the ball through his hands and in off the far post to provide that all-important two-goal cushion. Arsenal tried to get back into the game but the afternoon belonged to Spurs. They could look forward to an FA Cup Final against Nottingham Forest, who had beaten West Ham in the second semi-final.

The final whistle was greeted by euphoria by all in lilywhite as it contained all the ingredients of the most-perfect afternoon; a win in a semi-final at an iconic venue in front of a huge live television audience, with one of the greatest goals ever scored and against the deadly rivals.

For any Spurs fan or player, the victory remains one of the sweetest. Gazza's free kick will forever be immortalised in Spurs' history. The combination of the player himself (and his build-up to the game), the occasion, the venue, the opposition and most significantly the actual skill itself meant that this goal is perhaps not just the moment of the season but the moment of a generation that was not matched until Lucas Moura's heroics in Amsterdam 28 years later.

Winning a game as an underdog is infinitely more satisfying than winning against a well-matched opposition.

The denial of Arsenal's double featured on the B side of the club's official cup final single, 'We're off to Wembley 'cos we beat the Arsenal', which was naturally recorded by Chas 'n' Dave.

That the goal was Gascoigne's final goal in a Spurs shirt makes his Spurs legacy seem even more bittersweet.

Mike Leigh, co-host of *The Spurs Show* podcast, has fond recollections of the magnitude of this victory:

> Despite it not being a final, at the time and looking back all these years on it felt and still feels bigger than the actual final. Yes, I will watch the Gazza fouls and injury back and Stewart's goal from the final but will

> re-watch the semi-final much more, probably because it featured the greatest free kick ever seen at Wembley.
>
> The fact is that none of us thought we had much hope against a strong 'Plumstead' side going for the double but that first 20 mins is still mesmerising to watch.

Daniel Wynne, like many other north London-based Spurs fans, enjoyed the victory all the more owing to his friendship with many Arsenal fans:

> I've seen Spurs play in, and win, several finals but this victory, in a semi-final, is right up there among the greatest days I've enjoyed as a Spurs fan. Arsenal had run away with the league and were odds-on to win the double and we were so determined to stop them doing it. We were very much the underdogs and in my heart I hoped rather than expected that we might get a famous victory. I was at Wembley and despite the incredible opening ten minutes I remember how anxious we all were for most of the game when, at 2-1, Arsenal had us pinned back. That third goal provided sheer relief that soon turned to elation at the final whistle. The combination of THAT Gazza goal, the unexpectedness of the result and that it was against them made it one of the most glorious days to support Spurs.
>
> The day is particularly prominent for me – that evening it was my best mate's 21st birthday and he is a massive Arsenal fan. He was absolutely 'sick as a parrot' the whole evening and that was the beauty, but also the jeopardy, of such a big match against your biggest local rivals.

David Howells remembers the elation of beating Arsenal but felt the experience particularly, of Paul Allen and Gary Mabbutt, ensured that the players didn't lose focus for the final itself:

> It would have been easy for us to enjoy the semi-final and think that we'd already achieved what we wanted to but Mabbsy and Paul Allen were quick to tell the rest of us about how much they'd hurt in 1987 when they lost against Coventry. It was really important that we heard this and it helped focus minds on the real final.

It was implied in various media sources that Spurs' very survival chances were linked to their continued participation in the FA Cup; winning the competition would generate future funds through participation in the following season's European Cup Winners' Cup, but the positive attention could only help to secure a potential investor. Aside from the negotiations Venables was conducting, another proposal progressing in the background was that from the media mogul Robert Maxwell. Maxwell was well famed both in the business and media world – he owned Mirror Group Newspapers Ltd – but also within football as the owner of Derby.

Maxwell had secretly lent Spurs the money to cover the Lineker balance payment in summer 1990, though this information was subject to a strict confidentiality agreement. News had leaked in the financial press and so the connection between Maxwell and Spurs, via Scholar, was now in the public arena. Scholar had met with Maxwell on several occasions and sought a firm proposal to take over the club but as yet there seemed no solid substance to his interest. As the FA Cup Final approached, the uncertainty over Gascoigne and Spurs' future remained.

On the pitch, the league campaign continued in underwhelming fashion; Gascoigne was used sparingly and his performances were as lacklustre as those of the rest of the team. Spurs failed to win any of the five league games between semi-final and final, slipping down into 11th.

The final was full of intriguing side stories. Not least, would this be Gascoigne's final game in a Spurs shirt? On the other side the legendary manager Brian Clough, now in ill health but seemingly omnipotent at The City Ground, desperately wanted an FA Cup success to complete the incredible set of League Championships, European Cups and League Cup successes.

Clough's team had been one of Liverpool's main challengers of the late 80s but having won the League Cup in 1989 and 1990 were a highly polished cup team. Like Spurs, Forest had suffered an inconsistent league campaign, finishing eighth. However, fixtures between the two sides, and specifically while Venables and Clough were respective managers, were adored by the football purists. In the previous season Forest had knocked Spurs out of the League Cup after a five-goal thriller replay at White Hart Lane. Encounters between the two teams were always entertaining matches. Clough's team were considered marginal favourites by the bookies and pundits prior to the game and there was definitely a feeling that the neutral wanted Forest to win for their manager.

Venables was able to dedicate his time in the week before the cup final to the training pitch. His one big decision was whether to start with Samways or Nayim in midfield but he decided on the former, meaning it was the same XI that had started the semi-final at Wembley five weeks earlier.

Spurs wore a new kit in the final, having signed a deal with Umbro to replace the existing contract with Hummel. The Danish kit manufacturers had been synonymous with Spurs from 1985 onwards designing several iconic kits incorporating their trademark chevrons, which can still be seen being worn by Spurs supporters today. Umbro produced an innovative design of their own, with long shorts making a return after the minimalist versions during the 70s and 80s.

The match was expected to be Gascoigne's swansong in a Spurs shirt and having been the team's talisman through the previous rounds, his FA Cup Final lasted just 16 minutes in tragic circumstances. Venables reported that Gascoigne had been unusually subdued in the changing room pre-game, very much unlike his usual hyperactive demeanour.

Within the opening 60 seconds Gascoigne recklessly and needlessly raised his studs into the chest of Nottingham Forest midfielder Garry Parker, yet somehow escaped any disciplinary action. There was an audible gasp from the crowd, captured by the pitch-side microphones. The challenge looked worse on each replay and could quite easily have earned a red card from referee Roger Milford.

The game and Gascoigne then momentarily appeared to settle down, but just 13 minutes later he carried out his last act as a Spurs player. Having adopted the same system and personnel from the semi-final, Spurs had ceded territory in the wide areas, which allowed their full-backs to progress into advanced areas. Forest's right-back Gary Charles found himself on the edge of the Spurs penalty area drifting centrally until Gascoigne clattered him with an unnecessary and excessively forceful challenge that got nowhere near the ball. The collision damaged Gascoigne more than Charles and Spurs' physio was instantly called on.

After a three-minute delay, Gascoigne was eventually helped to his feet where he took his place in the Spurs defensive wall that could only watch as Stuart Pearce thundered the resulting free kick into the top corner of Thorstvedt's goal to give Forest the lead. John Sheridan, watching from the dugout, realised that Gascoigne was still in big trouble: 'From the restart Paul collapsed and fell to the floor as he tried to turn, and I immediately realised that something was seriously wrong.' Gascoigne, clearly distraught and in agony, was carried off on a stretcher and Sheridan recognised that this was a serious injury that might not only mark the end of the player's cup final but potentially his career.

With a quarter of an hour played Spurs had endured the worst possible start, going a goal behind and losing their best player, forcing Venables to make a change. Nayim, who had been unfortunate to miss out in the first place, came on, which allowed a shift in shape that nullified Forest's threats in wide areas but it was two of the players on field, including David Howells, who made the change:

> When Nayim came on Terry was understandably concerned about Gazza's condition; after a few minutes Paul Stewart and I decided to ask Nayim to play out on the left and let Vinny [Samways] come

> inside into Gazza's position. It changed the dynamic and gave Forest something to think about and allowed us to settle into the game.

As the first half progressed Spurs grew into the game and wrested back momentum and should have been at least level by half-time when Gary Lineker swept home Paul Allen's low cross but was wrongly adjudged to have been offside. Minutes later Lineker latched onto a Paul Stewart through ball and rounded Forest goalkeeper Mark Crossley before being unceremoniously brought down with an open goal in front of him. Referee Milford again showed leniency, issuing Crossley with just a yellow card, which allowed the keeper the opportunity to become only the second player in FA Cup Final history to save a penalty when he went the right way and palmed Lineker's attempt away for a corner.

Having ridden their luck throughout the tournament it seemed that destiny might be working against Spurs but Terry Venables's half-time talk resonated, as Howells recalls:

> Terry was brilliant at half-time. We were all concerned about Gazza and he told us the injury was bad. We could have become disheartened about the decisions that had gone against us but Terry reminded us that we had nothing to lose now – if Forest went on to win, everyone would say it's because Gazza got injured but we could prove that we were all good players and could do this for ourselves.

Ten minutes into the second half Nayim controlled a long kick from Thorstvedt and flicked the ball into the path of Paul Allen who galloped towards the edge of the Forest area; with Lineker distracting defenders to the left the ball was played in space to Paul Stewart just inside the box. Stewart settled himself before driving in a right-footed shot inside the far post. Spurs were level through the player who had scored their first goal in the competition back at Blackpool in the third round.

Momentum was now behind Spurs, though they had to wait until extra time for the decisive moment. It was Spurs' other sub, Paul Walsh, who played a significant role in what would be the winner in the first half of extra time. Van Den Hauwe's deep cross found Walsh who looped a header towards the back post that hit the bar with Crossley beaten, Pearce scrambling the loose ball out for a corner. From the ensuing kick, headed on by Stewart, Forest defender Des Walker, who grew up in Enfield just up the road from Tottenham in north London, dutifully got to the ball before Gary Mabbutt but, in doing so, got his angles wrong and headed into his own net.

Clough, clearly not a well man, appeared resigned to his team's fate and this mood appeared to have transmitted itself to his players; with 20 minutes to play they rarely entered the Spurs half and the final whistle seemed to be as much a relief for Forest as it was joyous for Spurs. The success provided Spurs with their eighth FA Cup win, more than any other club. Gary Mabbutt led his team, without Gascoigne who was by now at a central London hospital, up to the Royal Box and lifted the famous trophy aloft. Paul Stewart, who had seemingly always existed in Gascoigne's shadow having signed within weeks of him, was named Player of the Match, having scored the all-important equaliser.

The cup final success provided many individuals with their own career highlights. For Lineker it was his first and only domestic winners' medal, having lost in the 1986 FA Cup Final, despite scoring for Everton. Pat Van Den Hauwe had also been in the Everton team that day. David Howells and Vinny Samways had now won the FA Cup for the club whose youth ranks they had come through and Paul Allen and Gary Mabbutt were able to exorcise the demons of the 1987 cup final defeat to Coventry. Steve Sedgley, a boyhood Spurs fan, had been an unused sub for Coventry that day so could now say that he had played in, and won, a cup final.

Perhaps the biggest rags-to-riches story, though, belonged to Justin Edinburgh who just 12 months earlier had still been a Southend player in Division Four. Edinburgh was actually signed midway through the 1989/90 season, having impressed playing for Southend against Spurs in the League Cup, though he was loaned back to complete the season at Roots Hall.

Edinburgh joined the full-back stable at Tottenham along with Pat Van Den Hauwe, Mitchell Thomas and Terry Fenwick; the former two were capable of playing on both sides so Edinburgh had to wait patiently for his debut when he was picked to play in both legs of the League Cup second round against Hartlepool. His one and only league appearance in 1990 came as a sub at home to Wimbledon in November and he had to settle for League Cup action until 1991 when he started to establish himself as first-choice left-back – though largely this was down to fate when Terry Fenwick broke his leg in the warm-up ahead of the Portsmouth tie.

Edinburgh went on to play 26 times that season including both the semi-final and final. His one and only Spurs goal in what turned out to be a nine-year stint at the club came the week after the Arsenal semi-final away at Sheffield United in a 2-2 draw.

The squad wasted little time in curtailing their celebrations to visit Gascoigne in hospital where he was presented with a winners' medal. The deal with Lazio that might just be integral to Spurs' survival was now in jeopardy and Gascoigne, the best player in the world for the last 15 months, now faced an existential crisis for his own career. A scan revealed the worst possible news – that he had ruptured his anterior cruciate ligament, which was potentially a career-ending injury. Lazio initially reneged on the deal, concerned that he might never return to full fitness and in the best-case scenario would need 12 months to recover.

The following day the team paraded the FA Cup on a bus tour through the streets of Edmonton and Tottenham but still had one final league game to play at Old Trafford that took place the following night, ending in a 1-1 draw that pushed Spurs back up into tenth. It was a night of celebration for both clubs as Manchester United had won the European Cup Winners' Cup – the competition Spurs had qualified to play in the following season.

With the famous FA Cup trophy back in the White Hart Lane trophy cabinet, attentions now turned back to the club's continued existence. Speculation that the club might go out of business completely seemed a little hyperbolic but in hindsight the case of Leeds' fall from grace in the early 2000s is a reminder of football club's financial fragility when attempting to 'fly too close to the sun'.

Having masterminded the FA Cup success, Terry Venables, desperate to be part of a new ownership model, began dialogue with a renowned entrepreneur that would ultimately shift the dynamic of the club and play a part in changing the shape of English football as we knew it.

1991/92 – MANAGING THE ELEVEN

THORSTVEDT
VAN DEN HAUWE FENWICK MABBUTT EDINBURGH
P.ALLEN STEWART HOWELLS SAMWAYS
DURIE LINEKER

HOW I SAW IT:

I've always remembered this year 91/92 – and also my final one at primary school – as a particularly miserable one but I can only link this feeling to Spurs having such an underwhelming season. Maybe I was suffering from a pre-pubescent hormone imbalance but Spurs in particular seemed to make me particularly prone to bouts of tears.

Having witnessed Spurs lift the FA Cup I became particularly obsessed with the new Umbro kit, made revolutionary by the long shorts and also the very smart-looking navy socks with white tops. Throughout summer and autumn, I was incentivised to do chores and generally not to be mean to my sister in order to gain points that would earn me the different aspects of the kit.

It took a while to achieve this, because it turned out Spurs' merchandising division was as poorly run as the club's finances had been and so it took ages to get the replica kits out to the local sports shops. Even so, I was still one of the first kids at school to accumulate the whole kit. It was not because I was immaculately behaved – quite the contrary – but I think Mum just got fed up of me banging on about going to Henry Tilley Sports in Cheshunt 'just to see if they've got the shirts in yet'. Getting a player's name and number on the back of your shirt wasn't really a thing then but Henry Tilley provided kits for local amateur teams so was one of very few places that could print numbers. For Christmas I got a blue number seven added to the back of the shirt to reflect that Paul Stewart, after his cup final goal, had become my new hero.

For my birthday, in January, my QPR-supporting friends Matthew and Richard Koenig (well, probably their father Pete) bought me the book *Spurs – The Complete History*; a season-by-season guide through the club's history with every result from each season listed as well as player statistics. I was mesmerised by it and immersed myself in the club's history. I still have that book today.

The kit, and the book, proved to be just about the only good things about this season. Having hoped that the FA Cup victory would herald another glory era, I was brought to tears on several occasions. I'd got very bullish after the Arsenal semi-final and naively thought we would always beat them, so I was in for a humbling experience when we were comprehensively beaten 2-0 at Highbury in December. I was greeted the next morning with a rendition of 'We beat the scum 2-0' as I arrived at the school playground.

The defeat in the FA Cup to Aston Villa was also particularly galling. For a start my best friend Adam supported Villa and secondly, I'd spent the preceding ten days really enjoying Arsenal's shock defeat at Wrexham so received plenty of comeback. It didn't help that Mum made a point of asking my friends not to tease me too much when she dropped me at school the next morning!

The return league game against Arsenal in February was an opportunity for redemption. The game fell on Dad's birthday but he decided that instead of taking me to White Hart Lane we'd go and watch Maidstone against Wrexham in Division Four while my mum and sister could walk around the newly opened Lakeside shopping centre in Essex. I guess Wrexham were something of my second team following their win over Arsenal and perhaps this was further chance for karma to bite me on the bum.

As we got back to the car, we heard that Spurs were 1-0 up late into the second half. I waited what felt an eternity for BBC

Radio 2 (then the home of the Saturday afternoon football coverage) to announce the final score. It was well past 16.50. 'There's been a late goal at White Hart Lane …' I wasn't very worldly as an 11-year-old but I had learned that if there was going to be a late goal Arsenal would score it and that's exactly what happened. Not even a Burger King meal from Lakeside could cheer me up.

I managed to get to three matches all season – home and away against QPR and at home to Manchester City – and two wins and a defeat meant I had a 66 per cent-win record, which was considerably higher than the team, who languished in the bottom half for most of the season. What was memorable about the two home games was standing on the terrace in the Junior Spurs section of the North Stand, which only cost £3.

The European Cup Winners' Cup campaign brought an air of mystique, especially listening to Capital Gold's tinny radio coverage of away games in far-flung outposts that no doubt aided my knowledge of European geography; I was one of only a very few in Year Six who could place Porto or Split on a map. The quarter-final defeat against Feyenoord brought tears and ended any chance of seeing a second successive trophy success.

I was gutted to learn that Gary Lineker would be leaving at the end of the season and couldn't quite understand why he would want to play in Japan. With Gascoigne leaving as well and me coming to the end of my primary school years it felt like the end of an era for me and for Spurs.

SEASON COMMENTARY

With the FA Cup won, attention turned back to the club's existential crisis. The guarantee of additional income due to participation in the 1991/92 European Cup Winners' Cup provided some hope internally that perhaps the storm could be weathered. However, such was the uncertainty there were still questions raised as to whether the club could ethically sell season tickets in the knowledge that they could be put into liquidation. In the haze of post-FA Cup success, three options presented themselves. The first was the club would continue under its current ownership. Scholar remained confident that a deal could be reached with Midland Bank to gradually reduce the debt over a 12-month period, mostly through the sale of Gascoigne, other players and the sale and leaseback of White Hart Lane.

One of the options involved the sale of the club to Robert Maxwell, whose name kept being reported as being a prospective owner. Maxwell also curried favour with sections of the fanbase, and Scholar, having suggested that he would find the money to avoid Gascoigne's sale. Having initially come to the club's rescue to pay off the final Lineker instalment the previous August, Maxwell remained in advanced talks with Scholar.

Maxwell had previously owned Oxford United and oversaw their rise to the First Division in the mid-80s. Under Football League ownership rules Maxwell could only legally own one club and Spurs were clearly a far bigger proposition than either Oxford or Derby. He had negotiated to buy Manchester United in 1984 before eventually buying into Derby in 1987, though his son was named as the owner. His interest in buying Spurs seemed genuine enough.

Meanwhile Terry Venables had begun dialogue with a new party in the shape of Alan Sugar. As boss of Amstrad (the name is derived from 'Alan Michael Sugar Trading') Sugar was well known within the business world, but hadn't entered the public's consciousness in the same way that Maxwell had. Sugar had grown up close to Tottenham and while he maintains that Spurs were always his team, his attentions were focused on his business empire that began by selling car radios at Walthamstow Market and by the early 90s had grown into the global technology giant Amstrad.

It is worth reflecting on the wider landscape circa summer 1991; football had become fashionable again since the 1990 World Cup, and with talk of a breakaway league gaining momentum, commercial opportunities began to rise. Rupert Murdoch's BSkyB TV company were keen to get in on the act and there was already a strong relationship between BSkyB and Amstrad, who made and distributed their satellite dishes. For

Murdoch, having one of the leading clubs led by a business ally could open up great potential for a future venture into football TV markets.

In his 2010 autobiography *What You See Is What You Get* Sugar cites his intrigue at the club's situation as his main motivation for taking over the club. Learning of Spurs' perilous financial state in the newspapers and encouraged by his children, Sugar contacted Venables immediately after the FA Cup Final to discuss matters further. Although they had been brought up a few miles apart in London (Venables in Dagenham and Sugar in Stoke Newington) the pair had little in common and no previous relationship except for a brief advertising campaign in which Venables appeared in a commercial to promote one of Amstrad's products.

After a number of discussions Sugar agreed that he would put up £3m to match a further £3m that Venables would source that would enable the pair to buy out Scholar and Bobroff's shares and take a majority holding in the company. Sugar recognised his own lack of football knowledge but knew that Venables had been successful as a football manager and also owned a number of bars and clubs. By his own admission it had not dawned on him to question whether Venables actually had the money available.

The joint takeover would see Venables relinquish his role as first-team manager, instead becoming chief executive.

Spurs biographer and esteemed sports journalist Julie Welch had always held Venables in high regard dating back to his early days as a manager but had reservations about his new role:

> I'd just started my career as a football writer when Terry Venables's novel *They Used To Play On Grass*, which he co-authored with Gordon Williams, came out, and I was incredibly impressed – this was an ex-Spurs player and now he'd written a book! Then there were the Hazell detective thrillers that were turned into a TV series – all while he was a manager. When he was in charge at Crystal Palace, it was known as

> 'The team of the Eighties' and he was widely regarded as the cleverest coach in the country. Later there was his club, Scribes West, situated almost next door to the *Daily Mail* headquarters in Kensington. The press loved him, he was brilliantly quick-witted, amazingly versatile, and as far as the media were concerned, he was 'one of us'.
>
> As a Spurs fan I was bowled over when he and Alan Sugar got together. I thought it was the marriage made in heaven – Sugar to look after the business side and Venables to take care of the football. But now he was moving away from the training ground and more into the boardroom and I remember feeling a bit disappointed – he was such a great coach and I wished he'd concentrate on bringing us success on the pitch.

A meeting held on 21 June sealed the fate of the club. Sugar, in his typical straight-talking manner, persuaded Scholar and Bobroff that a deal with Maxwell would not be straight forward. Sugar by contrast had a banker's draft with him. Despite several counter-offers a deal was reached with Sugar and Venables that saw them take a controlling stake in the club. Selling the controlling stake to Sugar instead of Maxwell may have been one of the most significant 'sliding doors' moments in the club's history. Had Scholar and Bobroff decided to sell Spurs to Robert Maxwell in June 1991 it might at the time have been celebrated as the best possible solution to Spurs' problems.

Maxwell, a billionaire and one of the country's most renowned and seemingly credible business figures, was found dead in November 1991, having fallen from his luxury yacht off the Canary Islands. It would unravel that Maxwell's fortunes were built on a stack of deceptions and that he had used his companies' pension funds to desperately stave off bankruptcy. Had Spurs fallen into Maxwell's hands the club's future would have been even bleaker.

After an existential crisis that had been dragged out in the most public of domains the future of the club was finally secure. Most supporters hadn't been aware of the mounting problems that had built up until the press got wind of it. Now, the combination of Sugar in the boardroom and Venables overseeing the football provided genuine hope for the future even without Gascoigne.

The so-called 'Dream Ticket' combining local multimillionaire businessman to take control of the club's £11m debt and football genius to look after the '11 on the pitch' was unveiled the following week at a press conference at White Hart Lane in which Sugar and Venables were photographed on the pitch holding a Spurs scarf aloft.

The deal spelled the end of Irving Scholar's tenure as custodian at White Hart Lane. Scholar was undoubtedly a Spurs obsessive who only ever wanted the best for the club. He had innovative ideas for the club and football in general and may have been the right man but at the wrong time.

Scholar believed that, as part of the Sugar–Venables takeover, he had been offered a place on the club's board, though by September 1991 he discovered that he had been removed as a director. By March 1992 Scholar also learned that the club would not renew his corporate season tickets and so his ties to the club were cut. In the postscript of *Behind Closed Doors,* Scholar, in 1992, prophetically expresses concern that Spurs would abdicate their place as one of the big clubs in England and begin to share a more common purpose with the likes of Crystal Palace and Wimbledon than with Manchester United or Liverpool. He made a brief return to English football as a director of Nottingham Forest in the late 90s. Scholar maintained his love of Spurs having returned to live in Monte Carlo.

Paul Malshinger, a Spurs fan who had first attended White Hart Lane in the 60s, was a season ticket holder on The Shelf when Scholar was chairman. Paul provides a well-balanced take on Scholar's ownership of the club:

> When Scholar took over it felt a significant change from the Wale family who seemed still stuck in the 60s. He was a proper Spurs fan (albeit a very rich one)

> and seemed full of good ideas. At the time I felt him taking control was a good thing. Turning the club into a plc raised funds, and he instigated advertising and marketing strategies which were a first for Tottenham and maybe the league, although how much was his doing rather than Alexiou or Bobroff I don't know. He was instrumental in getting live football on TV while at the same time encouraging attendance at the Lane. (The strapline of 'It's not live unless you're there' is a phrase I still use today.)
>
> To be honest he seemed full of radical ideas but it appeared he had no handle on the cost of some of them.
>
> Becoming UK distributor for Hummel was a failure for one. The East Stand plans were what really alienated us. It was fine to replace the West Stand but to announce that the Shelf was to go was too much. He conceded that standing would remain on the 'Ledge, but it wasn't enough. So in some ways he was ahead of his time – I seem to remember he was investigating automatic ticket scanning but the technology was maybe not developed properly or too expensive?
>
> I felt he had the best of intentions but seemed to ignore the supporters which, while normal for the club, was a disappointment as he was a supporter himself. He seemed a bit naive with regards to finance.

With Venables taking on the role of chief executive, it created a vacancy in the dugout for a head coach to manage training and to pick the team. Venables turned to a former manager in the shape of Peter Shreeve, who had served Spurs with distinction as assistant manager to Keith Burkinshaw in the 80s. The pair had been responsible for Spurs' second-most trophy-laden period in history, winning two FA Cups, in 1981 and 1982, and the UEFA Cup in 1984 with an iconic team that included Hoddle, Ardiles, Villa, Perryman and Archibald among others. When Burkinshaw left the club somewhat acrimoniously in 1984, Shreeve was promoted to manager.

In a very promising first season, he led Spurs to a genuine title challenge but missed out to Everton. He also reached the quarter-final of the UEFA Cup but the following season (85/86) proved tough and Spurs finished in a lowly tenth position. Shreeve was replaced by David Pleat and would spend the next five years as an assistant/coach at QPR, Watford and on a part-time basis for the Welsh national team.

David Howells had made his debut, as a 17-year-old, during Shreeve's first spell and had fond recollections of him:

> Terry spoke to me about Peter Shreeve and I was very keen to work with him again; he had been a great coach and I had a lot of time for him. I had reservations about his credentials as a manager but as head coach he was perfect and I was delighted that he got appointed though I think we all assumed Terry would have greater involvement with team affairs; as it was we barely saw him all season.

Between Shreeve and Venables the first task was to work out how to fill the huge void created by Gascoigne's injury and pending departure. His move to Lazio had been deferred for 12 months provided he could prove his fitness and that the injury wouldn't affect him long term. While he would remain on the Spurs payroll and would receive regular treatment by Spurs' medical team led by John Sheridan, Gascoigne was essentially no longer a Spurs player.

Signing players was going to be an issue as Sugar had assured the club's bankers, The Midland, that money would not be spent on incomings until the overdraft had been significantly reduced. Sugar recalls making the point very clearly that he wouldn't authorise the signing of Chelsea striker Gordon Durie until he'd seen a very clear plan for the players that would be sold to generate the funds. According to Sugar, who was on holiday abroad, Venables then called him to assure his business partner that the deal would be financed by other player sales, which Sugar took at face value. He returned from holiday with Durie a Spurs player but no players had been sold. It was a sign of things to come. The transfer had to be financed through cash flow from season ticket sales instead. The friction between the two developed with Eddie Ashby, a loyal lieutenant of Venables who didn't have a formal title or position, and Tony Berry, a club director, often used as go-betweens.

Julie Welch feels that the partnership was always doomed:

> Hindsight is a wonderful thing – at first glance it seemed a marriage made in heaven but the Durie episode highlights that the dynamic between Sugar and Venables was just a ticking time bomb. Terry was a highly intelligent man – not just as a football man but academically, unnaturally so for the average professional footballer. He'd excelled at school and was intellectually very capable which he knew, but it was this hubris that was his ultimate downfall. By wanting to take on the role of chief executive he was stretching himself too far and it took him away from what he did best – coaching the team. He underestimated Alan Sugar – he thought he would be content to take a back seat and allow Venables to run the show, which proved not to be the case!

Venables had won the first battle, though, with the signing of Durie. The Scottish striker had spent six seasons at Stamford Bridge, scoring a modest number of goals for a struggling team. He had scored against Spurs in both league games the previous season and was powerful and quick and so, on paper, provided a good foil for Lineker. Durie was essentially a striker, though, and not a midfielder like Gascoigne. His arrival required a change in shape with Durie alongside Lineker in a more traditional front two and Paul Stewart dropping into a permanent deeper midfield role. The squad was otherwise unchanged with the takeover mitigating the need to make further sales.

As the previous season's FA Cup winners, Spurs played in the traditional season curtain-raiser, the FA Charity Shield, where they would play against Arsenal, the league champions, at Wembley just four months after the historic semi-final between the two teams. The heat perhaps played a part in a tired and largely forgettable match ending goalless. There was no extra time or penalties scheduled so the shield was shared between the two teams. Durie hadn't joined in time to play so didn't feature and Shreeve made just two changes from the team that had won the FA Cup Final. Nayim started in Gascoigne's position and Terry Fenwick replaced Justin Edinburgh (with Van Den Hauwe switching to left-back).

The opening day of the league season provided a trip to the south coast to play Southampton at The Dell. Having launched the new Umbro home kit in the cup final Spurs wore an intriguing yellow away kit known affectionately as the 'bird shit kit' owing to the strange asymmetrical sky-blue pattern on the right shoulder. Durie started alongside Lineker and, despite the team falling behind to the league's first goal of the season inside two minutes, the pair demonstrated an encouraging connection with both scoring, Lineker twice, in a 3-2 victory.

Autumn proved to be a promising start to the season with five wins and a draw from the opening seven games. The only defeat during the period came at home to Chelsea in the opening home game of the season. Lineker hit a purple patch with 11 goals before the end of September; this included four goals in an entertaining 5-3 win at Wimbledon who were now ground-sharing with Crystal Palace at Selhurst Park.

Spurs were third going into the final week of September but the good form was not sustained. Competing on three fronts, Spurs saved their best results for Europe and league results suffered.

Spurs having won the FA Cup, the European Cup Winners' Cup provided an opportunity for fans to see their team play on the continent for the first time in seven years. This was a competition Spurs had history in, having won it in 1963 and in doing so becoming the first English club to win any European club competition. As Bill Nicholson had once said, 'Spurs without European football were nothing.' Having seen Manchester United win the competition the previous season, there was hope that Spurs could win again to restore their name and pedigree on the continental stage.

Sparkasse Stockerau of Austria caused one of European football's biggest upsets of the era when they beat Rapid Vienna in the 1991 Austrian Cup Final, thus qualifying for European competition for the first time in their history. It was the Austrian outfit who Spurs were drawn against in the qualifying round with the first leg taking place in Vienna. Durie scored Spurs' only goal but all the credit for the win went to Erik Thorstvedt who saved a second-half penalty. The return leg, a week later, resulted in the same score – this time Gary Mabbutt, the only survivor in the squad from the successful 1984 UEFA Cup win, the goalscorer with a well-timed volley from outside the area.

If Sparkasse was a new name, Hajduk Split, still representing Yugoslavia which was embroiled in civil war, was a familiar opponent having faced Spurs in the semi-finals of the 1984 UEFA Cup. Just as had happened seven years earlier Spurs lost away from home but turned the tie around to win at White Hart Lane. Spurs blitzed Split from the kick-off with first-half goals from David Tuttle and Gordon Durie. The young Spurs defender, having been part of the 1990 FA Youth Cup-winning team, had made a handful of senior appearances in 90/91 and had only just come back into the team following a number of defensive injuries. His goal was a sweetly struck volley from inside the penalty area. It was the only goal he would score in his senior Spurs career that provided just two further first-team appearances.

The second round paired Spurs with more formidable opposition in the shape of 1987 European Cup winners FC Porto. The first leg at home was covered live on ITV – though strangely only the second half. Spurs were already 2-0 ahead by this point and the live TV audience had therefore missed one of the goals of the season. A series of neat, intricate one-touch passes was completed within a tight area on Spurs' right before Lineker poked home from close range. Durie then swept home a second. Porto scored an important away goal to reduce the lead only for Lineker again to restore the two-goal cushion with a cute finish. Back in Portugal the defence held out with resolve recording a 0-0 draw and 3-1 aggregate win.

Tyrone Foster describes the significance of the tie and outcome:

> I was only 14 at the time but it was the first occasion that I remember Spurs playing a game in Europe. Porto had been crowned European champions only four years beforehand so were glamorous opponents – I wasn't able to attend games at this point so having access to a Spurs game, in Europe, on TV was massive and it felt a really big deal to have beaten them.

With the quarter-finals not scheduled until March, focus could return to domestic matters but just as had happened the previous season Spurs' league form suffered.

Having briefly been as high as third in mid-September, Spurs only won one of seven league games before the end of November and fell to 15th. The only bright moment during the early winter period ironically came following a period of literal darkness. At home to Luton in mid-November Spurs fell a goal behind and trailed as the second half continued. The floodlights suddenly failed, casting White Hart Lane into partial darkness.

A delay of 15 minutes ensued, which appeared to bring Spurs back to life. Young winger Scott Houghton, another member of the 1990 FA Youth Cup-winning team, had made his league debut coming off the bench earlier that season and was turned to by Shreeve. His impact was almost immediate. Houghton scored twice, as did Lineker, as Spurs scored four goals within 15 minutes to record a first league win in two months.

Perhaps the floodlights should have failed more often – the following week the home crowd would have preferred darkness to the miserable 0-1 home defeat to Sheffield United. Houghton would go on to make only nine more appearances for Spurs before a number of loan moves and eventually joining Luton in 1993.

Spurs' poor run of results came despite Lineker's incredible goalscoring run – he had scored 19 goals in 22 games in all competitions since the start of the season. However, it was announced in November that he would be leaving the club in summer 1992 – a year before his contract with Spurs was due to expire. Now aged 31, Lineker had been giving serious thought to the end of his career. He had already announced his retirement from international football following the 1992 European Championships but now had also confirmed that he'd be seeing out the remainder of his club career in the newly created Japanese J-League as part of his wish to bow out of English football at the highest level. He would be leaving Spurs with everyone's best wishes and a transfer fee of around £1m was agreed.

Just days after his plans were revealed publicly, Lineker and family were devasted to learn that baby son George had been diagnosed with leukaemia and understandably the striker would be taking indefinite leave. Fortunately, Lineker Jnr was to make a full recovery.

With Lineker unavailable, Spurs were comprehensively beaten by Arsenal on 1 December; 2-0 flattered Spurs in another embarrassing defeat on live TV. It provided a stark contrast with the semi-final performance just seven months earlier. Naturally the departure of Gascoigne and unavailability of Lineker made an obvious difference to the quality of the team but the heart and belief just didn't seem to be there. Arsenal had invested £2.5m to sign striker Ian Wright from Crystal Palace earlier in the season; the dynamic all-action striker hit the ground running and recorded the first of many goals against Spurs in his first north London derby.

Following defeat at Highbury, December did at least prove to be slightly more fruitful with league wins over Notts County, Crystal Palace and Norwich. Spurs also recorded a creditable draw at Leeds and progressed to the quarter-final of the League Cup with a midweek victory at Coventry. By Christmas Spurs were mired in the middle of the table having won eight and lost eight. On Boxing Day Nottingham Forest recorded their customary annual win at White Hart Lane (meaning that seven of the last eight league games between the two sides had been won by the away team), yet there was some festive cheer as Spurs at least started 1992 well, winning 2-1 at Coventry for the second time in a month.

It was a well-established fact that Spurs won trophies in years ending in a 'one' but fans also remembered that in both 1962 and 1982 Spurs had retained the FA Cup and in 1972 won the UEFA Cup. Going into 1992 Spurs still had all three cup avenues available. Arsenal suffered the shock of the FA Cup third round when they were beaten 2-1 at Fourth Division Wrexham; the result was the major talking point as Spurs fans travelled to Aston Villa for their first defence of the FA Cup. A hard-fought goalless draw brought the tie back to White Hart Lane where an early goal by Dwight Yorke was the difference between the two teams. For the third time in four years Spurs had been knocked out in the third round.

The League Cup (now sponsored by the high street TV rental company Rumbelows) therefore provided Spurs' best route to success. Having beaten Swansea, Grimsby and Coventry before Christmas Spurs welcomed Norwich to White Hart Lane for the quarter-final tie on 8 January. Spurs went behind before half-time but fought back in the second half, roared on by the home crowd. Walsh equalised and then Lineker scored the winner with five minutes remaining to send Spurs to the semi-final stage for the first time since 1987. Lineker enjoyed a phenomenal goalscoring record against Norwich – his first goal in Spurs colours came at Carrow Road in September 1989 and since then had scored seven goals in four games against the Canaries.

Spurs were pleased to avoid Manchester United in the semi-final draw but instead faced a rematch of the previous season's FA Cup Final with a two-legged tie against Nottingham Forest. Clough's team took revenge on Spurs by winning 3-2 on aggregate. The two-legged semi-finals followed the pattern of recent league games by going the way of the away team. Spurs had the better of the first half at The City Ground with Lineker doing what he had failed to do at Wembley by converting a penalty past Mark Crossley. Forest rallied in the second half and equalised through Teddy Sheringham who hurt the club that he would join before the end of the year.

Such was the prominence of the League Cup that both semi-final legs were played on Sunday afternoons to provide ITV the chance to broadcast them live in a prime-time TV slot instead of a league game.

For the second leg at White Hart Lane on 1 March, north London had been hit by torrential rain all day which damaged the playing surface even further, but a bomb scare (this during the height of IRA tensions) caused the kick-off, and live transmission, to be delayed by over an hour. When the game did get underway the conditions played havoc – not least for Spurs' equaliser just five minutes after they had gone behind in the first half. Lineker's downward header from a corner didn't bounce as might have been anticipated and skimmed into the bottom corner.

As ever it was an end-to-end encounter that was decided in extra time just as the previous season's FA Cup Final had been – this time it was Forest's joy as Roy Keane rose to head powerfully past Erik Thorstvedt without reply.

Spurs' league form during spring 1992 continued to nosedive. They failed to win any of the ten games they played from New Year's Day through until the end of March. Spurs' best performance of that period was the home north London derby in which Paul Stewart looked to have headed Spurs a winner midway through the second half. However, it proved to be an agonising afternoon as Ian Wright equalised in stoppage time.

By the time of the European Cup Winners' Cup quarter-final tie against Feyenoord in March 1992 Spurs were at the nadir of their awful league form and had lost any of the momentum that had got them through the earlier rounds.

With no wins in ten and the emotion and physical exertion of having been beaten in extra time by Nottingham Forest just three days beforehand, Spurs put in a determined but fruitless performance in Rotterdam, going down to a scruffy second-half goal following a mix-up between Paul Allen and Thorstvedt. It would prove to be a costly mistake as that goal was all that separated the teams after the return leg at White Hart Lane. Sporting a new sky-blue third kit for the first time, Spurs were unable to break down a dogged Dutch defence.

Despite the disappointment, it had been an enjoyable return to European football, though sadly it would be the final game against continental opposition for seven and a half years.

David Howells played in six of Spurs' eight European games that season.

> I remember Spurs in Europe when I was here as a schoolboy in 1984 so knew what a big deal it was for the club. We really felt that we could go all the way and the home games were always incredible nights. If I'm honest, our league form suffered because we put so much into those European nights. We were unfortunate against Feyenoord – we let in a sloppy goal over there but just couldn't score at White Hart Lane.

In an attempt to freshen up the squad Terry Venables made two loan signings in March, bringing in two established First Division players from across London. Firstly, Crystal Palace's midfielder Andy Gray joined until the end of the season and played in every game. Towards the end of March Jason Cundy became the second player that season to cross London from Chelsea. The 22-year-old defender had recently been capped by England Under-21s and played regularly for Chelsea throughout the season so it was odd that he would be allowed to join Spurs.

Going into the home game with Coventry on 28 March Spurs were just one place above Luton who occupied the final relegation spot. Although Spurs had built up a bank of games in hand over their immediate rivals, the situation was seriously concerning. Perhaps it was connected or maybe it was just indicative of how badly Spurs played but the White Hart Lane pitch surface was badly affected by a diseased soil which meant it was awful to look at and not much better to try and play on. Either way a run of nine consecutive home games in all competitions without a win created a nervous and tense atmosphere at White Hart Lane.

No one individual mirrored Spurs' misfortunes through 1992 better than Gordon Durie. Having scored on debut at Southampton and netted twice more in his next three games Durie would score a smattering of cup goals through 1991. However, a league drought of 17 games without a goal meant that the Scot began to attract negative attention from a largely frustrated home crowd.

Coventry proved to be the perfect tonic for both Spurs and Durie, who scored a hat-trick in a deceptively scruffy 4-3 thriller. The result provided not only a very welcome three points but a springboard for the rest of the week – three days later Spurs recorded their second home win of the week with bottom-placed West Ham beaten 3-0 – this time Lineker bagging his final hat-trick for Spurs and in English football.

Lineker's three years at White Hart Lane will always be synonymous with the partnership he formed with Gascoigne for both club and country but even when Gascoigne was out throughout the 91/92 season Lineker continued to score goals for fun. In total Lineker scored 80 goals in 139 games in lilywhite, was part of the 1991 FA Cup-winning team, and remains one of the greatest strikers to have played for the club.

Alan Fisher has seen first-hand Spurs strikers including Jimmy Greaves through to Harry Kane, and explains what made Lineker so deadly in front of goal:

> Most of the time, you didn't really notice Gary Lineker, and I mean that as an ultimate compliment, because that was his secret. Defenders didn't notice him either, until he popped up in the box that is. He'd wait for space to appear, the smallest amount would do, or any loose ball, and he'd pounce. He didn't possess any style or grace, but his mind was the sharpest in any penalty area. Both feet, or a shin or knee would do, good on the turn, whatever was needed to get it on target. These days he trades laughs on being a 'goal hanger', and he scored almost every one of his goals from inside the area, but his movement was understated and shrewd. Attacks could

> begin with Lineker pulling out wide, stretching the defence, or darting inside with a little burst. A signal to Gazza determined whether the ball should be short or long, and Gazza delivered.

The successive home victories staved off immediate relegation concerns – there was now a ten-point gap between Spurs and Luton – but it wasn't the end of the bad performances. Easter Saturday produced a crazy home game with Aston Villa. Having taken a two-goal lead in 15 minutes through Lineker and an own goal, Spurs conspired to lose 5-2. That defeat was Spurs' 11th at home in the league all season – an unwanted club record.

April was an improvement but was riddled with inconsistency. Away wins at Notts County and QPR and a home win against Wimbledon sealed survival but defeats at Sheffield United and Oldham were reminders of how standards had slipped.

Lineker's final home game at White Hart Lane was against former club Everton. The crowd willed him to score but were content to see Spurs roar into a three-goal half-time lead. Another Spurs debutant from the youth ranks, Jeff Minton, was one of the goalscorers. However, just as Spurs had started the month at home to Villa by letting a two-goal lead slip, they went one better by conceding three in the second half to Everton.

The final game of the season took place at the same venue as the final game of the previous season – Old Trafford. Lineker's stoppage-time goal, in his final appearance in an English league game, was a nice moment and he was applauded by all four sides of the stadium although it was easy for United fans to be magnanimous having seen their team score three times beforehand in a very one-sided encounter.

Spurs ended the season in 15th place – the lowest they had finished since being relegated in 1977. Having completed a rigorous medical in Rome, Gascoigne did seal his long-protracted move to Lazio and with Lineker also leaving it felt very much like the end of an era.

1992/93 – HOPE SPRINGS ETERNAL

THORSTVEDT
AUSTIN MABBUTT RUDDOCK EDINBURGH
P.ALLEN SEDGLEY SAMWAYS
ANDERTON BARMBY
SHERINGHAM

HOW I SAW IT:

Not for the first or last time in my life, it felt as though my personal experiences and emotions mirrored Spurs' fortunes. My new secondary school in autumn 1992 was a lonely and confusing place as I felt completely overwhelmed by my new surroundings. Likewise Spurs seemed somewhat pensive and at times like a rabbit caught in the headlights in the embryonic stage of the newly formed Premier League. Much like at primary school I found that my new peers at secondary school provided a very even Spurs–Arsenal split. I made a new friend, Chris Edrupt, on my first day based purely on our Spurs allegiance and in the years to come we'd go to many games together.

Dad managed to get us tickets for the opening game of the season away to Southampton so I was there live for Spurs' first ever Premier League match, though the change of governance meant very little to me other than trying to work out whether Premier was pronounced 'Prem- ee – er' or, as Jimmy Hill referred to it, 'Pree – me – er'. Defeat at QPR in early October was particularly hard to take as not only was it a 4-1 mauling but I was sat in the home end and then the following day was driven on a long away trip for my youth football team by my QPR-supporting friends and their father.

The 1-0 win over Arsenal in December, which I was also at, felt like a coming-of-age moment for me and for Spurs as my white and blue scarf elevated me about a foot the preceding Monday. Having not learned my lesson from 1991 I was a little too quick to remind Arsenal supporters of the score through most of the season but lucked out that the semi-final defeat to them in April occurred at the start of the two-week Easter holiday.

The biggest change for armchair fans was that live Premier League games were only available on Sky Sports which felt, in 1992, as radical as the Channel Tunnel and the World Wide Web. Gone was ITV's free coverage of live top-flight football and without a Sky subscription, I, like many others, relied on Channel 4's Italian football coverage – featuring Gazza playing for Lazio – for my football fix on a Sunday afternoon. Dad finally succumbed in February and bought a satellite dish fitted at home along with a Sports and Movies package meaning I was the only one of my friends to be able to watch the Premier League.

As the season progressed, Teddy Sheringham became my new hero. I modelled my penalty technique on his; the very deliberate placing of the ball followed by confident backward steps diagonally towards the edge of the D; then the run-up and intention to curl the ball high up into the top-right corner. In a bizarre set of circumstances, I had the opportunity to take a penalty in an empty Wembley stadium (bar the 22 men who worked for the Football League who had just played a staff match that Dad had been a linesman for). Rather than roll the ball into an empty net just to be able to say that 'I'd scored at Wembley' I decided to go 'full Teddy' but alas got a bit too much under it and watched in agony as the ball sailed towards the famous players' tunnel behind the goal. This was the same end where Teddy should have had the opportunity to put a penalty past David Seaman in the FA Cup semi-final against Arsenal the following weekend had it not been for a terrible refereeing decision by Phil Don.

This was a period in my life immediately prior to puberty in which I was still largely living in a blissful ignorance of the world at large and my hopes for the future were sky-high, especially with Spurs having beaten Arsenal at Highbury and finished above them in the table. I watched with huge envy as Manchester United won the inaugural Premier League and in doing so ended a 26-year wait for the league title. As Bryan Robson and Steve Bruce lifted the trophy at Old Trafford following their final home game against Blackburn Rovers, I pictured similar scenes at White Hart Lane 12 months on, and with Terry Venables in charge it felt as though he would be able to repeat the success of Alex Ferguson.

Within a week of this epiphany, I was absolutely devastated to learn that Terry Venables had been sacked. Venables was one of the few constants in my relatively short period of following Spurs. To some extent he will always be up there with Mauricio Pochettino and Martin Jol in my affections as someone who just seemed to encapsulate what a Spurs manager should be. Needless to say, as an 11-year-old I really didn't understand the context to his sacking but believed in eternal hope that the High Court judge would reinstate him at Alan Sugar's expense. I made my point perfectly clear when attending a youth-team game Dad was refereeing at the Mill Hill training ground by taking an A3 card and writing in block capital letters 'SUGAR OUT'. It seemed to make little difference, at least not to the under-15s who were playing that morning.

I've since watched several documentaries about the fallout and reluctantly have concluded that Sugar had little choice but to sack Venables.

SEASON COMMENTARY

After the brief flirtation with relegation and very disappointing 91/92 season it was no surprise that Peter Shreeve was replaced in the summer. Terry Venables decided to take a more hands-on approach but made internal appointments in Doug Livermore and Ray Clemence, who became first-team coach and assistant first-team coach respectively. Livermore had been with the club since 1987, initially as a reserve-team coach. Clemence, having retired as a player at Spurs in 1988, had stayed at the club to begin his coaching career, working his way up through the youth and reserve teams. With several youth-team graduates now knocking on the door of the first-team it seemed a sensible appointment to help provide some continuity into the first-team set-up. Livermore, in his programme column for the opening home game of the season, explained the set-up:

> We no longer have a manager as such but Ray Clemence and I will be responsible for the senior squad in training and team selection and we are both delighted that Terry Venables has agreed to get back into his tracksuit and undertake a more direct role again in the coaching side.
>
> In a continental approach Terry will continue to deal with the administrative side of the job where he will take an overall view of things while Ray and I have the more specific coaching function.

As expected, Linker and Gascoigne left the club, but of more surprise was that Paul Stewart departed to head back to his native North West and join Liverpool for £2.5m. Even playing in a deeper position in midfield Stewart was still Spurs' third-highest goalscorer in 91/92. Spurs' other experienced forward, Paul Walsh, also left after a frustrating four years in north London, departing for Portsmouth as part of the deal that brought the highly promising winger Darren Anderton from Fratton Park in a deal worth over £1m. Anderton had starred in Portsmouth's surprise run to the FA Cup semi-final the previous season and had impressed with his athletic and technically proficient performances as a winger. Speaking on the 90s football podcast *Quickly Kevin*, Anderton explained that he was so impressed by Venables that he needed less than ten minutes to realise that this was the right move for him.

Anderton was the most high profile of a number of young players from the lower divisions that Venables brought to the club during the season. Right-back Dean Austin followed Justin Edinburgh from Southend to Spurs. Peter Beadle (Gillingham) and Gerard McMahon (Glenavon) also joined though neither would make an impact at White Hart Lane. During pre-season several youth-team players also staked their claim for first-team football with forward Nick Barmby and midfielders Andy Turner and Kevin Watson both featuring regularly in the first-team.

Coming back to White Hart Lane for £1m was Neil Ruddock, becoming the first player Spurs had ever re-signed. Ruddock had initially moved to Spurs from Millwall in 1986, making 11 appearances over two seasons. He failed to make an impression and was sold back to Millwall briefly before settling at Southampton and establishing himself as an imposing but good ball-playing defender. Following loan spells at the back end of the 91/92 season Andy Gray and Jason Cundy both secured permanent transfers to White Hart Lane.

The 1992/3 season was also the first under the new banner of the Premier League. Midway through the previous season all 22 First Division clubs had formally resigned from the Football League in what was a major shake-up to the system that had been in place for nearly a century. This meant that the Football League no longer controlled England's top division of clubs, who would be governed by the Premier League, operating initially under the auspices of the Football Association. Its stated purpose was principally to enhance the quality of football and the chances of the national team and there was a commitment to reduce the league down to 18 teams by the middle of the decade.

However, the subtext suggested that the new league would also be able to generate far greater commercial revenue in part because revenue would only be split between 22 clubs and not the 92 that existed within the whole Football League structure; hence it wasn't a universally popular move throughout the English football pyramid.

The first major commercial opportunity came in the form of live television rights. The previous arrangement had seen terrestrial station ITV securing a four-year-deal from 1988–1992 worth approximately £11m per season. It was widely anticipated that ITV would win the first round of Premier League rights and they were heavily backed by four of England's Big Five clubs' owners with the exception being Spurs, now owned by Alan Sugar.

As a leading manufacturer of satellite dishes through his company Amstrad some felt that Sugar had a conflict of interests and should not have the right to vote (as a member club) as to where the new league's TV rights would be sold. On the day of the vote Sugar, along with all 21 other club chairmen, met at a central London hotel to oversee a blind auction and determine the winners. Writing in his autobiography Sugar explained that he felt ITV were previously 'paying peanuts' for live rights and on the day were playing 'dirty tricks' and breaking the rules of the tender process. Sugar makes it clear that he wanted BskyB to win the process and called a senior executive at Sky urging him to raise their bid. In a significant moment in English football history some in the media have described Sugar's intervention as 'the phone call that irrecoverably altered the history of sport and media in Britain'. Sugar famously used the phrase 'blow them out of the water' in his advice. Having tabled an incredible £306m over a five-year period BSkyB won the battle with ITV by one solitary vote.

As well as a key moment in sport and media history, the episode also demonstrated Sugar's reluctance to act as part of a cartel with the other members of England's Big Five clubs. David Dein (Arsenal) and Martin Edwards (Manchester United) had particularly advocated for ITV's bid. The story dominated the back and front pages for several days and there were rumours that ITV would attempt to obtain a court injunction to block the BSkyB deal. As had been the case for much of Sugar's business career he had been an innovator and foreseen opportunities others hadn't. In his opinion the deal was good for Amstrad, good for all the clubs and good for Spurs, who'd get a healthy share of the new money coming in to the game.

This was the moment that Alan Sugar first made an impression on the national football audience. Having taken over at White Hart Lane he wasn't really discussed as a chairman, as in the football sense Venables was most commonly associated with the ownership of the club. If there was any doubt as to Sugar's vision, determination and bloody-mindedness, it came out during the TV rights process. The back pages would go on to learn a lot more about him in the years to come.

For fans to watch the Premier League they would require the installation of a satellite dish on the side of their home. This would come at a cost for which the Premier League clubs would ultimately be the benefactors. Sky Sports branded their coverage of the Premier League as 'a whole new ball game' and created a promotional advert with Simple Minds' 'Alive and Kicking' as its soundtrack.

Sky's proposal revolutionised the way that football could be consumed by a TV audience replicating many of the features of the NFL in the USA. There would be a live match every Sunday afternoon kicking off at 4pm. This was now considered the peak TV time and followed the enforced experiment of Spurs' match with Nottingham Forest the previous season kicking off an hour later than anticipated, which generated higher viewing figures.

Additionally, Sky, with its greater capacity and freedom in its schedule, also wanted to trial 'Monday night football' – an innovation that would see one weekend match held back until the Monday evening. Sky also experimented with other American style razzamatazz in the form of cheerleaders – 'The Sky Strikers' – inflatable sumo wrestlers at half-time and pyrotechnics (none of which lasted into the second season).

One major change, perhaps even more significant than the mass branding exercise of the Premier League, was the introduction of the 'back-pass law'. Until this point a goalkeeper could handle a pass played back to them by an outfield player, often to waste time. The new law instantly caused confusion among players, pundits and supporters. All sorts of hypothetical situations were questioned: for example, what if the defender passes a ball in a *forward's* direction and the goalkeeper picks it up: would that still be a *back* pass? The longer-term effect of the law was that it forced goalkeepers to be far more competent when using their feet to strike a moving ball.

Amid all the changes on and off the field, Spurs began the 1992/3 season at Southampton, the same ground as they'd started the previous one. Anderton and Ruddock both made debuts and were booed by the home crowd. The most eye-catching name on the Spurs team sheet was Andy Turner who, at less than 17½ years old, was barely known among Spurs supporters. In an interview in December 2019 with the Irish website The42, Turner recalled the reaction of Spurs fans when the team news was revealed over the PA system at The Dell:

> I was number seven that day and the announcer was doing the line-ups over the Tannoy. And he said, 'Number six, Gary Mabbutt.' And there was a huge roar from the Spurs fans. And then it was, 'Number seven, Andrew Turner' and it went deathly silent. There was just a murmur from the crowd of 'Who's that?' Then the announcer said, 'Number eight, Gordon Durie' and they started shouting and screaming again.

If the Premier League was supposed to herald a new era of a more exciting product compared to the tired old Football League it was not apparent at The Dell. There was little quality on display culminating in a drab 0-0 draw in the August sunshine. It was a tough opening week for Spurs. The draw at Southampton was followed up with a hugely disappointing 2-0 home defeat to Coventry.

Spurs' first Premier League goal came in their third game, but not a first win, Durie and Sedgley both on target in a 2-2 draw with Crystal Palace. The poor start was exacerbated with a crushing 5-0 defeat at champions Leeds in the following midweek. Just two points and two goals from the opening four games saw Spurs in the bottom three.

Despite initially being allocated the number 10 shirt (this was the last season that players were allocated a number 1–11 for each match before squad numbers were introduced), Darren Anderton was never bought as an alternative to replace Gary Lineker and so it was clear that a striker was on Terry Venables's radar. It was heavily reported that Teddy Sheringham was the preferred choice and a deal was finally done with Nottingham Forest in the final days of August for a fee in excess of £2m. The finer detail of this deal would later come under great scrutiny and set in motion a set of circumstances that would have fateful consequences for Venables and Spurs.

Sheringham had made his name scoring goals for Millwall initially in Division Two, but continued his good form in front of goal during the Lions' brief stay in the top division between 1988 and 1990. Despite being relegated with Millwall he became the club's record goalscorer the following year before moving on to play for Brian Clough at Nottingham Forest.

Sheringham made his debut away to Ipswich Town in Spurs' first televised game of the season but was unable to help the team record their first win of the season, in a 1-1 draw. The game is best remembered for a bizarre goal scored by Jason Cundy; the defender attempted to make a sliding tackle on the halfway line but he got such a good contact on the ball that it sailed into the top corner from over 50 yards.

Spurs had only won three home league games all season in 1992 to date but managed to win two within four days in early September. Sheringham scored his first in lilywhite in a 2-0 victory over Sheffield United. Next up Everton, who took an early lead, but were pegged back with goals by Paul Allen and Andy Turner, who at 17 became one of Spurs' youngest-ever goalscorers.

In autumn Spurs resumed relationships with Gascoigne as a Lazio player. As part of the long-protracted transfer negotiation it was agreed that the two clubs would play each other in home and away fixtures known as 'The Capital Cup'. The first leg in Rome proved to be Gascoigne's first appearance for his new club after being nursed back to full fitness and, despite being a friendly, was even televised live on Sky Sports.

In the context of the new Premier League, it already felt that Gascoigne belonged to a previous era but the wrap-around coverage of the first leg on Sky Sports was almost exclusively devoted to the former Spurs hero's recovery from injury. This seemed fitting as it was Gascoigne's performances, and tears, at the 1990 World Cup that had acted as the catalyst for the very formation of the Premier League and Sky Sports' huge financial resources thrown in to gain exclusive live coverage of the newly created league.

The money invested into the Premier League by Sky Sports would eventually wrestle power back to England from Italy as the most-watched European league. On the pitch, Gascoigne's new club came out as comfortable winners recording a 3-0 victory in Rome and winning at White Hart Lane 2-0. Gascoigne played in both and showed all his old charm when he mischievously yanked down his new captain's shorts as he held the Capital Cup trophy aloft pitch side at White Hart Lane.

The early part of the league season continued to generate inconsistent performances and results. No wins in the next six through September and October meant Spurs occupied 19th position as autumn became winter. Neither Sheringham nor Anderton immediately clicked, the latter having developed what turned out to be a hernia that required an operation. If only Spurs could have played Manchester City every week; a 1-0 victory at Maine Road in the League Cup third round was the first of four wins against the same opponents that season. There were good wins against Liverpool and league leaders Blackburn in successive weeks but defeats to Coventry, Sheffield Wednesday and Oldham. There was also disappointment in the League Cup where for the third time in four years Nottingham Forest knocked Spurs out – this time in the third round.

The team was continuing to evolve and further faith was put in young players; Kevin Watson and Sol Campbell both scored on their respective debuts to add to Andy Turner's earlier feat but none were able to make the same immediate impact as 18-year-old Nick Barmby who scored equalising goals in successive appearances against Middlesbrough and Wimbledon.

Barmby had been recruited by youth-team scout John Moncur (whose son – also John – graduated through the youth ranks making 24 appearances for the club) while playing for his local side in Hull and was enticed to relocate to north London where he signed his first professional contract while also representing England at youth level. He proved too good to be left out and was part of every match-day squad from the end of November until the end of February.

The first north London derby of the season went Spurs' way when Paul Allen scored the only goal of a bad-tempered match in which Ian Wright threw a punch at David Howells out of sight of the referee and was subsequently banned for three games. The victory was Spurs' first in a London derby all season after they had failed to beat Chelsea, Crystal Palace, QPR or Wimbledon. Spurs may have had north London bragging rights but it failed to trigger an upturn in results as they won just one of their next six league games and sat in 15th – where they had finished the previous season – by the end of January.

Having scored on his home debut, Sheringham had flattered to deceive at the start of his Spurs career. Of the eight goals scored so far only three were in the league and that hadn't been helped by Durie, Barmby and Anderton all coming in and out of the team. But all was about to change as Spurs' attack suddenly began to click. Starting with a 2-0 win at Norwich in the FA Cup fourth round, Spurs, and Sheringham in particular, enjoyed an incredible period beginning in late January and continuing throughout February, scoring 21 goals in eight games with the team winning six successive matches. Sheringham scored nine of them.

During that spring period Spurs were as vibrant in attack as they'd been since the 86/87 season and seemed to be able to score at will. Between February and early April they recorded championship-winning form, taking 23 points from the next ten games and also progressed to the semi-final of the FA Cup. The most remarkable moment in that spell came against Southampton at White Hart Lane. With Spurs trailing 1-0 into the second half, Sheringham equalised and then goals by Barmby, Anderton (his first league goal for Spurs) and Sheringham again gave Spurs a 4-1 lead, all within a spell of 289 seconds.

Home wins over Wimbledon in the FA Cup fifth round, a 4-0 thumping of Leeds in which Sheringham scored a hat-trick and a 3-2 derby win over QPR pushed Spurs up the table into eighth, above Arsenal, and within two points of fourth-placed Sheffield Wednesday.

Spurs' good results may have come mostly against teams in the lower half but it was still an extraordinary run of form with performances reminiscent of some of their most attractive sides of years gone by. Darren Anderton began to develop a telepathic relationship with Sheringham, and Barmby also contributed to form the triumvirate. However, through no fault of Spurs', the trio were soon to be split up. Barmby had been called up to join England's U20 squad for the FIFA World Youth Championships in Australia which would mean missing at least three weeks of the domestic season. It was an official FIFA tournament, meaning Spurs were powerless to stop Barmby travelling. The player then proceeded to aggravate a long-standing shin splint injury.

The only defeat during the period was a bizarre 6-0 reverse at Sheffield United, who started the day in the relegation zone; the result came out of nowhere as it was virtually the same side that played most of the previous games during spring. It capped a miserable season in Yorkshire, where Spurs had been beaten 5-0 by Leeds and 2-0 by Sheffield Wednesday. That defeat at Bramall Lane remains Spurs' joint-record defeat in the Premier League era and the largest since 1978, when they were beaten 7-0 at Liverpool.

Following that harrowing night in Sheffield, Spurs instantly recovered their mojo in one of the most iconic cup matches of the decade as they travelled to Manchester City for the third time in the season for an FA Cup quarter-final.

With Barmby now on England duty, Nayim was brought back into the team and he enjoyed his best afternoon in a Spurs shirt. One of the survivors of the 1991 FA Cup success, the Moroccan-born Spaniard had only ever been on the periphery of the starting XI largely owing to his enigmatic nature. He was able to offer moments of pure exhilaration – earlier in the season he'd scored a fine volley at home to Liverpool but then went 12 games without another goal. The emergence of Sheringham, Anderton and Barmby as a front three cost Nayim his place in the team, but with the latter now unavailable, Nayim came to the fore.

Spurs fell behind to an early goal but grew into the game and equalised when Nayim's low half-volley evaded City keeper Tony Coton. On the brink of half-time Sedgley smashed Spurs into the lead but it was Nayim who stole the headlines with two further goals to complete a memorable hat-trick for an eventual 4-2 victory. The end of the match was marred by ugly scenes in the crowd. The referee had to take the players off the field while mounted police restored order as City fans ran onto the pitch to goad the Spurs supporters behind the goal.

The semi-final draw paired Spurs with Arsenal again while both Sheffield teams would also play each other. In 1991 Spurs' very existence rested on the outcome of their cup run and the sheer force of nature that Gascoigne provided went a long way to securing semi-final success. Two years later the tables had turned somewhat; Spurs were now above Arsenal, who were not the same formidable force and were enduring their worst league campaign since 1986 when George Graham had taken over. It was difficult to work out why they had regressed since winning the league so comfortably in 1991 – the famous back five was at its peak and Ian Wright's goalscoring should have made them even more potent.

As had been the case two years earlier, the match was played at Wembley with the game a sellout. Spurs were the better team in the first half and should have been awarded a penalty when Anderton appeared to be fouled just inside the area, but Spurs were only awarded a corner. It was a game of few chances but the decisive moment went the way of Arsenal when Tony Adams headed the only goal of the game late in the second half.

Both Neil Ruddock and Teddy Sheringham in their respective autobiographies mention that it was a catastrophic mistake to have placed four players in the defensive wall for a wide free kick, which allowed Adams the extra space at the far post. There had been little between the two teams but on this occasion, it was Arsenal's afternoon. They had reached their first FA Cup Final in 13 years to play Sheffield Wednesday, whom they would also play in the League Cup Final.

Any defeat in the north London derby is a painful one but, on this occasion, Spurs had gone into the game as marginal favourites.

Paul Coyte, Spurs' match-day host and pitch-side reporter since 2004, attended the game with his father and remembers it as one of his lowest memories following Spurs:

> This match was such a huge disappointment I have essentially wiped my memory of anything that happened in the game; I'm told we should have had a penalty and I just about remember that Tony Adams scored the only goal of the game. Perhaps it was the hubris of having won the same match so spectacularly in 1991 that meant I just expected that we'd win on this occasion too. The feeling walking back out down Wembley Way afterwards was so miserable I don't think Dad or I said a word for the rest of the afternoon. Through some media contacts I'd already managed to get two tickets for the final assuming we'd be in it. I still took them and went to the final between them and Sheffield Wednesday where I could at least cheer on Chris Waddle; to our horror we discovered on arrival that our tickets were in the Arsenal end; there was a giant tifo motif organised for pre-kick-off and I'm pleased to say that if you watch this back closely there were two gaps in the red cannon where we refused to participate!

David Howells was a frustrated spectator watching on from behind the dugout due to a foot injury that ruled him out of action from February onwards.

> We felt we were the better team on the day but you always knew that Arsenal were canny so it wasn't a

> surprise that their only goal came from a set piece. We all felt that this was a huge disappointment as we backed ourselves to win the final.

The slow start to the league campaign had meant that even the spring resurgence left Spurs too far adrift to challenge for a UEFA Cup qualification which extended only as far as third. However, an Easter Friday 5-1 thumping of Norwich, who were still in with a faint chance of winning the league, at White Hart Lane served as a reminder of how potent Spurs were in attack and how much they had improved over the season. Sheringham netted twice and Nayim scored a magnificent solo goal in what would prove to be his final appearance for Spurs.

The win temporarily lifted Spurs up to fifth but it proved to be a false position. Two days later, on Easter Monday, a defeat at the hands of relegation-haunted Nottingham Forest, in which Kevin Dearden made his one and only Spurs league appearance in goal following injuries to both Walker and Thorstvedt, dropped Spurs back down to ninth.

Sheringham scored two penalties in a home win over Oldham but it was away from home that Spurs were struggling. Middlesbrough, staring into the abyss of relegation, beat Spurs 3-0 on Teesside – it meant that Spurs had failed to win away from home on five successive occasions.

Having only taken a single point from home games with Wimbledon and Blackburn in early May, Spurs had their hopes of a top-six finish extinguished. On what should have been the final weekend of the season, Liverpool scored three late goals to inflict an emphatic-looking 6-2 defeat over Spurs but there was one match still to play.

Just as had been the case in 1990, local bragging rights were up for grabs going into the final game of the season. Arsenal's success in reaching both domestic cup finals came at the expense of their league form. They had very briefly topped the table in November but lurked around mid-table through much of 1993.

Owing to the semi-final taking place on the same day that the league fixture had been scheduled, the match at Highbury was moved beyond the final weekend of the Premier League season to Tuesday, 11 May – just four days prior to Arsenal's FA Cup Final appearance. They began the evening in ninth spot, just above Spurs on goal difference, meaning that nothing less than a victory would leapfrog Spurs above Arsenal (as well as Chelsea and Manchester City).

Arsenal prioritised their cup final as reflected in their team line-up, which saw wholesale changes made. Spurs, though, had team selection issues too – Barmby had been out since mid-April and youngsters David McDonald (right-back) and Danny Hill (midfield) were selected in only their second league starts in lilywhite. Another youth-team graduate, Lee Hodges, was named as a substitute, having appeared in the last few match-day squads.

Highbury was in physical transition during the inaugural Premier League season. The famous North Bank was being converted into a two-tier all-seater stand with the work taking place over a 12-month period. To avoid the eyesore of a construction site a giant mural was erected with 15,000 faces in red shirts painted onto it. Those 15,000 faces looked on as Spurs recorded a 3-1 victory – their first in the league at Highbury since 1985. Sheringham scored his final goal of the season to cap a fantastic year which secured the Premier League Golden Boot award ahead of Ian Wright.

Spurs' other goals were scored by John Hendry, who was making only his sixth Spurs start. The Scot had been no more than a peripheral member of the playing squad since joining in 1990 but had achieved a remarkable feat of having scored four goals in those appearances, which also included an equaliser at Old Trafford. Not until 2010 would a Spurs player repeat the feat of scoring a winner in an away north London derby.

Spurs had secured north London bragging rights though QPR ended the season as London's top club. The spring of 1993 had provided grounds for optimism with a young, developing side – Spurs had played for a spell with swagger in an attack spearheaded by Sheringham, Anderton and Barmby. In defence Neil Ruddock looked to be the imposing figure Spurs had missed since Richard Gough departed. Having improved his disciplinary record, Ruddock was being talked of as a possible England call-up.

There had been similar optimism in summer 1990 but then the squad hadn't been added to. Now, three years later and on a far more secure financial footing – largely down to the financial promise the Premier League offered – the club had the opportunity to build on the platform that had been created. There were strong rumours that players including Tim Flowers, Des Walker and Roy Keane had all been earmarked as summer signings with the appeal of working under Venables said to be a major factor.

Two days after the victory at Highbury the football world was rocked by the news that Terry Venables had been sacked by Alan Sugar. News had leaked at the evening's Football Writers' Dinner by Venables's camp and by the morning Sugar was hounded by a gaggle of media and angry fans baying for blood outside White Hart Lane.

The reasons for Venables's sacking were entirely non-football ones. What had seemed like the perfect partnership when the pair came together had turned sour very quickly. Both had underestimated the other. Sugar failed to realise the affection held for Venables among supporters and the media and, by his own admission speaking on Channel 4's *Dispatches* programme in 1993, was lured by Venables's reputation as a football genius who seemingly had invested his own funds into the club.

Venables in turn hoped that Sugar would become a silent partner, allowing him omnipotence in the boardroom. The relationship had got off to a bad start with the signing of Durie just weeks into the new regime. Writing in his autobiography, Sugar also noted that as the new season started, he had been allocated tickets at White Hart Lane in the back rows of the directors' box while Venables's family, friends and associates occupied the front rows. Sugar wrote that he confronted Venables, telling him that 'you must think I'm some wally with a load of a money who's come in here to rescue the club and let you do as you wish'.

For Julie Welch it was inevitable that the so-called 'dream ticket' would end acrimoniously:

> When everything erupted between him and Sugar, it was obvious that Venables would have the media on his side, and through them the fans. But with hindsight, I think Venables had always been used to being cleverer than everyone else he dealt with and had completely underestimated Sugar. While Venables was gifted at a wide range of things Sugar was focused on one thing only, at which he was supreme. You don't get to be a multimillionaire without being many moves ahead of everyone else. I was always pretty sure there could only be one winner.

In August 1992 Sugar was also deeply concerned to learn about the nature of the deal to sign Teddy Sheringham from Nottingham Forest. He was livid to learn that Venables had instructed one of the club's accountants to go to the local bank and withdraw over £50,000 in cash that would be gifted to the player's agent as an 'arrangement fee', which if not officially recorded was illegal. For wider context English football was embroiled in several high-profile 'sleaze' cases during this period and Sugar was keen to avoid any wrongdoing.

Sugar revealed that Venables was equally as suspicious of him. When Sugar's Amstrad company quoted £4,000 to supply a new set of computers, Venables felt this was a conflict of business interests. Sugar points out that Venables, likewise, would host official club events at his West End nightclub, Scribes West, for which the club would foot the bill.

It was an ugly few weeks for the club, which played out throughout the summer on the front pages, back pages and financial pages of the media as the case was taken to court. In an unedifying episode, Venables was initially reinstated, by a judge, to his position of chief executive. The case soon went to court with a mob of angry Spurs fans spitting and snarling at Sugar, who would later remark that the reaction made him think that he had 'just killed Bambi' (though of course students of the Disney-animated story will recognise that it was actually Bambi's mother who was killed!).

The legal dispute culminated in Venables's sacking being upheld and so Alan Sugar now found himself cast as the villain among Spurs supporters and across the back pages where Venables had many allies.

Fans mobilised quickly to side with Venables and protest at his sacking. Not only were they in open revolt, but Sugar also alienated several of the senior players who were very loyal to Venables. Neil Ruddock and Nick Barmby both handed in transfer requests and club captain Gary Mabbutt spoke glowingly in court about Venables's importance to the football club.

David Howells reflected the mood of the squad:

> We were all stunned, the news came totally out of the blue and we weren't prepared for it. Many of the lads had only ever known Terry as manager and felt he was our future. We all loved playing for him. By this point I'd only met Alan Sugar on a couple of occasions and really didn't have any feel for him so it was natural that we all backed Terry. One of the directors, Tony Berry, called me and I'm sure most of the lads to try and explain the situation from the chairman's point of view. Razor [Neil Ruddock] really went out on a limb for Terry and while I'd have to say I wasn't immediately pacified I realised that there were, as ever, two sides to the story but don't get me wrong: we all wanted Terry to stay.

Writing in his 2014 autobiography *Born to Manage*, Venables remained adamant that he was on the cusp of delivering a league title to White Hart Lane but reflects that his relationships with both chairmen, Irving Scholar and Alan Sugar, dominated his time at the club. Venables also suggests that there was a campaign in certain sections of the media to present him as unscrupulous and incompetent in his role as chief executive and his wider management of business. Venables believes that these persistent insinuations were wide of the mark but influenced Sugar's judgement of him.

A number of documentaries shown on terrestrial television circa 1993 are available to watch now online and the narrative of each highlights Venables's naivety in many business dealings, most notably allowing a former bankrupt, Eddie Ashby, to sit on the club's board of directors. While it had always been Venables's ambition to run a football club and become a successful businessman, it is regrettable that his undoubted abilities as a football manager and coach could not continue at Spurs where he had started to build a young, vibrant team of real potential.

There is an alternative view of Venables's time as Spurs manager. Mark Jacob, a lifelong Spurs supporter, would later in the decade go onto form the Tottenham Action Group (TAG) – a movement that mobilised supporter protests and criticism against Alan Sugar's stewardship of the club – but in summer 1993 Jacob felt that Sugar was right to sack Venables:

> I was genuinely underwhelmed by Venables since he joined us in 1987 and could never quite understand the faith that Scholar had put in him – he managed QPR against us in the 1982 FA Cup Final and the replay, which were two of the most boring games on record and even his Barcelona teams weren't great to watch; his success in 1991 was built solely around the genius of Gascoigne. His style of play was far more pragmatic than his reputation would lead you to believe and his default transfer strategy was to buy average players. People will talk about Gascoigne and Lineker but the team around them was littered with the likes of Fenwick, Van Den Hauwe and Cundy. Over the six-year period he was in charge, it was hard to see evidence of progress or that Spurs were going to challenge.

Venables's ties with Spurs were severed. The outcome of the court case required him to resign as a director and to sell all bar some nominal shares. Venables's legacy at Spurs was tainted – his achievement of being the only person in the club's history to have won an FA Cup as both a player and a manager should have seen him recognised as a club legend. Venables passed away in November 2023 aged 80. The club remembered him before kick off with a tribute. Alan Sugar also reflected his sadness and sympathies for the Venables family via his social media account.

For Spurs and Sugar, summer 1993 was a turbulent one; having appeared to be on the cusp of a prosperous future, Spurs were back to the drawing board and seeking a new manager.

1993/94 – OSSIE'S NIGHTMARE

THORSTVEDT
AUSTIN MABBUTT CALDERWOOD CAMPBELL
SAMWAYS
ANDERTON DOZZELL
SEDGLEY
SHERINGHAM BARMBY

HOW I SAW IT:

I became a teenager midway through the 1993/4 season and experienced significant changes physically as I hit puberty full on and emotionally where, for the first time, I started noticing girls. My first crush, a girl in my form, lived literally within the shadows of Highbury Stadium which I only knew by using the only method available to teenagers in the early 90s, looking her up in the BT Phone Book – though I was never brave enough to phone her.

I desperately hoped that Terry Venables would somehow regain his position as manager but even without him still believed we could emulate Manchester United's success to win the league title under new manager Ossie Ardiles. I was too young to remember him as a player but I knew of his legend and that his vision for the way football should be played resonated with me.

We were on a family holiday road trip driving up the country to the Scottish Highlands in August and actually called in at St James' Park the day before Spurs played there on the opening day of the season. The city was brimming with positive energy but I listened to the game in the car somewhere over the Scottish border and remember the agony of the second-half onslaught on our goal, which was hard to keep up with as we dipped in and out of MW frequency.

Forty-eight hours later, for the north London derby, we tried in vain to find a pub in the Scottish Highlands broadcasting English football but alas I sat alone in Dad's car outside our holiday cottage and listened in horror to the description of Ian Wright's late winner.

Being one of the very few households to have a Sky subscription meant that my bedroom became a venue for old and new friends to come together to watch Spurs games. Darren Caskey's late winner in the home game against Everton in October caused several breakages and chairs being knocked over in my bedroom.

Despite the terrible performances and results, I enjoyed going to many new away grounds. Dad took me to my first visit to Old Trafford in October for the fateful game in which Sheringham got injured and our season effectively ended. We were sat in the away end and it was the first time I could recall that sense of collective comradeship among fellow travelling Spurs fans. I also went to four other away games – at Sheffield United for a 2-2 draw in September, my regular visits to QPR and Wimbledon, and to Everton in March. Away games were far more fun and fruitful than home games where, like many others, I didn't see a Spurs win all season.

The terrible results in 1994 kept coming. Going to school on a Monday morning became more and more daunting. Our school had many historical and personal connections to Arsenal; one of the science teachers, a big Arsenal fan, managed to arrange for the FA Cup and League Cup – both in their possession that season – to be brought into school with students able to have their picture taken with them. Needless to say, I draped my navy and white-bar scarf across the red and white ribbons.

Following Spurs was a chastening experience but once Teddy Sheringham got injured, I developed a fascination for Micky Hazard when he returned to Spurs in November. I recognised something in his ability to pass the ball quickly and to pass and move with finesse; my own playing career with

Cuffley Youth Under-13s rarely saw me make any appearances, mostly through a series of growing injuries, so most of my Hazard-esque performances were restricted to playground football.

At school I found that football was my route to notoriety and having been inspired by the new innovation of a Fantasy League – initially in the *Daily Telegraph* and then the late-night TV show presented by David Baddiel and Frank Skinner – I organised a Year 8 Fantasy League competition and presented the concept to all my peers in a full-year assembly which generated a modest level of interest with 26 people signing up to take part and the money collected going to charity.

Without access to the newly created internet there was only limited information available to know which players had scored what fantasy points so I would religiously record, and carefully watch back, Saturday night's *Match of the Day* to record the goal scorers, the assister and which defenders had played to generate either clean sheet points or minus points for goals conceded.

This meant there was no escaping Spurs' horrific performances and results. I would spend many a Sunday evening totalling up participants' points and then carefully hand-writing a league table that would be posted on the noticeboard in our block. Much of Monday was spent confirming whether Jeremy Goss or Ian Crook had assisted Efan Ekoku's third goal for Norwich at Wimbledon though this didn't resonate as much with any of the girls in my class I was now consciously trying to impress.

I used my newly found fame as a platform to support Alan Sugar's cause to have the draconian punishment levelled against Spurs at the end of the season by the FA overturned. I produced a handwritten petition that I took into school, leaving a space for fellow students to write their name and the team they supported in solidarity. This list became populated quickly, with most thinking they were merely signing up for the following season's Fantasy League. The list and accompanying letter I posted to the FA was as spurious as the charges levelled against Spurs. I did actually receive a response from them thanking me for writing to them and assuring me that they would take into consideration my views.

Despite the valuable life experiences gained, these distractions resulted in my end-of-year results nosediving as much as Spurs' had in a 12-month period. Both Spurs and I had gone from offering promise to mediocrity.

SEASON COMMENTARY

Having defeated Venables in the High Court, Alan Sugar was public enemy number one to large cross-sections of the fanbase and now had the challenge of appointing his first new manager. The two leading candidates were both former Spurs players and legends in Glenn Hoddle and Ossie Ardiles and either offered the opportunity to provide some positive PR among angry fans who only three weeks earlier had been symbolically burning shirts and season ticket books.

Glenn Hoddle, perhaps the greatest player in the club's history, had enjoyed a glorious 14-year career at Spurs as boy and man. Regarded as the most gifted English player of his generation and the most gifted player ever produced by Spurs, Hoddle oozed class in midfield and was symbolic of all the club stood for. Hoddle had been part of two great Spurs teams in the 80s but left in 1987 to test himself in France with Monaco.

By his early 30s a series of injuries had forced Hoddle into thinking more seriously about his future in the game as a coach and he returned to England in 1991 to become player-manager of Swindon Town, then in Division Two. Within two years Hoddle had Swindon playing an innovative and attractive style of football that saw them promoted to the Premier League via a thrilling play-off final at Wembley in which Hoddle himself scored.

By the time of the vacancy at White Hart Lane, however, Hoddle had already agreed in principle to take over at Chelsea and in his 2021 autobiography *Playmaker* he references Spurs' interest in him at the time but explains that he felt it was too early in his managerial career to take the job that, ultimately, he felt would be his destiny at a later point.

This left the path clear for Ossie Ardiles, Hoddle's former midfield partner, to become Sugar's top target. Ardiles had been part of the Argentina 1978 World Cup-winning team before being the subject of a major transfer coup when he and compatriot Ricky Villa joined Spurs, who had only just returned to the top division after a one-year hiatus in Division Two. Ardiles was the subject of the iconic 1981 FA Cup Final record 'Ossie's Dream' which preceded Spurs' victory over Manchester City at Wembley. The Falklands War meant that Ardiles had to relocate to Paris for a season but he returned to White Hart Lane once hostilities ceased, to play his part in the 1984 UEFA Cup success and continued to link Spurs' midfield with Hoddle until 1987.

Post-retirement Ardiles had been quick to turn his attentions towards management, and he was offered his first opportunity, also like Hoddle, at Swindon in 1989. Ardiles should have achieved promotion with Swindon at the end of his first season but after they had beaten Sunderland in the play-off final it was discovered that, unbeknown to Ardiles, the Wiltshire club had been guilty of financial irregularities relating to payments made to players as part of signing-on fees.

The draconian punishment set by the FA would see Swindon demoted back to the Second Division for the 90/91 season with Sunderland taking their place. Ardiles remained at Swindon for the majority of the 90/91 season until he was lured in late March to take over at Newcastle who were struggling at the foot of Division Two. He briefly consolidated Newcastle but the following season (91/92) was a disaster. Newcastle sat bottom at one stage and lurched dangerously above the relegation zone until Ardiles was sacked less than a year after being appointed.

The Argentine would not have to wait long for a new job though he did have to drop a division to take over at West Bromwich Albion in summer 92. Under Ardiles West Brom played good football and were promoted, via the play-offs, from the third tier at the first time of Ardiles's asking. Having been turned down by Hoddle, Sugar turned to Ardiles, who eagerly accepted the post, taking the first available flight from Argentina to sign a contract, on 19 June at White Hart Lane.

Ardiles had wanted Keith Burkinshaw, his former manager at Spurs and assistant at West Brom to rejoin him at White Hart Lane, but instead Burkinshaw remained in the West Midlands. Ardiles had no hesitation in turning to another Spurs legend, Steve Perryman, to become his assistant. Perryman held the record of most appearances in a Spurs shirt in a career that spanned 19 years and an incredible 867 senior games in lilywhite. He was simply 'Mr Tottenham' and epitomised the role of captain particularly during the trophy-laden early 80s. Ardiles and Perryman had remained great friends since departing White Hart Lane as players and Perryman too had gone into management with stints at Brentford and then Watford before returning to Spurs in summer 1993.

Doug Livermore retained his role within the first-team set-up and Pat Jennings, another club legend, joined the new-look coaching team to work with the goalkeepers. Ray Clemence was the most high-profile departure from the management and backroom team with scout Ted Buxton and physio Dave Butler, both Venables loyalists, also leaving.

The move to appoint Ardiles may have gone some way to appeasing fans upset that Sugar had ousted Venables, but both chairman and manager had several players to try and win round. Sugar described in *What You See Is What You Get* that there was a clique of players who made life difficult for the new manager initially and this view is shared by more than one new player to join the squad that season.

Neil Ruddock had been Venables's most ardent supporter and while the rest of the squad eventually backed down, Ruddock appeared at a Spurs testimonial match with a sign stating 'Venables must stay – without Sugar' and even went live on BBC Radio voicing his disgust at the situation. His then wife Sarah even staged a protest outside Sugar's Essex home holding a sign that stated: 'We want T – not Sugar.'

Writing in his 2001 autobiography *Hell Razor*, Ruddock states that he felt he had become a one-man crusade backing

Venables but that he was open to staying at Spurs if he was offered the contract that Venables had promised him. Ardiles was caught in the crossfire between Ruddock and Sugar but the ugly episode played out in public until Liverpool signed Ruddock for £2.5m.

Spurs now needed a central defender and Ardiles went back to one of his old clubs, Swindon, to make Colin Calderwood his first signing as Spurs manager. The saga played out through most of the summer meaning that the squad that toured Ireland and Scandinavia consisted of the same players that had finished the previous season as Ardiles looked to instil his new ideas into the team.

Calderwood's signing was one of the last where the transfer fee was decided by an independent tribunal. In 1993, when a player's contract expired his previous club were still entitled to a transfer fee and if the buying and selling club were unable to agree a price the decision was made by a panel of three people appointed by the FA.

The eventual fee agreed was £1.25m and Calderwood, a guest on an October 2022 episode of *The Spurs Show* podcast, recalled being in the car back from the hearing with club secretary Peter Barnes who had the unenviable task of calling Alan Sugar to tell him that the fee would be considerably more than the amount Spurs had wanted to pay. Calderwood jokes about hearing Barnes having to confirm with Sugar that it was too late to pull out of the deal at this point!

The new signing was available to play in a pre-season four-team tournament known as the Makita Cup, which would be held over a weekend at White Hart Lane before the league season began. This international tournament had been a feature of English pre-season since its inception in 1988 pairing at least two English clubs with high-profile continental opposition.

White Hart Lane hosted the 1993 version that provided an opportunity for Paul Gascoigne to make another return for Lazio who would make up the quartet alongside Spurs, Chelsea and Ajax. Spurs defeated Lazio 3-2 in the first semi-final in an enjoyable game that provided glimpses of Spurs past, present and future; Sheringham and Anderton both scored, while Gascoigne earned a penalty with a trademark dribble and then capped the scoring with a fine jinking run and curler into the top-right corner which, drew as much applause from the Spurs crowd as any of the home goals. The weekend's joy was short-lived, however, as Chelsea comfortably won the final the following day 4-0.

The second transfer of the summer was completed shortly before the start of the season with Jason Dozzell joining from his hometown club Ipswich in a deal worth £1.75m. Having made his first-team debut as a 16-year-old in 1983, Dozzell established himself as an attacking midfielder with an eye for goal. He had starred in Ipswich's promotion to the Premier League in 1992 and scored seven times during the 92/93 season, impressing in both games against Spurs.

Ahead of the season the Premier League replaced the traditional numbering of players' shirts from 1–11 with the US sport concept of squad numbers, which meant that each registered player would be allocated a number that they would retain throughout the season. Players' names were also added to the shirts, which opened up new merchandising opportunities in the club shop.

This provided fans with a definitive roster of players in the manager's plans and the 93/94 squad list included several young players for the first time. The youth team had once again won the South East Counties League, in 92/93, and three Spurs players, Darren Caskey, Chris Day and Sol Campbell, had featured for England in their victorious UEFA Under-18 summer tournament.

Campbell, having scored on his senior Spurs debut against Chelsea the previous season, had seen no further first-team action and had felt underappreciated until Ardiles and Perryman arrived and recognised the attributes that he could bring to the squad. Though Campbell had scored as a forward he was ideally suited to playing in defence or midfield and featured as a left-back in the Makita Cup match against Lazio.

Darren Caskey had been one of England U18's most eye-catching performers during the summer and, having trained regularly with the first-team for over a year, was now being readied to play for the senior team. Both Caskey (number 20) and Campbell (23) were allocated squad numbers for the upcoming season along with Andy Turner, Danny Hill, Kevin Watson and Stuart Nethercott who had all made their debuts in 92/93.

The fixture list provided Ardiles with an intriguing start to the season and an opening-day trip to his former club Newcastle who were riding on the crest of a wave after their promotion back to the top division. When Ardiles left in February 1992, Newcastle were second from bottom and staring relegation in the face. Keegan managed to stabilise the club though it took a win on the final day of the season to retain their second-tier status.

During summer 1992, with financial backing by new club owner Sir John Hall, Newcastle embarked on an incredible rise to become one of the dominant forces in 90s football and with Keegan in charge added the romance and cult following that created national intrigue. Newcastle roared away with the second tier (at this point known as Division One to reflect the inception of the Premier League) and the spending continued during summer 1993 with Peter Beardsley returning to his native North East to partner sharpshooting Andy Cole in attack.

Having been outside the top division at the time of the vote in 1991, neither Newcastle nor Blackburn had been among the clubs to sign up to the Premier League but both appeared to have leapfrogged Spurs in terms of relevance, ambition and spending power.

Both Calderwood and Dozzell started and Campbell was selected at left-back. Nick Barmby and Darren Anderton were both unavailable – the former still feeling the effects of his shin splints and the latter due to a minor injury. Ardiles picked Gordon Durie to start alongside Sheringham.

In a febrile atmosphere, Spurs contained the home team for the opening half an hour and then went ahead through Sheringham just before half-time to silence the home crowd. Newcastle rallied but found Thorstvedt, selected ahead of Ian Walker, in inspired form to preserve the lead and a clean sheet

– something Spurs hadn't achieved in the final 12 games of the previous season. The Ardiles era began with a win.

Just two days later Arsenal were the visitors to White Hart Lane for Ardiles's first home game in charge. In a tight match there was heartache when Arsenal scored a late winner to win 1-0.

The early season continued with a run of good results – Spurs lost just once more in the first ten games and the highlight was a rare win at Anfield in which Sheringham scored twice in a 2-1 victory.

Gordon Durie scored his final Spurs goal in a home game with Oldham in mid-September. Spurs won 5-0 but were three up inside eight minutes following two identical goals caused by terrible goalkeeping errors from Oldham's goalkeeper Paul Gerrard. The game was also notable for a nasty injury sustained by Dean Austin that would rule the full-back out for several months, requiring Ardiles to return to Swindon for another former player in David Kerslake to fill the right-back berth.

On his way out was Paul Allen who had been at Spurs since 1985. Allen, the cousin of Clive Allen and nephew of Spurs double winner Les, had been a stalwart in the team under three separate managers. He had proved his versatility, operating anywhere across the midfield and often acting as a balance to the likes of Hoddle, Gascoigne and Anderton. Allen moved to Southampton where he would spend the next two seasons.

Despite scoring in the 5-0 win against Oldham, Jason Dozzell had made a slow start to his Spurs career, being selected to play on the left of a midfield diamond. He was not utilised in the same way that he had been so effectively at Ipswich. It was written in the stars that his first meaningful Spurs contribution came at Portman Road. With Spurs 2-1 behind and down to ten men following Colin Calderwood's red card, Dozzell pounced to slot into an open net after a mix-up in the home team's penalty area and secure a draw.

The following week Spurs played out one of the more entertaining games of the season, again live on Sky, at home to Everton. When Spurs trailed 1-0 and then 2-1, it appeared that Everton would gain a rare win at White Hart Lane. With two minutes remaining, Anderton volleyed an equaliser but Spurs weren't finished. Darren Caskey, on his full debut, demonstrated incredible composure as the ball fell to him inside a crowded penalty area to carefully stroke the ball into the far corner. It would prove to be Caskey's best moment in a Spurs shirt and also the pinnacle of a Spurs season that was quickly to descend into chaos.

With the team up into fifth in the embryonic league table, it appeared Ardiles might be able to continue the trajectory he had inherited. With Barmby's return imminent there was every hope that Spurs could make a statement win in their next game at Old Trafford in mid-October, but then crisis hit.

Spurs played neat possession football in the opening exchanges but midway through the first half the complexion of the game and season turned. Sheringham, who had been in tremendous form having already scored 11 in 12 games, had to be substituted after two particularly robust tackles from Bryan Robson, both of which went unpunished but had hurt Sheringham.

Spurs' top goalscorer emerged out of the dressing room in the second half on crutches by which point Manchester United had scored twice, though Caskey would score what turned out to be a mere consolation. Sheringham's absence in the match and for what proved to be most of the season was a sliding-doors moment which nearly led to fateful consequences.

Sheringham's injury was initially believed to be a minor one but such was his importance to the team that his unavailability caused immediate issues. Durie was sold to Glasgow Rangers in November, having actively sought a return to native Scotland for personal reasons. It left Spurs without a senior striker to link up with Barmby and Anderton.

Over the course of the winter Ardiles toyed with various options including Howells and Campbell out of position, and Paul Moran and John Hendry made fleeting appearances from the reserves but with no joy. The following week's home game resulted in a very underwhelming home draw with newly promoted Swindon.

Spurs won just one of their next eight league games before the customary victory at Manchester City in December. To add to Sheringham's injury, Spurs were also denied the services of Gary Mabbutt who was on the receiving end of an elbow from John Fashanu during the midweek draw at home to Wimbledon in November. Mabbutt suffered a fractured eye socket and was inches from losing his sight. Howells also picked up an injury that denied Spurs his experience for another four months.

Micky Hazard made a surprise return to White Hart Lane in early November. The 33-year-old had made his initial Spurs debut in April 1980, having joined the club as a teenager. Hazard was a fine, technically gifted midfielder, but rather unfortunately was too stylistically similar to Glenn Hoddle to play as regularly as his talent should have allowed. Having been part of the 1984 UEFA Cup-winning team, Hazard eventually moved away to join Chelsea in 1985. He spent five seasons in West London before playing under Ardiles, and then Hoddle, at Swindon.

Having been both a team-mate in his playing days and then his manager at Swindon, Ardiles was aware of the qualities that Hazard could bring to his Spurs team and, after Kerslake and Calderwood, became the third player to swap Wiltshire for north London.

Speaking as a guest on *The Spurs Show* podcast in October 2022, Hazard recalled that the move came out of the blue but he was desperate to make a return to White Hart Lane, having regretted leaving almost instantly upon signing for Chelsea. Hazard signed for Spurs for his great friend Ossie Ardiles on exactly the same money he had been earning at Swindon and was so excited about agreeing the deal that he had to rely on his wife to negotiate the lease of a club car as he'd had to give his previous one back to Swindon!

Upon overcoming the initial excitement, Hazard was quick to pick up on the palpable tension that he sensed had permeated the club from the messy divorce between Sugar and Venables that Ardiles had unfortunately walked into. Hazard suggested that while there were no obvious factions within the playing squad itself, there was a sense of unease that hung like a cloud above the club.

During the summer Alan Sugar had appointed Claude Littner as the club's chief executive. Littner was a loyal lieutenant for Sugar and was renowned as a troubleshooter. Interviewed in The Athletic in December 2020, Littner revealed that Sugar had told him: 'It's like World War III there. Just go in and sort it out.' What Littner found when looking beneath the surface was what he described as 'the wild west … where everyone was just doing their own thing.' Many club operations were scrutinised, in part to cut unnecessary costs.

While Littner was invariably concerned with the non-football operations, he clashed with Steve Perryman. Littner discovered that a crate of milk was being delivered to the stadium every day just in case the first-team trained at White Hart Lane. The stadium milk deliveries were promptly cancelled but the media, presumably via some of the pro-Venables factions in the playing squad, jumped on the story and it hit the headlines after a defeat.

'With a normal company, you can do more or less what you want without being under the glare of the newspapers … Here, when anybody said anything, it immediately got into the newspapers. It was always putting a negative slant on us, making us look bad,' Littner told The Athletic.

Hazard made his second debut away at Southampton in early November and was picked to start every game until an injury in mid-January. His impact contributed to an upturn in performances for a brief period in late November and December. He was involved in what was arguably Spurs' goal of the season – a passage of one- and two-touch play eventually set up Anderton to score an equaliser at QPR in late November.

That game at Loftus Road also saw a fleeting appearance from youngster Steven Robinson, who rather ignominiously came on as a first-half substitute for the injured David Howells only to get injured himself and be replaced by Stuart Nethercott.

Hazard continued to roll back the years and dictate the tempo of the midfield; his pirouette and neat turn set up a move that resulted in Darren Anderton scoring the opener at Highbury – a game that Spurs played well in, though they had to settle for a 1-1 draw. Liverpool came to White Hart Lane in mid-December and Hazard's penalty provided the necessary momentum for Spurs to come back from 1-3 down to gain a 3-3 draw. Then, in a busy Christmas period that saw most teams play twice in successive days, Hazard capped a magnificent display at West Ham by starting and finishing a lovely team goal that contributed to a 3-1 victory.

Holistically these bright moments were all too isolated and not sustainable. Either side of the win at West Ham, Spurs suffered home defeats to Norwich and Coventry – the latter on New Year's Day and a harbinger of what 1994 was to bring.

The FA Cup, so often the salvager of Spurs' seasons, saw the team travel to second-tier Peterborough United in the third round. Dozzell spared Spurs' blushes at London Road with a late equaliser and then it required extra time and penalties to defeat the lower-league opponents back at White Hart Lane. Sedgley, who had taken on the captaincy since Mabbutt's injury, also assumed responsibility by scoring the winning penalty.

The fourth round sent Spurs to Ipswich, a team they were yet to beat since the Suffolk club had returned to the top flight. Spurs were well beaten 3-0 and dumped out of the FA Cup before the end of January.

The League Cup also failed to provide any respite. Having beaten Burnley, Derby and Blackburn, Spurs were drawn to play at home to Aston Villa in the quarter-finals in mid-January. Ron Atkinson's team had been a regular thorn in Spurs' side and enjoyed decent form at White Hart Lane, having lost just once in ten meetings since the turn of the decade. It was a classic cup atmosphere under the lights and Spurs played with a higher tempo and intensity than was on display in league games.

All the goals came within 12 second-half minutes. Ray Houghton put Villa ahead only for Caskey to equalise. With Spurs looking to have wrestled the momentum back in their favour, Earl Barrett rose unmarked to head home from close range from a corner. Despite a late siege on the Villa goal a second equaliser couldn't be found and Spurs' season now was entirely focused on trying to address the concerning slide down the league table.

Spurs' striking problems persisted with no sign of Sheringham returning. Publicly reported return dates came and went as it became clear the initial prognosis had not identified the full extent of the injury. The uncertainty prevented Spurs from seriously seeking an external replacement, though results would make this a necessity. Out of both cups, Spurs ended January in 15th place, having lost four on the spin in the league, which included a dismal 2-1 defeat at bottom-placed Swindon, who had won just once up to that point.

The solution was identified as Liverpool's Israeli forward Ronny Rosenthal, who had initially made a positive impact at Anfield since joining at the back end of the 1989/90 season. He was a quick and powerful forward who could also deputise as a left-winger but could be very erratic in front of goal; for every great goal there was an embarrassing miss and his time at Liverpool was mostly remembered for hitting the crossbar from eight yards with an open goal gaping in a game against Aston Villa.

With Mabbutt and Howells still missing, Ardiles signed another of his previous players in the shape of Newcastle defender Kevin Scott, who had become surplus at St James' Park.

Both Scott and Rosenthal came straight into the starting XI for the home game with Sheffield Wednesday on 5 February. Rosenthal partnered Barmby in attack and scored a good headed goal from a corner midway through the second half, but by this point Spurs were already three goals behind. Spurs lost at home the following weekend too – this time at the hands of Blackburn. This defeat created an unwanted record – a sixth successive league defeat, now the worst run in the club's history.

Relegation fears were very much looming and the live Sky Sports *Super Sunday* encounter at Stamford Bridge was billed as a six-pointer. Spurs went into the game in 16th and on 30 points one place, and three points, above opponents Chelsea.

Under Hoddle, Chelsea had also endured a challenging season. They had won just once in 11 games at the back end of 1993, which included a six-game losing streak, and had dropped to second from bottom on Boxing Day. However, the turn of the year had marked a turnaround in fortunes, particularly with their new striker Mark Stein, a £1.5m signing from Stoke City, suddenly finding his feet. Having not scored in his first seven appearance Stein scored ten in 14 games which helped Chelsea to climb out of the relegation zone and into Spurs' slipstream.

Spurs could at least call upon Gary Mabbutt who, having undergone successful surgery and rehabilitation, was finally able to return to the starting XI. Wearing a *Phantom of the Opera*-like facemask, he slotted into an unfamiliar role just in front of the two central defenders, Kevin Scott and Stuart Nethercott. Mabbutt's inclusion was countered by injuries to Barmby and Caskey, who both missed the game. In one of the games of the season (for the neutral) Spurs were edged out in a topsy-turvy seven-goal thriller.

Spurs led 2-0 only to go in 3-2 down at half-time. Andy Gray, a forgotten man at White Hart Lane, came off the bench for only his second appearance of the season to equalise from the penalty spot but then missed a second after Rosenthal had been fouled with just minutes remaining. The match reached its crescendo when Chelsea were awarded a penalty of their own that Stein converted with the final kick of the game.

Daniel Wynne remembers the fear that enveloped many fans that evening:

> We'd been on a terrible run but always felt as though Teddy would come back and it would turn around. In a funny way this game encapsulated the whole season – we started well and went 2-0 ahead and then suddenly we were behind. The drama of those three penalties in the second half was so hard to take and it was even more upsetting seeing Glenn Hoddle, our Glenn Hoddle, my first Spurs hero, celebrating this dramatic win against us for Chelsea! Coming away

> from this game, for the first time I genuinely thought we could get relegated – you suddenly couldn't see where the next win was coming from and other teams, including Chelsea, were leapfrogging us.

While many fans like Daniel feared the worse there was also a feeling of apathy as evidenced when just 17,452 turned up for the following home match – a rearranged midweek game against bogey team Aston Villa. Having been the villain at Chelsea, Andy Gray dropped back out of the match-day squad never to be seen in a Spurs shirt again. However, his inability from the penalty spot had spread to the rest of the squad. A goal-down Spurs saw two penalty kicks saved – once from Barmby and the other Anderton – though Rosenthal did equalise to rescue a point and end the seven-game losing streak. Spurs were now just four points above the relegation zone, having played more games than their adversaries.

The next two home games yielded only draws against Sheffield United and Ipswich before a first win of 1994 was eventually recorded on 26 March, a 1-0 victory at fellow-strugglers Everton. Sedgley's second-half strike was the difference between the two teams, allowing Spurs to leapfrog Everton and put a little more daylight between them and the relegation trap door. It was a fitting contribution from Sedgley, who would leave the club that summer. During his Spurs career he had rotated between defensive and midfield responsibilities – often in-game – and had also stepped up into the captaincy role with both Mabbutt and Sheringham out.

That win and the long-awaited return of Sheringham eased the unrest for an Easter Saturday match at Norwich. Entering the game as a half-time substitute with the score 0-0, Sheringham scored within 11 minutes of his return as Spurs went on to record a 2-1 win, and back-to-back league victories for the first time since August.

However, Spurs' frailties were once again exposed when West Ham won 4-1 at White Hart Lane on Easter Monday. Further defeats at Coventry and Leeds by mid-April dropped Spurs right back into the mire and they were now in their most precarious league position since being relegated in 1977; sitting in 18th place, Spurs were just two points ahead of Oldham in 20th but having played two games more. Of Spurs' final four games, two were against teams immediately around them, in Southampton and then Oldham.

Southampton travelled to White Hart Lane on 23 April with both teams on 39 points. The Saints had looked doomed all season and had never been out of the bottom six, but came into the game in much better form than Spurs. Ardiles made three changes, bringing back Barmby, Nethercott and Samways for Scott, Rosenthal and Dozzell. Once Sedgley scored after just five minutes – his final goal for the club – Spurs played with greater freedom and then added two more after the break to record their first home league win in 15 games dating back to the victory over Everton in October.

Once again, no momentum could be built when they lost the next game at Wimbledon on the same day that Sheffield United, Southampton and Oldham all picked up points. Spurs were now just one point above the trap door and, aside from already doomed Swindon, were one of seven teams in very real danger of occupying the other two relegation places going into May – and they faced one of them, Oldham, in their penultimate game of the season.

Boundary Park was not a happy hunting ground for Spurs, who had lost on their last two league visits, and the game was billed as a 'relegation shoot-out'. Oldham knew that defeat would all but relegate them but a win would leapfrog them above Spurs. To add to the drama the game was in danger of postponement following torrential rain throughout the day but was deemed playable, though the pitch was in a terrible condition.

Barmby and Anderton both missed out again through injury, meaning Ardiles's attacking options were limited. Sheringham was partnered in attack with Rosenthal but it was Spurs' two homegrown central midfielders, Vinny Samways and David Howells, who scored the decisive goals. Samways scored what proved to be his final, and arguably his most important, Spurs goal towards the end of the first half.

The goal gave Spurs something to hold onto but they dominated possession throughout the second half and therefore restricted the home team. Spurs continued to look assured and deservedly scored a second through Howells 15 minutes from time. The goal provided an impregnable cushion in the match and Spurs saw out the remaining time to record a win that ultimately kept them in the division.

Howells, who scored the all-important second goal at Oldham, always felt confident that Spurs would survive:

> I'd been out injured from November and only got back into the team at the start of April but I don't ever recall being particularly worried that we'd go down. Both Teddy and Mabbsy were out for so long that once they returned we suddenly had a lot more experience and quality in the team. I do remember Alan Sugar hosting a meeting for us at one point and he was great, to be fair. He was good in those situations.
>
> The motivation for the Oldham game was easy – we knew that if we won, we'd send them down and there was an air of confidence as soon as we got out on the pitch. We played really well that night and kept the ball away from them even though the surface was dreadful.

The final game of the season – a home match against QPR – provided a moment for careful reflection and collective relief. In a fitting end to the season Spurs were beaten 2-1 on a cold and wet afternoon in north London. It was yet another home defeat – the ninth of the season, and a measly four home league wins was by a considerable margin the worst total in the club's history (six was the previous worst in 1975/6). Spurs finished the season in 15th place with 45 points – seven less than they had achieved two years earlier. Their opponents on the final day, QPR, managed by Gerry Francis, had now finished above Spurs for three consecutive seasons despite having far less resources available.

Mike Leigh summarises the combination of apathy and concern as the season culminated in near disaster:

> We were bang in trouble particularly as we failed to beat other teams near the bottom like Sheffield United and Ipswich before a big win against Southampton at home who also just avoided the drop. Also, the attendances, despite now being in the Premier League era, were poor for us. We got as low as 17k for a couple of home games. We went into the Oldham away game knowing that a defeat would mean we would go into the last game of the season needing to probably win (we lost that game at home to QPR who finished 15 points ahead of us!).
>
> Oldham were two points below us too so it felt like a relegation decider as they went down. I have interviewed Vinny Samways, Gary Mabbutt and Darren Anderton for *The Spurs Show* and they were all aware of the importance of this game. It was incredible how low we had sunk despite all the razzmatazz of the new league and how we were so off the pace as a club despite Sugar being part of its inception.

The previous summer had created off-field drama the moment the season had ended and 1994 would prove to be equally as unsettling. Following the fallout from the Venables court cases, internal investigations launched by Sugar uncovered a number of irregularities relating to alleged illegal payments made to players under the previous regime. All records were proactively submitted to the FA who conducted their own investigation. The alleged illegal payments in question related to 40 cases of malpractice between 1985 and 1989.

On 12 May 1994, less than a week after the end of the season, the FA formally charged Spurs with misconduct for the alleged irregular payment to a number of players and revealed that relegation was a very real punishment available to them; there were contingencies already in place to reinstate Sheffield United. After an agonising four-week wait the FA Commission gave their verdict in mid-June. The punishment wasn't outright relegation but it might well have been for the following season. A 12-point deduction was issued for the upcoming season, Spurs were banned from participating in the FA Cup and also fined a record £600,000.

Despite the turmoil, the situation did provide an opportunity for Alan Sugar to demonstrate to supporters his qualities as chairman to fight the perceived injustice. Sugar described the outcome as evidence of a clear vendetta against the club and him, and instantly submitted an appeal. By mid-July the FA's Appeal Panel had determined that the points deduction should be halved to six, though the FA Cup ban was upheld and the fine more than doubled to £1.5m. Sugar was adamant that he would continue to fight the very premise of the punishment and was bullish in his assertion that the punishment would be overturned, as David Howells remembers:

> He was very clear from the outset that the punishments wouldn't be enforceable and that was persuasive enough for us. As a result, we never really thought too much about it but I understand the uncertainty of the fans who were reading all about it in the news.

The fact remained that Spurs had suffered their worst league performance in a generation. It is unfathomable looking through the prism of top-flight football in the 2020s that a Spurs manager could survive such a horrific season but perhaps the frequency of significant injuries to key players saved him. Ardiles would therefore have a new season to prepare for and 1994/95 would be no less dramatic than the previous campaign.

1994/95 – WALKING IN A KLINSMANN WONDERLAND

WALKER
AUSTIN MABBUTT CALDERWOOD CAMPBELL
ANDERTON POPESCU HOWELLS BARMBY
SHERINGHAM KLINSMANN

HOW I SAW IT:

This season, coinciding with my Year 9 at school, continues to be one of my most vividly remembered. My memories are full of technicolour and produced a range of emotional highs and lows as I looked to raise my profile at school with some startlingly ill-conceived plans to impress girls that were as ineffective and unsustainable as Ossie Ardiles's Famous Five experiment.

In 1994 the most accessible source of football information came from Teletext, the primitive form of the internet that was available via a TV set. During the off-season I would regularly check in, hoping to learn of a new transfer, and to my pleasant surprise I discovered that we had agreed a deal for Ilie Dumitrescu, a player who had impressed me during the World Cup, for Romania. When I checked back the following day looking for further news about the Dumitrescu deal, I was gobsmacked to read the headline:

SPURS IN SHOCK KLINSMANN SWOOP

I remember there had been some speculation that Klinsmann might be available, but it seemed inconceivable that one of the best and most well-known strikers in world football would be tempted to join Spurs. On reading the Teletext report it was clear that this was not mere speculation and that the deal had actually happened.

I was glued to all the local news reports over the next few days. Pictures showed Klinsmann being mobbed by fans as he arrived at White Hart Lane for his press conference and unveiling. All the pain and anguish of the previous season was forgotten amid unbridled optimism. There was nowhere in the world that I wanted to be other than soaking in every moment of Klinsmania, so was somewhat aggrieved at the timing of our family holiday to America right over the start of the season.

We were in Manhattan for the opening game against Sheffield Wednesday and having waited patiently until 5pm UK time, I demanded that we ring home to find out the score. Using a payphone in Battery Park with the Statue of Liberty as a backdrop, Dad was writing out the scores as my grandad relayed them to him: 'Sheffield Wednesday 3 …' – oh, not again! 'Spurs 4' – what? Spurs 4? I spent the next five days picturing how each of the seven goals might have played out. The Empire State Building and Statue of Liberty were merely distractions. New York City is an amazing place but I really didn't appreciate it. Our flight back to London coincided with the home game against Everton. Dad and I were invited up to the cockpit mid-flight but rather than question what any of the hundreds of dials and gadgets were for, I asked whether the first officer could check in with ground control about the Spurs result. Sadly, no one knew.

On arriving at Heathrow my first stop was WHSmith to turn to the first back page available. I forget which newspaper it was – almost certainly a tabloid – but Klinsmann was again the headline, 'WUNDERBAR', with his incredible acrobatic volley and dive caught perfectly on camera. At least I'd picked up some German vocabulary.

My first live experience of Klinsmann came at Selhurst Park for the away game at Wimbledon. He didn't score but we won. Later that month I suffered my most galling experience following Spurs. It was October half-term and we had our annual family break in the North West which Dad usually looked to try and coincide with a League Cup match. With

Spurs away at Notts County the only thing available in the Manchester metropolitan area was Oldham, who had been drawn at home to Arsenal. My cousin Gary Lewin had been able to get us two tickets so while Mum and my sister went to watch *The Lion King* at a nearby cinema, Dad and I went to Boundary Park, met Gary to collect the tickets and then took our seats … in the Arsenal away end.

The game I was watching was a 0-0 bore draw but most Arsenal fans were more excited about the news filtering through from Meadow Lane. Someone immediately behind me shouted, 'TOTTENHAM ARE LOSING' which generated a huge cheer. At half-time the Oldham PA announcer endeared himself to the away crowd introducing the half-time scores by saying he would leave one score until last that 'our friends from Arsenal might be interested in.' I can still hear it now … 'Notts County 2, some team called Tottenham 0'. Cue rapturous cheers, applause and laughter – "oh and someone called Dumitrescu has been sent off too.'

Midway through the second half the same idiot sat behind me had told everyone that 'THEY'RE 3-0 DOWN!' For once Dad read my mood and agreed that we should leave. I listened to the final result and angry fans on the radio phone-ins.

I was also behind enemy lines on the day that we beat Liverpool away in the FA Cup quarter-final. Mum and Dad were long-term friends with a West Ham director and we were invited to watch their league game against Norwich from the directors' box at Upton Park. I had no comprehension of the rivalry between Spurs and West Ham so didn't think anything of celebrating in the Directors' Lounge when Teletext revealed Klinsmann's last-minute goal.

In February I was allowed to attend my first home game without Dad and booked to go and watch the home match against Wimbledon with a friend. Dad had given me the responsibility of booking my own ticket and I recall coming home from school very excited to find his credit card details left out for me. I joined the telephone queue for the ticket office and went through the process of booking two seats for the Paxton upper tier. I had been planning the journey for months, using public transport, which involved a train from Cuffley to Enfield Chase, a walk through Enfield to Enfield Town and then another train to White Hart Lane. I had developed a real joy in planning and travelling on public transport but the excitement was dashed when Mum told me that one of her friends was going and had offered a lift instead.

Having not attended the FA Cup semi-final at Elland Road I don't have any particular memories of the huge disappointment other than being convinced that we would go on to win the competition – I blame Dad for jinxing the result by enquiring with his contact at the FA, in the days beforehand, about potential FA Cup Final tickets.

Jurgen Klinsmann announced that he would be leaving Spurs, in a press conference from The Comedy Club in London. I was told just before going into bat for the school's cricket team. My season-best of 39 runs was about as good as it got all summer. By the final game of the season – at home to Leeds – our campaign had ended in disappointing fashion but I was now attending games independently with friends. I used that much-planned and well-rehearsed journey via Enfield. Going to Spurs was now something I had control over.

SEASON COMMENTARY

While the legal battles between Alan Sugar and the FA continued, the 1994 FIFA World Cup, taking place in the United States, provided something of a distraction. England failed to qualify for the 1994 tournament – the first occasion since 1978 – which cost Graham Taylor his job. Amid popular acclaim, Terry Venables was appointed new manager in February 1994, nine months after his acrimonious departure from Spurs.

The only Spurs player involved in the World Cup finals that summer was Erik Thorstvedt, who started all three of Norway's group games. Thorstvedt, who had joined Spurs in 1989, had remained Spurs' first-choice goalkeeper in 93/94 despite strong competition from Ian Walker.

By 1994 the Premier League was beginning to assert itself commercially and with Arsenal and Manchester United both having won European competitions in the decade, English football was ready to emerge out of the shadows. Italy, and Spain to a lesser extent, were still able to monopolise the best talent playing in Europe. The famous AC Milan side, which also provided many of the Italian team that reached the summer's World Cup Final, had been built on the Dutch triumvirate of Marco van Basten, Ruud Gullit and Frank Rijkaard. The stars and top goalscorers of the World Cup in 1994 played almost exclusively within those countries – Gabriel Batistuta (Fiorentina), Roberto Baggio (Juventus), Dennis Bergkamp (Inter), Hristo Stoitchkov and Romario (both Barcelona).

Without the distraction of England, or any of the home nations, the World Cup provided an opportunity for British supporters, managers, chairmen and scouts to identify talent that might be suited to play in the Premier League. One of the major early stories of the World Cup had been Diego Maradona's ban for failing a drugs test after the second group game against Greece. Argentina's tournament lasted only until the second round when they were surprisingly beaten by a vibrant Romanian team that was centred around their playmaker Gheorghe Hagi – who would go on to sign for Barcelona later that summer. Hagi scored what turned out to be the decisive goal but it was a skilful winger, Ilie Dumitrescu, who also drew attention. The 25-year-old had been with his hometown club Steaua Bucharest since turning professional.

Spurs had previous for making audacious international signings following World Cup tournaments, most famously with the signing of Ossie Ardiles himself in 1978. Relocating to England with his team-mate Ricky Villa, the Argentinian would make a huge impact at Spurs but it did not herald an era of other exciting foreign players coming to England in any great numbers. Ipswich dabbled in the Dutch market to bring Arnold Muhren and Frans Thijssen to Suffolk, and Newcastle surprisingly tempted Brazilian forward Mirandinha to the North East briefly but these were real outliers.

With virtually every top division club managed by British coaches and owned by local businessman, there was still an unspoken general scepticism about foreign players who, it was deemed, would not be able to handle the unique physical nature of English football. By 1994 minds were beginning to change and the world seemed smaller and better connected – literally with the Channel Tunnel crossing completed in May 1994 and politically with the historic signing of the Maastricht Treaty the previous year that tied the UK closer to their then European partners.

Spurs had started their transfer business by generating income through the sale of Steve Sedgley to Ipswich for £1.5m and a few weeks later Vinny Samways was sold to Everton in a deal nearing £2m. The funds were soon invested into the purchase of Dumitrescu, who joined Spurs in the final week of July for a fee of £2.6m. This was an exciting transfer and an exotic name that fans had been familiar with throughout the summer. However, the deal was overshadowed 24 hours later when Spurs and Alan Sugar shocked the football world with a deal that nobody had foreseen.

Sitting on his yacht in Monte Carlo, no doubt focusing on the ongoing dispute with the FA, Alan Sugar was alerted to the fact that the German superstar striker Jurgen Klinsmann, who had scored five goals at the World Cup, was potentially available for transfer from Monaco. By chance Klinsmann was in his apartment no more than 200 yards away from the marina and a meeting was agreed between the two to take place on Sugar's yacht.

Sugar may not have known a great amount about international footballers, but was wise enough to know that Klinsmann was a world-class talent who would bring goals, experience and prestige to Spurs. The deal between Sugar and the player was done in a matter of hours on Sugar's yacht. Klinsmann had received several offers that summer from both Italy and Spain but was sold on the move to London, favouring a new life experience in a league that he felt was growing in prominence.

The news broke on Friday, 29 July around lunchtime, with most Spurs fans stunned to learn via radio bulletins or that evening's newspapers that one of the best players in the world would be coming to White Hart Lane.

Theo Delaney recalls the sheer unexpected elation of hearing the news:

> I was driving down the Bayswater Road in London in slow-moving traffic when the news broke on the radio that Spurs had signed Klinsmann. It's just as well that we were sat in traffic as if it had been free-flowing I'd have almost certainly crashed the car. I just couldn't believe what I was hearing – one of the world's best and most well-known players was joining Spurs despite the fact we'd effectively done nothing in the best part of a decade and weren't playing in Europe. I was in the car with my then girlfriend and we were in a rocky patch – she despised football anyway but seeing how delirious I was pushed her over the edge – we didn't last until the start of the season!

Using his media contacts, Sugar had phoned Sky Sports, imploring them to send a photographer down to his yacht immediately for a major transfer story, which had the dual purpose of preventing any other clubs making an 11th-hour bid. It was perhaps Sky Sports' first major exclusive transfer scoop. Far from it being a mere PR exercise, Sugar had, in signing one of the world's greatest and most-renowned footballers, gone a long way to winning back supporters who 12 months previously had identified him as public enemy number one.

Klinsmann quickly endeared himself, not only to the Spurs fans, but also to the English media who had, for years, perpetuated the narrative that he was a cheat. This stemmed from World Cup 1990 when Klinsmann had on several occasions, particularly in the final against Argentina, showed histrionics in tumbling and rolling over multiple times to exaggerate a foul against him. He had developed a reputation as a diver but the sentiments against him were also laced with xenophobia. During his unveiling at a press conference at White Hart Lane Klinsmann opened proceedings in a packed auditorium to ask whether anyone 'knew of any diving schools in London'! It was met with good humour and instantly defused any animosity towards him.

Speaking on *The View from the Lane* podcast in October 2022 Klinsmann revealed that Sugar had been very straight with him about the predicament Spurs were in. Klinsmann said that he knew of Spurs but was not aware of the size of the club and the level of support. He was astonished that 12,000 fans had turned up for a pre-season friendly in Ireland.

The World Cup winner was also quick to impress his new team-mates with his down-to-earth character, exemplified by the fact that he drove his classic Volkswagen Beetle to training.

How Klinsmann would be incorporated into a starting XI that already included Sheringham, Anderton and Barmby and now record signing Ilie Dumitrescu remained to be seen. Sheringham recalled asking Ossie Ardiles, who simply told him that all five would play. In the mire of the previous season's relegation-haunted campaign it wasn't necessarily obvious what the desired style of play was. Now, with an embarrassment of riches up front, Ardiles could install his core principles of attack.

A pre-season friendly at Watford, in which Klinsmann made his Spurs debut on English soil, had to be delayed due to the sheer number of fans who wanted to come in and see him. Fans were astonished that Klinsmann patiently signed autographs amid being mobbed. Though he didn't score in the 1-1 draw he was the star attraction, drawing comparisons to Gazzamania four years earlier. It wasn't uncommon for fans of other clubs to attend Spurs games just to see Klinsmann in action.

The opening day of the season sent Spurs to play Sheffield Wednesday at Hillsborough. Spurs hadn't won, or even scored, there in three outings since 1990. As anticipated, all 'Famous Five' forwards were selected to start. Anderton started on the right; Dumitrescu nominally on the left with Barmby tucked behind Sheringham and Klinsmann.

In goal, Ardiles went with Ian Walker ahead of Erik Thorstvedt who had returned from the World Cup with a knee injury. The Norwegian had been first choice throughout most of 93/4 having started 32 of 42 league games but with a series of chronic injuries creeping up on him it was time for Walker, who was primed to make the position his own.

Experience was overlooked in favour of youth in the centre of defence too. Stuart Nethercott and Sol Campbell, in partnership, had starred for England U21 during the summer and were selected ahead of Gary Mabbutt. Colin Calderwood was asked to sit in front of them in an unfamiliar midfield role. This was particularly perplexing as David Howells played in that position naturally and had done so during pre-season, even captaining the team. Equally disappointed on opening day was Dean Austin who had been overlooked at right-back. David Kerslake was selected with Justin Edinburgh at left-back.

On paper this was a 4-1-5 formation but in reality, it was all-out attack. As Colin Calderwood told *The Spurs Show* podcast in October 2022, "It was 4-1-5 and I was the "1". When the players questioned Ardiles on what the plan was out of possession, he simply told them that they were great players and shouldn't lose the ball in the first place!

The encounter at Hillsborough, a match between two teams who had finished the previous season seventh and 15th respectively, was the main attraction on opening day. It produced one of the games of the season and most memorable of the decade.

While all the talk was of Klinsmann, it was Sheringham who opened the scoring for the season, he and Anderton both scoring before half-time to provide a 2-0 lead. Sheffield Wednesday contributed to an all-out attacking game and scored twice themselves midway through the second half, the first a goal from their debutant Romanian, Dan Petrescu, and the equaliser an unfortunate own goal by Calderwood.

Barmby then put Spurs back in the lead but the stage was set for Klinsmann to announce his arrival. Hazard, on as a substitute, angled a pass wide to Anderton who delivered an inch-perfect cross towards the edge of the six-yard box. Klinsmann anticipated perfectly by pulling behind his marker Des Walker and leapt to thunder a header past Kevin Pressman.

However, it was not the goal that made the headlines. In a premeditated move Klinsmann sprinted towards the touchline in celebration and launched a forward dive ten feet across the turf, which was replicated by outfield team-mates.

Klinsmann's orchestrated dive celebration continues to be replicated today. It has gone into Premier League and Spurs folklore.

Theo Delaney was at the game:

> The fact that the celebration is as memorable as the goal itself tells its own story. It was just a phenomenal moment especially as all the players joined in; just when you thought it was impossible to feel even more in love with the bloke, he pulls off this celebration that completely disarmed all the criticism that had, mostly unfairly, been aimed at him by the media.

The home side scored again to make the remainder of the game interesting but it was not the end of the drama for Klinsmann that afternoon. In an aerial battle with Des Walker the pair accidentally clashed heads and Klinsmann was knocked unconscious and had to leave the field on a stretcher. Seven goals, a win for Spurs, spectacular goals and added drama – this was the epitome of not just Ossie Ardiles's vision for free-flowing football but was everything Spurs were supposed to be about.

Mark Jacob was at Hillsborough:

> This was exactly what Spurs were all about – it was the club that I had fallen in love with all those years ago and made me fall back in love with them. We were brought up on the notion that 'the game is about glory' and to win 4-3 with the best striker in the world scoring the winner was football utopia; it was as good as it could get. It is our DNA.

In the midweek Everton came to White Hart Lane and were dispatched by another Klinsmann masterclass. Midway through the first half with the ball bouncing around in the Everton penalty area Klinsmann leapt and acrobatically scissor-kicked a stunning volley. He then added a second with a carefully placed header. Klinsmann repeated his diving celebration with all players joining in. Everton did pull one back early in the second half but it was a second successive win – the first time Spurs had won their opening two games of the season since 1980 (when Ardiles had been a player).

The only disappointment was Sheringham's penalty miss. With the crowd imploring him to let Klinsmann take it to mark his home debut with a hat-trick, Sheringham, the captain in Mabbutt's omission, and designated penalty taker since he joined the club, ballooned his effort over the bar.

Three days later champions Manchester United came to White Hart Lane in a game that would give a better indication as to Spurs' credentials. Although United won 1-0 Spurs played well and deserved something from the game. Klinsmann had a goal wrongly ruled out for offside and Sheringham had a second-half penalty saved, but Spurs couldn't force an equaliser.

Despite the defeat the vibe among the home fans had changed completely since the end of the previous season though only 24,000 fans were there to see the visit of United. The reason for this was that the South Stand had begun its significant rebuild over the summer of 1994. The previous structure, first built as a terrace in 1905 and remodelled to incorporate seats in the upper tier in 1961, had been razed to make way for a new purpose-built two-tier cantilever stand to match the height of the East and West Stands. It meant that the south end of the stadium was a building site for most of the season.

Next was a trip up the A12 to Ipswich on Tuesday, 30 August. Ipswich had been a bogey team for Spurs since returning to the top flight, remaining unbeaten in five meetings (which included the FA Cup humbling earlier in 1994). Sadly, the game wasn't televised, meaning only the travelling fans at Portman Road were able to savour a quite majestic performance. Spurs led 3-0 at half-time through two more Klinsmann goals and the other by Dumitrescu. Darren Anderton recounts in his autobiography *Takenote* that it could have been 10-0.

Alan Fisher was at the game and recalls the feeling of excitement at the performance and what many Spurs fans felt would be one of many mouthwatering results on the way to better things:

> On a Tuesday night in late August 1994, I sat spellbound right at the very back of the away end at Portman Road as Tottenham destroyed Ipswich with an exuberant display of attacking brilliance. The first half was dazzling. It's not the goals themselves I remember as much as looking down from on high at mesmerising patterns of movement and pace that tore our opponents apart; Darren Anderton out wide, Nicky Barmby and Ilie Dumitrescu dropping into space created by Teddy Sheringham, the master of the mobile, intelligent centre-forward role and years ahead of his time. And Jurgen Klinsmann up front, eager and predatory, looking like he hadn't enjoyed football this much since he was a kid. They were made for each other. I watched open-mouthed in astonishment, then leapt to my feet as, yes, my eyes did not deceive me and yes, we kept this incredible football going until tiring later in the game. Honestly, six or seven would not have flattered us. This was a Spurs side in Ossie's image, skilful, attacking and hard-working. I was witnessing a new dawn at Spurs; what could possibly go wrong?

An international break followed that game at Ipswich with Spurs sitting pretty in third having gained nine points from four games. It wasn't the points on the board that were most satisfying; the team were playing a combination of highly aesthetic and winning football which felt true to the core of all that Spurs stood for.

Inevitably it would prove to be a false dawn.

Spurs' next fixture – a home game against Southampton on Monday night – would be the first time that a live television audience could see what all the fuss was about. Klinsmann answered that question within six minutes sweeping Spurs ahead from close range but couldn't force a second.

As the second half developed the visitors grew in confidence. With 15 minutes remaining Sol Campbell lunged to make a last-ditch challenge as Neil Heaney skipped through to the edge of the area. It appeared that Campbell had just played the ball but referee Alan Wilkie adjudged that it was a foul, awarding a penalty and sending Campbell off. Le Tissier scored from the spot and then in the dying moments capitalised on Stuart Nethercott's air-kick inside his own six-yard box to inflict a hugely frustrating defeat.

The post-game analysis was full of the sense of injustice over the Campbell red card/penalty decision though it papered over the cracks of a less-than-fluent performance in which Southampton got to grips with the limitations of a front five that had little interest in defending. The following weekend those very same limitations were badly exposed away to newly promoted Leicester City, who ran out 3-1 winners despite another Klinsmann goal. It meant Spurs had now won three and lost three of their opening six but had a negative goal difference.

Ardiles was able to bolster the squad with the much-anticipated arrival of Gheorghe (Gica) Popescu, an international team-mate of Dumitrescu who had also starred for Romania in the World Cup. Popescu was a classy midfielder, who could also play in the centre of defence, and was signed to add some balance to the attack-heavy team. He joined from PSV Eindhoven for £2.9m but had not been available to play at Leicester. Watching on from the stands he must have been perplexed about how he alone might be able to prevent opponents attacking in droves through an otherwise vacant central midfield. It was the final occasion that all members of the Famous Five started a game together.

With the FA Cup ban still in place, Spurs' only hope of silverware was in the League Cup. The second-round draw provided a local derby against second-tier Watford with the first leg at Vicarage Road – the same venue where Klinsmann had made his first appearance on English soil some five weeks earlier.

Popescu was immediately drafted into the starting XI in place of Colin Calderwood, and Micky Hazard came in to replace Barmby, who had suffered a minor injury. Popescu must have wondered what he'd let himself in for as Watford took the lead within 30 seconds but the lead lasted less than three minutes with Anderton immediately equalising at the other end. Klinsmann then scored a hat-trick before half-time to give Spurs a 4-1 lead. The scoring was not over – both teams scored twice each in the second half producing an incredible 6-3 victory. Even by Ardiles's standards this was pure fantasy football.

Overpowering second-tier Watford was one thing, but it was league points that would determine the effectiveness of this radical approach. The same XI started the next league game at home to Nottingham Forest who, like Leicester the week previously, had just been promoted back to the top division. Sheringham missed another penalty but Dumitrescu equalised Steve Stone's opener. However, Spurs' defence fell apart after the break, conceding three times. It was only 25 days since that scintillating performance at Ipswich but it felt very much as though, Spurs and Ardiles had been found out.

By the end of September, Spurs were back in mid-table and with a negative goal difference. If the six-point deduction was included Spurs were in the relegation zone.

The next three league games produced more conservative performances – a 2-1 win at Wimbledon with a goal from Popescu and also the first sighting of the famous Anderton–Sheringham corner. It was a routine that had been worked on in training. Anderton would shape to cross the ball deep but instead would roll the ball low diagonally across the penalty area. Sheringham, who was the master of deceiving markers, dropped short and arrived to hit the ball cleanly, finding the bottom corner.

Two draws then followed, at home to QPR and away at Leeds, while in between Watford won the second leg 3-2 at

White Hart Lane (8-6 on aggregate to Spurs) but it was only to be the calm before the storm.

Manchester City had been a happy hunting ground for Spurs during the 90s. They had won there three times in 92/93 alone. City were also kicking around in mid-table but took Spurs apart. Paul Walsh, who had spent two seasons at Portsmouth since leaving Spurs, had moved up to the North–West and took particular delight in scoring twice in a 5-2 win – although Spurs had created enough chances that the result could quite legitimately have gone the other way. Dumitrescu scored both Spurs goals either side of half-time.

The nadir was yet to come, though. Spurs had been beaten comprehensively by Nottingham Forest in the league and now their neighbours Notts County, sitting bottom of the Second Division, inflicted the final nail in the coffin for Ardiles in the League Cup third round. Thorstvedt had come back in for Ian Walker, who had suffered criticism for his role in Spurs' defensive calamities, but was unable to prevent a horrific evening in which Spurs were comprehensively beaten 3-0. Dumitrescu was also sent off in what must go down as one of Spurs' bleakest nights of the decade and sections of the away crowd were becoming more vociferous in wanting Ossie Ardiles out. Not only had they been humiliated but their only route to cup success at that point had also been extinguished.

Julie Welch summarises the internal conflict most supporters felt:

> We all so wanted Ossie to succeed. Not only was he a lovely man, a true gentleman, but he encapsulated everything we wanted Spurs to be about – panache, style, grace. As a player he could be spoken about in the same breath as Blanchflower, Greaves and Hoddle and as a manager he wanted his team to play with the same level of style. Tactically, football was, by the mid-90s, more pragmatic and more cynical. Playing beautifully didn't necessarily generate results and sadly it seemed that Ossie's admirable approach to the game was being found out with disastrous

> consequences. Even Steve Perryman couldn't convince him to change his approach. The Notts County game was the final straw and heartbreaking as it was it was probably the right time to make a change.

It was clear that Ardiles's days as manager were numbered. Rumours about his future had become more prominent throughout October. He surprisingly lasted the following weekend – a 3-1 home victory against West Ham in which Sheringham was dropped to the bench but came on at half-time to give Spurs a lead. Sheringham had suffered the same fate as many others who found themselves in and out of the starting XI. After only 13 separate players had been used for the opening six games, 22 had appeared in the subsequent nine. Only Klinsmann had played in every game. On the Monday Ardiles was summoned to Sugar's house and was sacked. It was a crushing end to his Spurs managerial career but one that he handled with great dignity.

Ardiles specifically requested the opportunity for a press conference, alongside Sugar the following day. He spoke eloquently and passionately about his love affair with the club and recognised that results just weren't good enough. Klinsmann, speaking on *View from the Lane* podcast in 2022, felt that Ardiles had ideas ahead of his time but just couldn't work out the way to balance the team. For example, Klinsmann felt that with more instruction he and Sheringham could have been coached to defend from the front and alleviate pressure on the defence.

Micky Hazard's role had become more peripheral since Popescu arrived but recalls with great affection the brief period of Ossie Ardiles and the Famous Five. Hazard told *The Spurs Show* that he'd never enjoyed such a wonderful period throughout his playing career; every morning he would wake excited about the day's training that was exclusively ball work – even the warm-up was a circle of players around the outside attempting to keep the ball away from two defenders.

The net result was that Sugar now needed to appoint a new manager and he needed to make the right choice quickly. Spurs sat in 11th position but with the six-point deduction were just a point above the relegation zone. For the next game, away at Blackburn, Steve Perryman took temporary control of the team but could do little to prevent a 2-0 defeat. This would prove to be Perryman's final act as a coach at Spurs as he duly left the club but would later team up with Ardiles in Japan.

Meanwhile the search for Ardiles's replacement had presented an opportunity for Sugar to act quickly. Across London at QPR Gerry Francis had unexpectedly become available following a terminal disagreement with his chairman. Francis had worked wonders at QPR and it hadn't gone unnoticed that on a limited budget they had finished above Spurs in each of the previous three seasons even ending 92/93 as London's highest-placed club. After several conversations Francis agreed to become Spurs manager on 15 November.

Gerry Francis explains his move across London:

> I'd never wanted or expected to leave QPR but my exit had been manufactured as they wanted to install Rodney Marsh as a Director of Football behind my back. I had fond memories of Spurs going back to my childhood years – the Glory, Glory Nights, the double-winning team and so on. Bill Nicholson was president at the club – it had big appeal for me but I also had reservations – I'd finished above Spurs, with QPR, in the last three seasons and they had struggled in the league. At this point in time, they were disqualified from the FA Cup and also had the points deduction in place.
>
> Initially Alan spoke to me about coming in as a coach alongside David Pleat who he wanted as a Director of Football but I told him that wouldn't work for me. I thought that might be the end of it but a few days later he called me back having had a change of heart and offered me a traditional manager role. The chairman was very upfront with me – I was told that there was no money to spend but crucially that I wouldn't have to sell players as had always been

> the case at Bristol Rovers and QPR. I think he was surprised that I wasn't interested in a formal contract – I never had been. I was happy to take the job until the end of the season to see if we could work together.

In Francis's first address to his new squad, he reinforced the importance of hard work on the training ground and togetherness. He soon discovered the difference in media attention from QPR to a bigger club like Spurs and recalls that, the following day, mugshots of players whom it was suggested he wanted to sell were listed in the daily newspaper. Bearing in mind the importance of squad harmony and spirit this deeply concerned Francis and meant that his demeanour in future media outings had to be more guarded.

Making the step up from QPR, a club with a natural ceiling and with fewer expectations and demands than those at White Hart Lane, could have caused an issue for Gerry Francis. Not only were expectations that much higher, but he was also working with a higher calibre of player.

David Howells recalls how Francis made an immediate impression on the squad:

> There was no doubt that Gerry belonged at this level. No disrespect to QPR who had finished above us in the last three seasons, making the step up to Spurs could have been an issue for some managers but not Gerry. It was instantly obvious that he was very confident in his own ability and methods. After all he had captained England in the 70s. As players you need to see that conviction in your manager and he quite clearly had the aura about him to succeed with us.

While the football was never going to be as cavalier as under Ardiles, Francis is keen to highlight his football principles:

> I always wanted my teams to attack. I loved playing with two wingers. In my system everyone had to take responsibility for defending and attacking. It was

> about the whole team and not just compartments doing their own thing. Over a number of years managing against Spurs under a variety of managers I always knew they were a team that, if you let them play, could tear you apart but if you could put them under a bit of pressure you could get at them. As new manager this is what I wanted to put right and bring a real consistency level to the team. We had some fantastic players but a lot of work was needed.

Although the Famous Five hadn't played together in the same side since September, Francis's arrival marked the end of Dumitrescu's Spurs career. For his first-team selection for the home game with Aston Villa on 19 November Francis reinstated Calderwood to the centre of defence, moving Campbell to left-back. In midfield Barmby was surprisingly left out for Caskey though this proved to be the only time Barmby wasn't selected when available.

If defensive stability was what this team needed, it was not apparent as Aston Villa stunned the 26,899 fans at White Hart Lane by strolling into a three-goal lead within half an hour. Sheringham pulled one back just before half-time which changed the complexion of the game. Francis ripped into the team during the interval telling them in no uncertain terms that what he had seen was well below the standard he expected.

The talk paid instant dividends and within half an hour Spurs were level and, roared on by a raucous home crowd, pressed for a dramatic winner. By pushing forwards Spurs were exposed at the back and were exploited in stoppage time as Dean Saunders, ever the antagonist having scored against Spurs in the past for both Derby and Liverpool, found a stoppage-time winner. The drama of the match and its conclusion seemed a fitting legacy of the Ardiles era.

Francis promised a more stable and consistent approach, which ultimately would negate some of the attacking instincts of the team. He recognised the need to get the team fitter; under Ardiles, training had been exclusively with the ball in small-sided games but Francis included a notoriously gruelling running session quickly known as 'Terror Tuesday'. It generated an immediate upturn in performance; Dean Austin replaced Kerslake at right-back and Barmby returned on the left side of midfield; his role was to be fluent, making runs into the space that Sheringham would pull defenders out of.

The next two games produced good draws against Chelsea and away at Liverpool before what was perhaps the most complete performance of the season, relative to opponent, with a 4-2 victory at home to Newcastle in which Sheringham scored a hat-trick.

More significantly, Alan Sugar had won his battle against the FA. The case against the club had been referred to an independent tribunal who, on 25 November, agreed that the FA could not deduct Spurs points nor remove them from the FA Cup. Under Francis Spurs had recorded eight points and Sugar's perseverance had ensured that six would not be taken away. The outcome of the hearing, just four months after the sensational signing of Klinsmann, proved to be Sugar's most popular period as Spurs chairman – a startling contrast to being spat on by supporters following Venables's departure 18 months before. White Hart Lane was rocking – an appreciation from the stands to both the players on the pitch and to the chairman for a euphoric victory over Sheffield Wednesday on 10 December in which Klinsmann scored another emphatic goal.

The FA Cup third-round draw had also been kind. Spurs were drawn at home to non-league Altrincham. That game, played on 7 January, was the sixth successive game that Spurs kept a clean sheet – a club record. The run, which began in mid-December with a goalless draw at Everton, included a resounding 4-0 victory at Coventry on New Year's Eve and then a 1-0 home victory over Arsenal on a freezing-cold Monday night; Popescu further endeared himself to the home crowd with a first-half winner.

Popescu was by now the only Romanian at the club. Having been the club's record signing only five months earlier, Ilie Dumitrescu had made two brief substitute appearances during Francis's first week but hadn't featured since. Several players have since referenced Dumitrescu's lack of interest in defending and it became clear very quickly that he wasn't going to fit into Gerry Francis's plans. On New Year's Eve a deal was reached with Sevilla for the player to play the rest of the season on loan in Spain.

Spurs' run of form moved them up into sixth place for the first time since September. With the points deduction now cancelled there was genuine hope that qualification for European football could be achieved via the league. Spurs won the next game at West Ham though the defence was finally breached after 513 minutes of league football. This was a remarkable run and was evidence of the organisation Francis brought to the team, but they were still scoring goals too.

The turnaround at Upton Park – largely down to second-half goals from Sheringham and Klinsmann – extended the unbeaten run to 11.

Aston Villa provided a symmetry: having been the last team to inflict defeat on Spurs, in Francis's first game, they recorded a league double in late January to end Spurs' run with a 1-0 win at Villa Park on the same night that Eric Cantona infamously kung-fu kicked a Crystal Palace fan, having just been sent off. The incident at Selhurst Park dominated the front and back pages and distracted from a horrific challenge by Aston Villa's goalkeeper Mark Bosnich on Klinsmann. The two players collided in mid-air on the edge of the Villa penalty area. Bosnich's knee landed into the temple of Klinsmann, knocking him unconscious. Not even a foul was awarded. Saunders inevitably scored Villa's winner.

Miraculously Klinsmann was able to return four days later – the fact that the BBC had selected the fourth-round FA Cup tie at Sunderland for live transmission on Sunday provided a crucial 24-hour additional recovery time. Klinsmann scored twice in a 4-1 win with Sheringham and an own goal making up the goals – the scoresheet was completed by ex-Spurs youngster Phil Gray scoring for Sunderland. The draw for the next round provided a home tie with Southampton.

The feel-good factor continued into February. Blackburn were top of the table and with the most expensive strike force in

English Football (Alan Shearer and Chris Sutton) seemed well equipped to end Manchester United's dominance. For Spurs it was an opportunity to test their credentials and measure their ability to beat the best teams.

They didn't disappoint and produced a thrilling 3-1 victory that provided genuine hope that European qualification might be the least of Spurs' ambitions. Klinsmann and Anderton had given Spurs a half-time lead but the pick of the goals was Barmby's stooping header to round off the scoring in the second half. It was a beautiful team goal that Ardiles would have been proud of. That Spurs would finish the game so strongly vindicated the additional fitness work that Francis had introduced.

However, the victory over Blackburn proved to be the only win in February. Draws at Chelsea and then at home to Southampton in the FA Cup were followed up by a disappointing home defeat at the hands of Wimbledon, which was made all the worse by a double injury to Sol Campbell and Popescu in the same phase of play. Campbell would not play again until May and Popescu until April.

The 1-1 home draw against Southampton resulted in a replay at The Dell on 1 March. There was a growing feeling that, having been initially banned from the competition, Spurs' name might just be on the cup. Gerry Francis was keen for his team not to get carried away in the hype. Francis had been so concerned about Le Tissier that he had selected Stuart Nethercott to play in midfield to man-mark him. The plan backfired and Spurs still found themselves 2-0 down approaching half-time. With just over 45 minutes to salvage a desperate situation Francis made a radical decision to rip up his game plan and replace Nethercott with Ronny Rosenthal in what proved to be one of the most inspired substitutions of the decade.

The Israeli had been no more than a peripheral figure that season. Virtually forgotten completely under Ardiles he had made some fleeting appearances as a sub and occasionally deputised on the left side of midfield for Francis. His reputation before joining Spurs had been that of an inconsistent player capable of anything between the sublime and ridiculous.

Twelve minutes into the second half he pulled a goal back with a sweet left-foot half-volley at the near post. Within two minutes he had equalised with a thunderbolt shot from 25 yards that flew inside the near post.

The final 31 minutes were end-to-end with both teams going close to a winner. Instead, the game went to extra time but the night was Rosenthal's. Just before half-time he picked the ball up just inside the Southampton half. Untracked, he progressed towards the edge of the area before unleashing a swerving effort from 30 yards. The ball seemed to deceive Bruce Grobbelaar in the Southampton goal, as he almost waved it into the top corner. The jaw-dropping look on Rosenthal's face was as much in astonishment as it was delight.

The home team chased the game in a frantic final period but on three occasions Spurs were able to pick them apart on the counterattack. Sheringham, Barmby and finally Anderton scored to produce an emphatic 6-2 victory. Rosenthal had to convince the referee that he had indeed scored a hat-trick before obtaining the match ball at full-time. He had entered Spurs folklore.

Victory over Southampton produced a quarter-final tie away to Liverpool. Between the two cup games Spurs recorded a draw at Nottingham Forest before a comfortable home win against Ipswich. The four points pushed Spurs into sixth place, just one position off a UEFA Cup qualification spot. European football was therefore available down two avenues as the season entered its final quarter.

The Nethercott man-marking experiment was not used again. With Popescu out, Rosenthal won a starting place, which allowed Anderton to play centrally alongside Howells.

Historically a graveyard even for the best Tottenham teams, Anfield had been more welcoming recently. Spurs had won and drawn the last two meetings and travelled to Merseyside on 11 March in good confidence and with a huge away following that took the whole lower tier of the Anfield Road stand.

Just as he had in the league game back in November, Robbie Fowler put Liverpool ahead, in the 39th minute. Spurs fought back instantly and just on the stroke of half-time Teddy Sheringham scored one of his best Spurs goals. Klinsmann controlled a forward pass on the edge of the Liverpool penalty area. The ball initially got stuck under his feet so by the time he had it under control he was facing away from goal. Sheringham had made a run to his left and the ball was laid off just to the edge of the D where the England striker placed the ball perfectly, using the inside of his right foot to guide the ball in off the near post. The goal was scored in front of the away end amidst scenes of jubilation.

The second half was a cagey affair; the home side dominated possession but failed to create any clear chances. Spurs' superior fitness began to take effect and with two minutes remaining the crucial moment occurred. Spurs won possession from a Liverpool throw-in deep inside their own half. Anderton's forward pass was deftly flicked by Sheringham into the penalty area and into the path of Klinsmann, who controlled the ball with his first touch and swept the ball into the corner with his second for a famous winner. The raw emotion of the goal almost caused Klinsmann to be sick. He has since listed the goal as his favourite in a Spurs shirt. In a touching gesture, even the Kop stand remained behind at the final whistle to applaud Spurs.

For many Spurs fans the win at Anfield was as spectacular as the 1991 FA Cup semi-final had been. Spurs fan Steffan Chirazi, now co-host of *The Game is About Glory* podcast, was at the game:

> I was going through some deep personal stuff, and remember vividly hoping upon hope that MY Spurs could deliver a slice of escape, happiness and glory. This was Anfield. Such things didn't really happen for us there. I can still replay the Sheringham equaliser like a YouTube clip. We were behind that goal, just above the top-left (our perspective) of the goal, so Klinsmann's lay-off for Teddy to curl that superlative equaliser into said-corner postage stamp played out at 2/3 speed, a thing of beauty. As for

> the winner, it happened in a flash, so fast, so slick, such a brilliant finish on reflection, and we absolutely exploded. MY personal prayers had been answered, much against my expectation I must admit, and WE had silenced Anfield. I clearly remember how respectful the Liverpool supporters were afterwards; in my case I was meeting some Liverpool-supporting friends outside. As I walked up to them, I was literally vibrating with delight, and my friend's dad looked at me, smiled, and said in his broad Scouse accent, 'Go on lad, let it out, Spurs played really well.' I screamed 'YEEESSSSSS' punching the air, and passers-by either ignored me or smiled. There was not one person leaving the away end who did not think we would lift the cup in May.

It really did begin to feel as though destiny was with Spurs. Klinsmann had spoken of his desire to play in an FA Cup Final just as his previous manager Ossie Ardiles famously had when he came to Spurs. Ardiles had of course gone on to win the competition in 1981 and been the focus of the Chas 'n' Dave cup-final record titled 'Ossie's Dream'. After he had scored the winner at Anfield, the song had colloquially been changed to 'Jurgen's Dream'.

The final four in the FA Cup were Manchester United – still battling with Blackburn for the league title – Everton, who were enjoying their own renaissance under Joe Royle, and either Crystal Palace or Wolves (the latter of the second tier) who had drawn in the first tie at Selhurst Park. The draw paired Spurs against Everton – a team they had not lost to since August 1989 and who sat ten places and 12 points below Spurs in the table. It raised the possibility of a dream final for the neutrals in which Spurs could play Manchester United. BBC Sports' Jimmy Hill described the prospect as a 'people's final'.

Before the semi-final Spurs had four league games to negotiate. Just four days after the euphoria they returned to the North West and became the first-team that season to prevent Manchester United from scoring at Old Trafford. Rosenthal cleared one off the line as Spurs took a creditable point from Old Trafford. Leicester arrived at White Hart Lane bottom of the table and nearly managed to frustrate an understandably tired Spurs team. In front of the newly opened South Stand upper tier over 30,000 fans saw Klinsmann execute an acrobatic volley in the 83rd minute to give Spurs a narrow victory.

A gruelling March came to an end with the visit of Liverpool in a league game that could very well have been the FA Cup replay had it not been for Klinsmann's late intervention. On this occasion, though, it wasn't the German's night. His 72nd-minute penalty was saved and the game ended goalless. Liverpool may not have got their FA Cup revenge but following an international break, Southampton, who fell to Spurs in the fifth round, did. At The Dell in the first week of April another incredible thriller played out with seven goals to add to the eight in the previous month's cup tie. This time Southampton edged Spurs out, winning 4-3 to alleviate their relegation concerns.

The semi-final, taking place at Elland Road for the first time since 1961, was supposed to be Spurs' final hurdle en route to a destined cup final appearance. The arrangement of supporters in the ground was a cause of concern. Rather than splitting the ground into two ends with each set of fans occupying one stand behind each goal and taking approximately half of each touchline as is the usual arrangement, the FA decided that all 18,000 Spurs fans would be located in the huge East Stand along the side of the ground. While numerically this matched the number of Everton fans, it meant that they had their fans behind both goals as well as on the main touchline.

Everton had narrowly avoided relegation at the end of the previous season and having started the 94/95 season just as badly, replaced Mike Walker, father of Ian, with their former hero Joe Royle who ironically had suffered relegation with Oldham to Everton and Spurs' benefit. They had rallied under Royle and were notorious for their tough tackling and determination. While still languishing in lower mid-table, Everton were, on their day, a formidable opponent, especially with their towering centre-forward Duncan Ferguson.

In hindsight the omens were already working against Spurs. In the Grand National, run the day beforehand, the race was won by a 40/1 outsider Royle Athlete – what were the chances that the outsider in the FA Cup semi-final, managed by Joe Royle, would cause another upset the following day?

Going into the game Spurs had an injury crisis; Popescu had just returned to full training and was only just fit enough to start the game but the big issue was at left-back. Campbell had been out since February and was nowhere near fit; Justin Edinburgh was suspended and David Kerslake was injured. There was little alternative but to play the right-footed Stuart Nethercott on the left.

For Gerry Francis it was a particularly traumatic build-up to the game:

> My son had been very poorly and been in hospital the week before the game so personally it was a tough time. I really didn't like the constant talk about 'our name being on the cup' – everyone in the media was suggesting it was written in the stars for us to just turn up and we'd win but football is never like that. Everton were a good team, a really tough team to play and they'd given us a real game at Goodison before Christmas. Picking the team was a challenge – Sol, our best defender, was out injured and Justin was out so we had no natural left-back. Darren was struggling and could only play with heavy strapping so however we tried, the balance was never going to be right.
>
> There were heated rows between all parties in the lead-up to the game. We just couldn't understand why the game wasn't being played at Wembley as all semi-finals in the last two seasons had. Spurs and Everton were massive clubs with huge supporter bases so playing at Wembley would have allowed more fans to see the game. We made this point very clearly to the FA but they, and Everton, were adamant that the game should take place at Leeds for a midday

> kick-off and that our fans would only be on one side of the ground.

While all in lilywhite, except Francis, expected the game to be a procession, it was Everton who settled much the quicker. They were first to every loose ball and the only team capable of stringing a sequence of passes together. Nine minutes before half-time they took a deserved lead via a corner that Matt Jackson glanced home at the near post. After the break Spurs looked to be improving but were hit on the counterattack following a miscued goal kick. Everton scored a second. It now required a Ronny Rosenthal-sized miracle.

The deficit was halved before the midway point in the second half. Sheringham was fouled inside the area and Klinsmann converted the penalty. Game on. Spurs pushed and pushed and came agonisingly close when Nethercott's shot from inside the area cannoned off the post. The ball rebounded outside of the area to Anders Limpar who had been part of the Arsenal team that famously lost to Spurs in 1991. The Swede carried the ball upfield before Graham Stuart's cross found substitute Daniel Amokachi who headed past Walker with eight minutes remaining. The Nigerian striker who, like Klinsmann and Dumitrescu, had impressed during the 1994 World Cup was not even supposed to be on the pitch. He had been warming up and, without his manager's knowledge, had told the fourth official that he was coming on for Paul Rideout. Before Royle knew anything about it Amokachi was on the field and he would then score his second and Everton's fourth to complete an unlikely comprehensive defeat for a shell-shocked Spurs.

Gerry Francis summarises the result:

> You can't hide from the fact that we just didn't play well enough on the day. We got nowhere near the levels we were capable of … the way we'd played at Liverpool or when we'd beaten Blackburn in the months before. At half-time I tried to put things right and we talked about what we needed to do but then inexplicably ten minutes into the second half

> Ian [Walker] shanked a goal kick and they ended up scoring a second goal. We were always chasing the game from then on so had to take risks. We scored and then hit the post but left ourselves vulnerable.
>
> Let's remember that Everton were also a very capable team. They went on to beat Manchester United in the final don't forget!

It was a desolate feeling for all at Spurs, backed so heavily to win a game that it appeared was destined to go their way; you can't help but to apply the dreaded expression 'Spursy'.

Many Spurs fans had already been preparing for an FA Cup Final appearance. Co-presenter of the *Extra Inch* podcast, 'Bardi' had not even been in the country but was stunned to learn the result:

> I was on a school trip to Greece and my Spurs-supporting mates couldn't think of anything else that day but there was no way of knowing the result. We'd been on a sightseeing tour and when we got back to our accommodation three of us managed to scramble enough drachma together and piled into a public telephone booth where one of my mates rang his dad. We were expecting to hear how Klinsmann had led us to Wembley only to see my mate turn as white as a sheet to inform us that we'd lost 4-1! How could this be?
>
> I was in denial and just didn't believe him. So much so that I rummaged through my pockets, threw in whatever coins I had and rang my dad who of course told me exactly the same chilling tale. It wasn't until three days later that the English newspapers turned up that we were able to discover the full horror of what had happened. I've still got a grudge against Daniel Amokachi!

Nine points off a European qualification spot, the rest of the season contained no more than a distant hope of salvaging any sort of redemption, though Gerry Francis had a particularly poignant memory of the subsequent league game – a midweek victory over Manchester City at White Hart Lane:

> I know the fans were just as gutted as all of us travelling back from Leeds. After that sort of defeat, you just want the next game to come around quickly and we played Manchester City in the midweek. I was so impressed with the crowd – they were right behind us from before the game and we were so pleased to be able to deliver a win that night. It was a reminder of the size of the club and the passion of the supporters.

That win, however, failed to give the team a lift as they looked to qualify for the following season's UEFA Cup competition that only a sixth-place finish would secure. Spurs won just one of their remaining seven league games though that run did include an exciting 3-3 draw at Newcastle and a great display at Highbury where Klinsmann equalised in front of the North Bank to ensure that Spurs would finish the season as north London's top club.

Defeat at QPR in early May extinguished any hope of European qualification but worse news was to follow. It was announced on 12 May, two days before the final game of the season, that Klinsmann had exercised the clause in his contract to leave Spurs at the end of the season.

Alan Sugar had agreed to a clause when the contract had been signed in Monaco the previous summer that would allow Klinsmann to leave midway through his two-year contract although the chairman believed that this could only be activated if Spurs had been relegated. By his own admission he hadn't checked the small print in his excitement to get the deal done.

Klinsmann and his wife were loving life in London and would have been happy to stay for the second season until he received a call from his former German national team manager Franz Beckenbauer who was now president of German giants Bayern Munich. Beckenbauer, perhaps the greatest footballer in German history, convinced Klinsmann that he should join Germany's biggest club to give him the opportunity to win a major European trophy and explained that he was their number one target.

Sugar was furious and his mood hardly improved when he learned that Francis would make Klinsmann captain for the day in an emotional send-off for the final game of the season at home to Leeds. The fans, while equally distraught at the loss of Klinsmann, were more sympathetic and willed him to score but to no avail. Sheringham did score a sweet volley but Leeds equalised to draw 1-1 and secure the final European place. Klinsmann received a standing ovation with many renditions of the 'Walking in a Klinsmann wonderland' song from all four stands at White Hart Lane.

Klinsmann's incredible spell in England culminated in being named the Football Writers' Player of the Year. Just 12 months prior, the prospect of him playing in England was fanciful enough but he instantly won over the media in his first press conference and his humble demeanour only further endeared him to the wider public. He was able to challenge the outdated perceptions about foreign players playing in England.

Later that summer Sugar gave an incendiary interview to BBC *Sportsnight* when he famously brandished Klinsmann's number 18 shirt, which the striker had personally given to him, and stated that he wouldn't even want to wash his car with it.

Spurs finished the season in seventh position but ten points behind sixth-placed Newcastle. The FA Cup run had produced moments of sheer elation but ultimately heartache. It was the most dramatic campaign of the decade with so many subplots along the way.

The boom-and-bust days of Ardiles's Famous Five seemed a lifetime ago and under Gerry Francis Spurs had shown that, on their day, they could compete against the very best.

Players and supporters alike will, however, recall the season as being one of the most enjoyable. Both Anderton and Campbell have also described the season as their most enjoyable at the club.

Chris Slegg who co-wrote *The Team that Dared to Do* with Gerry Francis explains why this season is remembered so affectionately:

> I lived through the season as a supporter and was mesmerised by the signing of Klinsmann. For anyone studying this season where they would see that we finished seventh, were knocked out of the League Cup by Notts County and lost in the semi-final of the FA Cup to Everton you wouldn't think there was much to be excited about but that couldn't be further from the truth – it felt like a lifetime following Spurs crammed into a nine-month period.
>
> Being able to go back through the season with Gerry and several of the players and supporters, to pull the book together brought back many of those visceral emotions. There is a universal affection for the season. There were just so many highs and lows – the Famous Five playing at full throttle, the euphoria of winning at Anfield, to the heartache of knowing Ossie's football wasn't going to work and ultimately seeing Klinsmann leave … but there was never a dull moment – we were either the best team in the league or the worst.
>
> I know I'm not alone in remembering this season as one of the most enjoyable in a generation and that is up against years in which we've won trophies and played in the Champions League.

1995/96 – IS IT GOING A BIT PONY?

WALKER
AUSTIN MABBUTT CALDERWOOD CAMPBELL
FOX DOZZELL HOWELLS ROSENTHAL
SHERINGHAM ARMSTRONG

HOW I SAW IT:

I spent most of the summer term telling Arsenal supporters at school that we were going to sign Bergkamp to replace Klinsmann so had egg on my face when he ended up at Highbury and we made the incredibly underwhelming, by comparison, signing of Chris Armstrong instead. It really felt that Spurs lost their pizzazz that summer; even changing kit manufacturer from Umbro to PONY felt like we were becoming less relevant.

I got more football joy this season through playing and had my best season in youth football as a central defender for Cuffley Youth Under-15, playing in the second division of the Cheshunt League, and I also got a call-up into the school's Year Ten 'A' team squad. It meant that football continued to dominate my weekends with school matches on Saturday mornings, Cuffley Youth matches on Sundays and, whenever I could afford to, attending Spurs games on Saturday afternoons.

I managed to negotiate a pocket money increase and used all my funds to buy Spurs tickets. I got to nine home games during the season with a variety of school friends. I loved the planning and booking the tickets as much as I did the actual match-day experience. I felt very grown up when four of us from school travelled from Potters Bar to Enfield on the 313 bus before getting the train from Enfield Town into White Hart Lane for the home match against Wimbledon in September. It was a 3-1 win and we sat in the Paxton upper. I have a vivid memory of Dean Austin making a miraculous goal-line clearance down in front of us.

As a Junior Member I had the option of sitting in the East Stand or behind the Paxton Road goal and rotated between them.

The highlight of the season was beating Arsenal in November. Armstrong seemed to come of age with the winning goal but I then suffered a really heavy cold and was off school the next week so missed out on gloating.

Having lost the flair and creativity of Klinsmann, Barmby and Popescu, the style of play was understandably more functional and seldom exciting and my friend Gamey missed Jason Dozzell's winning goal against Southampton as the programme quiz was more engrossing than the game.

Following the heartache of the penalty shoot-out defeat to Nottingham Forest we were walking through Enfield when I spotted a Wimpy milkshake cup that had been left on top of a concrete bollard. The frustration inside me boiled to the surface and I could think of nothing other than volleying the cup, preferably full of milkshake, high into the air. I always thought that my ball-striking technique was pretty good but, on this occasion, I misjudged the height of the bollard and, with some force, crashed my right foot straight into hard concrete leaving the offending Wimpy cup unmoved. The pain was nauseating but the adrenalin was flowing through me and allowed me to get back home before placing a pack of frozen peas on the bruise. I was very fortunate not to have done more damage and managed to play the next morning.

Dad did take me to a few away games – I have a bittersweet memory of the away win at QPR in September which Spurs won 3-2 having been two goals behind at half-time, but it was the day before my nan's funeral.

Having learned of Spurs' elimination from the League Cup among Arsenal fans at Oldham the previous year I was at least with Spurs fans to see us knocked out this year; Dad took me up to Coventry where, in a reversal of the game at Loftus Road, Spurs roared into a 2-0 lead but lost 3-2. I swore out loud in front of Dad listening to Coventry manager Ron Atkinson's post-match interview on BBC Radio on the way home and was told in no uncertain terms that I wouldn't be taken again if I couldn't control my language.

SEASON COMMENTARY

The epic 94/95 season ultimately ended in disappointment, with Spurs missing out on an FA Cup Final appearance and, following a disappointing end to the league campaign, falling short of qualification for the UEFA Cup. The departure of Klinsmann had been bad enough but Gica Popescu was also reluctantly granted a transfer away from White Hart Lane. Popescu had announced to team-mates after the final game of the season that he would be leaving, with Barcelona paying just over £3m to take him to the Nou Camp. There had seemed an air of inevitability that Popescu would want to leave. A solid season in the Premier League following his performances for country at the World Cup had put him on the radar of the continent's best teams.

The story of Spurs' incomings in the early part of summer 1995 was just as much about who they didn't sign as who they did. Once it became clear in early May that Klinsmann wanted to leave, Alan Sugar received multiple calls from various agents and intermediaries across Europe. While Klinsmann was an established name in world football even before his five goals at USA '94, the tournament had highlighted the finesse and ability of the Dutch striker Dennis Bergkamp. Then of Inter Milan, Bergkamp impressed and scored three times for the Netherlands including a goal against Brazil in their quarter-final defeat. The Dutchman had developed a reputation as a play-making striker, was a classic Spurs player and had even grown up idolising Glenn Hoddle.

Bergkamp was offered initially to Spurs via an intermediary but the idea was taken no further. It seems likely that Spurs would have been quoted a transfer fee in the region of £10m plus higher salary demands than any current player. This

Lineker is unveiled as a Spurs player at White Hart Lane in summer 1989 where the mouth-watering prospect of an attack alongside Gazza and Waddle lasted for less than a week when the latter was sold to Marseille.

Gascoigne and Lineker returned from the 1990 World Cup as national heroes. They scored all Spurs' three goals in the opening-day-of-the-season victory over Manchester City.

Gazzamania extended into the new season – a hat-trick against Peter Shilton and Derby in September is enjoyed by the jubilant home crowd.

Beating Arsenal at Wembley in the 1991 FA Cup semi-final remains a highlight for both players and supporters.

Gascoigne and Lineker took the headlines scoring all three goals against Arsenal in the 1991 FA Cup semi-final.

On-field celebrations following the 1991 FA Cup Final victory. Meanwhile Gazza was in hospital with a ruptured knee ligament.

Gazza's rash challenge on Gary Charles in the FA Cup Final proved to be his last action as a Spurs player. He ruptured his anterior cruciate ligament and was stretchered off.

Alan Sugar and Terry Venables – the supposed 'Dream Ticket' as new owners of the club. The harmony barely lasted beyond this unveiling at White Hart Lane in June 1991.

Gazza and Lineker flank manager Terry Venables in April 1992 pitchside at White Hart Lane to commemorate their achievements as Spurs players.

Durie (goalscorer) and Thorstvedt (penalty save) ensure Spurs' return to European football resulted in victory at Sparkasse Stockerau (Aug 1991).

All outfield players mob Jason Cundy after his fluke goal against Ipswich in August 1992.

Cult-hero Nayim celebrates an incredible hat-trick in an eventful FA Cup quarter-final victory at Manchester City in March 1993.

Fans gather outside Alan Sugar's Essex mansion to protest against the sacking of the ever-popular Terry Venables in summer 1993

Neil Ruddock was the most outspoken member of the playing squad about Venables' sacking. His then wife Sarah joined the protests outside Sugar's mansion.

Club legend Ossie Ardiles returned to White Hart Lane to become new manager in 1993.

Ossie appointed his former Spurs team-mate and club legend Steve Perryman to act as his assistant.

In one of the decade's biggest transfer coups Alan Sugar enticed Jurgen Klinsmann to come to England. The pair walk through Heathrow Airport ahead of his unveiling at White Hart Lane in August 1994.

The iconic Klinsmann 'dive' celebration following his debut goal at Sheffield Wednesday in August 1994.

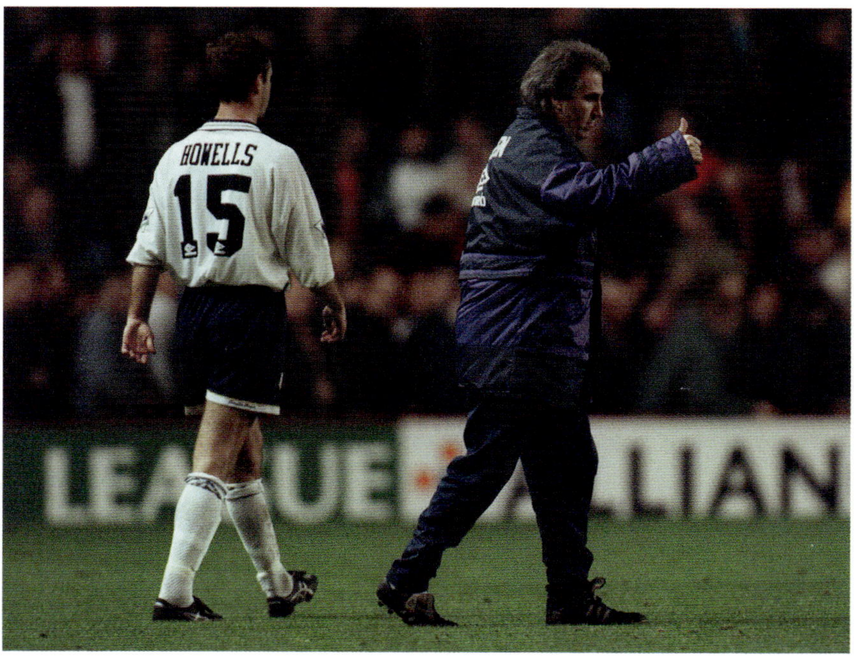

Gerry Francis made an immediate impact as manager with David Howells reinstated to the midfield.

was more than they had paid for Klinsmann, Dumitrescu and Popescu combined. In perhaps the biggest sliding-doors moment in north London since the 1987 League Cup semi-final, Bergkamp went on to become Arsenal's record signing for an eventual fee of £7.5m.

Contrary to popular myth Gerry Francis never turned down the opportunity to sign Bergkamp and explains:

> The figures quoted – both the transfer fee and the wages – were always going to be well out of our reach so it was never a consideration. In fact, Alan spoke publicly about how Arsenal were crazy to pay so much money! However, if you look at his playing style, he was a number 10 and we already had a world-class player in Teddy Sheringham who in my opinion was a better goalscorer. I wanted an out-an-out centre forward, with pace, who would complement Teddy in the same way that Jurgen did but of course you couldn't replace Jurgen!

Sugar gave a brash interview to *The Sun* newspaper before the season began stating that 'Arsenal have taken an almighty risk … there's no way that he [Bergkamp] is going to make the same impact as Klinsmann … Arsenal got him because they needed a bit of cosmetic marketing.' Sugar went on to say, 'I don't think Tottenham could ever sign a superstar like a Klinsmann or a Bergkamp again,' and described them as 'floaters' who would 'go anywhere, play for anyone who pays them the most'.

For Mark Jacob this was a seminal moment in the club's trajectory and signalled a significant lack of ambition. Along with friend and fellow spurs fan Joff Wild, Jacob set up the Tottenham Action Group (TAG) to act as a voice for fans disenfranchised with the direction the club was heading in:

> I'd backed Sugar during the toxic Venables episode in 1993 but by summer 1995 it was clear we were going backwards. His interview on *Sportsnight* when he

> brandished Klinsmann's shirt not worthy of washing his car was deeply disrespectful to one of the best players who'd ever played for us and lacked dignity; his behaviour did so much to besmirch the name of Tottenham Hotspur especially on such a public platform. Joff and I got talking and we realised that there was a lot of discontent so we created TAG as a platform to galvanise fellow supporters who felt disenchanted with the direction Sugar was taking us in. Bergkamp was in every sense a Spurs player, Hoddle was his idol; he oozed class and grew up a Spurs supporter; letting him sign for Arsenal was a disgrace; we were letting them steal our DNA. His comments about Bergkamp and how he perceived he would get on in the Premier League lacked complete class and foresight … you're fired!
>
> We wanted to articulate how so many other Spurs fans were feeling but this was an era before social media so we had to rely on some good contacts we had in the mainstream press to start getting our message out which essentially was to publicly challenge the lack of direction coming from the top. In the very early days of the internet, I created the website www.sugarout.com as a platform; amusingly Tate and Lyle wanted to buy the domain name from us!

It wasn't just Arsenal stealing a march on Spurs as, across London, Glenn Hoddle was able to attract another Dutchman, Ruud Gullit, to join Chelsea. Although he was 33, Gullit was as stellar a name as Klinsmann, having captained the Dutch team to their glorious Euro '88 campaign and then being part of the famous AC Milan side that won three Serie A titles and the European Cup twice.

Both Bergkamp and Gullit would have a profound effect on their respective new clubs – the latter becoming a player-manager within 12 months – while Spurs continued to seek value in the transfer market and stuck to a predominantly British squad with little innovation.

In many ways Spurs were ahead of the curve with the three foreign signings in 1994 but 12 months on – Klinsmann and Popescu had departed at the first opportunity and Dumitrescu had not worked out – it felt as though Spurs were reluctant to continue with an innovation they had started. This oversight, in hindsight, feels the same as if Christopher Columbus, having discovered the New World, had decided to return from across the Atlantic and explore the Channel Islands instead.

In summer 1994 Blackburn had broken the British transfer record with the £5m signing of Chris Sutton. This seemed an extraordinary amount of money but the striker's arrival had contributed to Blackburn's league title. The initial commercial success of the Premier League meant that money was more readily available to spend on transfers and wages with strikers, as ever, commanding the biggest fees. Domestically strikers were in high demand. Stan Collymore, who had scored 22 goals for Nottingham Forest and won his first full England cap, joined Liverpool for a new British record fee of £8.5m.

Les Ferdinand was another forward on the move. Having played for Francis at QPR, the striker, a boyhood Spurs fan, was the manager's first choice but the £6m price tag was too much and he instead joined Newcastle.

Spurs fans hoped that Klinsmann would be replaced by a Bergkamp, Ferdinand or Collymore so were hugely underwhelmed when it was revealed that they bid a club-record £4.5m for Crystal Palace's Chris Armstrong. The 25-year-old had begun his professional career at Wrexham in the Fourth Division and via Millwall ended up at Palace a few weeks into the 1992/93 season. At Selhurst Park Armstrong continued to develop his reputation; despite his 15 goals he was relegated with Palace but then netted 22 times to help them secure instant promotion the following year. In 94/95 Armstrong was once again playing in a struggling team who would get relegated again and scored eight goals in 40 league appearances but added ten cup goals in a campaign that saw Palace reach the semi-finals of both domestic cups. However, Armstrong made the headlines for the wrong reasons; in March 1995 he became the first Premier League player to receive a doping ban, having tested positive for cannabis use.

Gerry Francis was delighted to land Armstrong:

> Les Ferdinand was my first choice but he was always going to be too expensive for us and went to Newcastle instead for over £6m. Chris was a player I admired. He had all the attributes that I was looking for as a partner for Teddy. He was young, a top goalscorer and could get better.

As a supporter, Tyrone Foster was also intrigued by Armstrong's arrival:

> I used to read *Match* and *Shoot* magazines and can remember at some point around the mid-90s reading a feature about who the quickest players in league football were. It always stuck with me that Chris Armstrong, who was then at Crystal Palace, was able to run the 100m in 10.6 seconds which was incredibly quick. We always seemed to have really slow and often immobile players so to have this injection of pace was promising.

Spurs' only other signing of the summer was the free transfer of 33-year-old QPR left-back Clive Wilson, whom Francis had previously worked with. Wilson's career had taken him from Manchester City and Chelsea to QPR and he added experience and versatility, having also played in midfield. That Francis had been forced to use his fifth-choice left-back in the crucial semi-final against Everton had convinced him that he needed to add reinforcements.

In the postscript of Irving Scholar's 1992 *Behind Closed Doors,* the former chairman, ever the Spurs romantic, had shared his concern over some of the underwhelming transfers Terry Venables had made. Referring to Venables's previous stints at Crystal Palace and QPR, he described his transfer strategy of trying to create a 'Crystal Park Rangers' at White Hart Lane. How prophetic that three years later Spurs' only incomings came from both Crystal Palace and QPR.

Leaving the club during the season was crowd-favourite Erik Thorstvedt. Though the Norwegian played his final senior game for Spurs in 1994, he formally retired during 1995–96. Signed by Terry Venables following a brief but successful trial at the back end of 1988 he made an inauspicious debut howler against Nottingham Forest in 1989, failing to deal with a routine shot from range, spilling it like the proverbial bar of soap into his own net. This error proved to be an outlier in a memorable Spurs career that saw him achieve cult-hero status with the nickname 'Erik the Viking'.

Thorstvedt played a key part in the 1991 FA Cup success and would have played many more games had it not been for a number of knee and back injuries. Ian Walker provided some genuine competition and following Thorstvedt's injury sustained during the 1994 World Cup played all but two games in 1994/95.

Thorstvedt's Spurs career was followed closely by fellow Norwegians and ensured that the club has always generated a big following in Norway. In retirement he has become a TV pundit and was one of the club legends paraded on the pitch at the White Hart Lane send-off in 2017.

Bardi, as a young aspiring goalkeeper in the 90s, remembers Erik Thorstvedt affectionately:

> Erik Thorstvedt was my hero. I modelled my goalkeeping on him. Not only did I have the kit (my favourite was the yellow Umbro one with the purple and black patterns) but I tried to copy everything he did from the way he dived even to this really unique technique he had when drop-kicking the ball from his hands from a low position and then this bizarre follow-through jump!
>
> By the mid-90s Ian Walker was very much the man, though, and Erik seemed to age considerably.

The first team was depleted during pre-season. Thorstvedt was one of many who spent much of summer in the treatment room. In addition, with England competing in a summer international tournament – the Umbro Cup, designed as a small-scale precursor to the following summer's European Championships being staged in England – several players including Sheringham, Anderton, Barmby and Walker were all given an extended break. Both Dumitrescu and Caskey, previously out of the first-team reckoning, were gaining regular minutes.

While the first-team endured a challenging pre-season, a strange combination of youth and reserve-team players and a bizarre collection of non-contracted and loan players were representing Spurs in Europe.

The Intertoto Cup was originally a non-UEFA competition set up by a group of clubs that were not participating in pan-European tournaments, largely from Scandinavia and East Germany. It was a relatively unknown competition and received little widespread support or interest until UEFA decided to take it over for the summer of 1995. The competition, all contested before the beginning of the new domestic seasons, provided a back-door route for teams who had narrowly missed out on automatic qualification to the UEFA Cup in their domestic leagues, via an initial group stage, and then knockout rounds, until two teams remained. They would become 'Intertoto Cup Winners' while also being entered into the UEFA Cup.

When the Intertoto Cup was first discussed at a Premier League meeting, there was little interest in participating. The first group stages were due to begin in June when players would still be on summer recess. However, UEFA were insistent that the Premier League must nominate three teams to participate. As the highest-placed team not to automatically qualify for the UEFA Cup Spurs were nominated to participate along with Sheffield Wednesday and Wimbledon. There is no obvious logic why the latter two were nominated or chosen ahead of Arsenal, Chelsea, QPR and Southampton who all occupied higher positions at the end of the 94/95 season. The Spanish league was the only high-profile one not to enter any teams.

Spurs agreed that they would participate, representing the Premier League, on the basis that they could field under-strength teams and that home games could be staged away from White Hart Lane largely because the pitch was being re-laid as a result of the American Football taking place over the summer. The short-lived NFL Europe series included a London franchise, the London Monarchs. Initially based for two seasons at Wembley, their crowds steadily diminished and so White Hart Lane was used as their home venue for the 1995 series despite the fact that the playing area wasn't long enough. Five matches were played throughout May and June.

After clarification from the FA, it was agreed that Spurs' Intertoto Cup games would be played at Brighton's Goldstone Ground and that they could field a weakened team. The competition was made up of 60 teams with 12 groups of five. Aside from Spurs, the most high-profile names were FC Cologne and Bordeaux but otherwise some of Europe's minnows were included like Ton Pentre – the third-placed team in Wales – Partick Thistle, who had finished eighth in the Scottish Premier League, and Farul Constanta – the 11th best team in Romania.

Gerry Francis was first consulted about the competition in late summer:

> The Chairman had been reassured by the Premier League that we could field any team that we chose. It was a ridiculous schedule, especially to learn about it so late. We'd already planned our pre-season; we had five players in the England squad that summer and we didn't have a home ground as the pitch was being re-laid at White Hart Lane. We chose to leave the games to Des Bulpin (reserve team manager) and Chris Hughton (reserve/youth-team coach) and didn't really give it much thought beyond that as we were in Scandinavia on pre-season when most of the games took place.
>
> With more notice, and had the competition taken place closer to the start of the season (as opposed to

> starting before pre-season even began), I would, of course, have loved the opportunity to have a go in Europe with Spurs.

The club cobbled together a squad in time for the opening game against the Swiss side Luzern on 25 June – a full month before even the reserve team played their first pre-season fixture. The squad consisted of reserve and youth-team players and was supplemented with older, experienced players signed on short-term loans. The most high profile of these was the 34-year-old Alan Pardew who had starred for Crystal Palace in their 1990 FA Cup run. Pardew had just come to the end of his contract with second-tier Charlton and, speaking to *The Guardian* in 2015, revealed that he was approached to play for Spurs in the four Intertoto Cup games. He explained: "We literally had the youth team, a couple of reserves, and some mercenaries – I was one of them. I still enjoyed it. It was a great experience.'

In addition to Pardew, short-term loan deals were agreed for David Byrne (St Mirren), Mark Newson (Barnet) and Ian Sampson (Northampton) just for the four-game competition. The rest of the Spurs squad was made up of reserve and youth-team players like Owen Coll, Simon Spencer, Robbie Simpson, Simon Wormull and Chris Day, whose only registered senior Spurs appearances came in these fixtures.

Spurs won just one of their four games – away to the Slovenian side NK Rudar. The final game was a chastening 8-0 defeat at the German outfit Cologne, who had taken the competition seriously. The four matches are not registered by Spurs as official first-team matches, though they are recorded by UEFA. The 8-0 defeat in Cologne is listed as Spurs' biggest defeat in European competition.

The Cologne team consisted of several players that had appeared in previous World Cup tournaments, most notably Bodo Illgner, who had played in goal for West Germany at the 1990 World Cup and earned a total of 57 international caps.

Europe's governing body took a dim view of Spurs' disregard for the competition and charged them with fielding an under-strength team. The draconian punishment was a one-year European ban meaning that Spurs would not be eligible to qualify for any 1996/97 European competition. However, this was eventually overturned. The fine that was issued to both Spurs and Wimbledon was shared between all Premier League clubs – another victory for Alan Sugar.

Wimbledon took a similarly blasé approach to the competition and, like Spurs, played their home games in Brighton, finished fourth in their group, and were subjected to the charge of fielding an under-strength team. Sheffield Wednesday did at least play at their actual stadium and narrowly missed out on qualification to the knockout stages. Bordeaux were one of the two eventual winners and qualified for the season's UEFA Cup in which they got all the way to the final where they were beaten by Jurgen Klinsmann's Bayern Munich. The example of Bordeaux encouraged UEFA to develop the Intertoto Cup further with three teams subsequently qualifying for the UEFA Cup by 1997.

Back with the first-team, Gerry Francis endured a difficult pre-season. They won only two of their nine fixtures which included a four-game tour of Scandinavia and Gary Mabbutt's testimonial at home to Newcastle the weekend before the start of the season. The squad was laced with injuries which Gerry Francis referenced in his first programme notes of the season. He listed 15 players that had required treatment.

Francis's plans were further scuppered with the very reluctant sale of Nick Barmby in early August. The sale of Barmby had not been foreseen. He had signed a new four-year deal only months beforehand and was considered a huge part of Francis's plans and been involved in the first-team friendlies throughout the pre-season right up until a game at Derby just two and a half weeks before the season started.

Now 22, Barmby had signed for Spurs as an 18-year-old from his hometown club Hull City. Gerry Francis explained that Barmby, and his girlfriend, came to see him during early pre-season to say that they were both homesick and desperate to relocate back to the North East.

There was no shortage of interest and a deal was reached with Middlesbrough for Barmby to join the Teesside club for £5.25m – a record fee received by Spurs and over four times the amount generated from selling Klinsmann. In joining Middlesbrough, Barmby was part of the revolution on Teesside. Backed by highly ambitious local businessman Steve Gibson, Middlesbrough had just been promoted back to the Premier League and were just about to move into a brand-new 30,000-seater stadium. The purchase of Barmby was a real statement of intent and would prove to be the first of many high-profile signings over the next 18 months.

One player who did remain at White Hart Lane was Darren Anderton. Over the summer of 1995 Alex Ferguson had orchestrated a charm offensive to bring Anderton to Old Trafford to replace Andrei Kanchelskis.

Anderton revealed in his autobiography *Take Note!* that he had been contacted directly by Ferguson and was interested in making the move. Sugar and Francis were able to make a compelling case for him to stay and Anderton signed a new contract.

With Klinsmann and Barmby both departing and Anderton convinced to stay, Ilie Dumitrescu, the forgotten member of the Famous Five, returned to the club following a loan spell at Sevilla. He had scored once in 13 games and while the Spanish club were keen to sign him permanently, they weren't prepared to pay the fee that Spurs were looking to recoup. The Romanian featured regularly for Spurs in pre-season along with Darren Caskey and Danny Hill who had both previously been cast aside by Francis.

Commercially Spurs had been busy throughout the spring of 1995 to secure two new major sponsorship deals. The kit deal with Umbro and shirt sponsorship with the German beer manufacturers Holsten were both due to finish at the end of the 1995 season. Holsten had been synonymous with Spurs since the very inception of shirt sponsors in the early 80s. The new deal with technology company Hewlett Packard represented the changing consumer market in Britain in which it was becoming more common for households to possess a personal computer, printer and other domestic technology. Hewlett Packard signed a four-year deal to become the club's new shirt sponsor and their branding would feature prominently around White Hart Lane.

The deal to replace Umbro with the American sports brand PONY was not so well received. Umbro had been manufacturing Spurs kits since 1991 and they were well established as a leading sports and leisure brand, also partnering with Manchester United and the England and Brazil national teams. PONY, by contrast, were largely unheard of in the UK. They had begun to get involved in English football in 1993, having secured a deal to manufacture Southampton's kits. The following year they signed contracts with Coventry and West Ham but they saw Spurs as a breakthrough. Unfortunately for them, Pony was colloquially a term, in cockney rhyming slang, used to mean 'crap' ('Pony and trap' = crap). The deal to replace Umbro with PONY in a summer in which Spurs had replaced Jurgen Klinsmann with Chris Armstrong seemed symbolic of a regression that the team and brand were undergoing.

As the season approached it was difficult not to reflect on what was happening the previous summer. After all the fanfare of Klinsmann's arrival in August 1994, the opening day of 95/96 felt a far more subdued affair for the visit to Manchester City on 19 August.

Francis's starting XI was arranged largely through necessity. Calderwood (suspended) and Campbell (injured) were unavailable but the back four in front of Ian Walker at least initially looked balanced, consisting of Austin, Mabbutt, Nethercott and Edinburgh. Anderton had suffered a new abdominal injury during pre-season and so full-back David Kerslake was picked to play on the right side of midfield alongside David Howells, Ilie Dumitrescu and Ronny Rosenthal. Sheringham partnered Armstrong in attack.

Sheringham opened Spurs' scoring for the season, just as he had in the previous two seasons, but Spurs had to settle for a 1-1 draw. Two home defeats followed, to Aston Villa and then Liverpool. The latter was met with a chorus of boos at full-time, directed mostly at the chairman who had not helped his relationship with the fans over his outspoken comments about Klinsmann and how he saw Bergkamp's arrival at Arsenal.

On that afternoon Liverpool were majestic and well worth the 3-0 lead they kept until a late John Barnes own goal provided Spurs with a mere consolation. The prominent feeling of what had been lost was difficult to ignore – less than six months beforehand Spurs had been applauded by the Anfield crowd after that thrilling FA Cup victory.

A draw at West Ham did at least stop the rot and then the first international break of the season allowed precious time to regroup and nurse players back from injury. The first game in September provided a repeat of the final game of the following season with Leeds returning to White Hart Lane. Darren Anderton, who had come on as a second-half sub at West Ham, was available to start on the right of midfield. From his corner David Howells headed Spurs ahead before half-time. Leeds equalised through Tony Yeboah, an explosive striker who had already scored the goal of the season earlier in August against Liverpool – another example of a foreign striker making his mark in England – but Sheringham scored a magnificent winner, guiding Armstrong's deep cross from the left expertly into the far corner. It was Spurs' first win in ten games dating back to the previous Easter but set the wheels in motion for a spectacular run of results throughout autumn.

Though Armstrong didn't score, he contributed to three subsequent wins in September; the middle of these was a winning return to Loftus Road for Gerry Francis where Spurs trailed 2-0 just after half-time but goals by Sheringham (2) and Jason Dozzell proved Spurs, post-Klinsmann, could still produce exciting comebacks and performances. For Dozzell, it marked a turnaround in fortunes. He had fallen well down the pecking order following the acquisition of Popescu and then the re-emergence and consistency of David Howells, meaning that the former Ipswich man had been named in just one match-day squad since November 94. He had undoubtedly benefitted from Francis's training and been repurposed to sit deeper in midfield alongside Howells.

The win at QPR was marred by another injury to Darren Anderton, who had to come off midway through the second half. It was clear that the hernia surgery he had received in the summer had not worked. It began an unfortunate period that lasted the best part of three years in which Anderton struggled with a series of injuries that he has blamed on the poor diagnosis and treatment received from Spurs' medical team. He would start only 27 of the next 107 league games – a situation that afforded Anderton the nickname 'Sicknote', which he deeply resents. He rightly points out in *Take Note!* that he managed over 600 games in a career spanning nearly 20 years. Until Hugo Lloris surpassed his record in 2021, Anderton was Spurs' leading appearance-maker in the Premier League.

A replacement was found in the shape of Ruel Fox who joined in the first week of October for £4.25m. Fox, an out-and-out right-winger, had become surplus to requirements at Newcastle and his signing solved the immediate issue on the right of midfield but in the long term provided an option for Anderton to play centrally. Fox made his debut in Spurs' only league defeat between August and late December, a 1-0 home reversal against Nottingham Forest at White Hart Lane.

The new strike partnership of Sheringham and Armstrong began to take shape. Armstrong had provided five assists for Sheringham before scoring his first league goal for Spurs away at Everton in his ninth full appearance. He had scored his first goals in lilywhite against Fourth Division Chester City in the League Cup. Armstrong's goalscoring run coincided with Spurs' excellent form throughout October and November. Most notably he scored the winner in a 2-1 victory in the north London derby at White Hart Lane. By scoring the winning goal in a game in which Bergkamp was on the losing side (albeit that the Dutchman had opened the scoring), Armstrong may have vindicated Sugar and Francis's transfer decisions of the summer.

Three days later Spurs became the first away team to win at high-flying Middlesbrough's new stadium. The late goal pushed Spurs up into fifth and began another run of five games without conceding a goal. The football was less spectacular but was highly efficient and with Sheringham and Armstrong in form, a top-six league finish looked well on the cards.

In the final game before Christmas, Spurs had the opportunity to move into second, ahead of Manchester United, if they could beat bottom-placed Bolton Wanderers at White Hart Lane. Sheringham and Armstrong both scored after the break to provide a commanding 2-0 lead. White Hart Lane was buoyant but turned to jubilant when the giant Jumbotron screen, built into the roof of the new South Stand, showed a close-up of former Spurs cult-hero Nayim, who was a guest of the club, sitting in the West Stand.

Nayim had further endeared himself to the Spurs crowd by scoring what is perhaps the most famous non-Spurs goal of the decade. In the closing seconds of the 1995 European Cup Winners' Cup Final against Arsenal for Real Zaragoza, Nayim launched a 50-yard volley high into the air of the Stade de France stadium in Paris. It was surely no more than a speculative effort but sailed over David Seaman and into the far corner.

Any game in which Arsenal conceded a last-minute winner was always going to be well received at White Hart Lane but to do so in a major final and to an ex-Spurs player ensured that the incident enjoys special cult status. The goal even had its own song that became one of the most frequently heard at White Hart Lane; Arsenal fans adopted the tune of 'Go West' by Village People and, later, the Pet Shop Boys, applying the words '1-0 to the Arsenal' to reflect their most frequent winning score. This was adapted by Spurs as 'Nayim from the Halfway Line'.

Upon seeing Nayim on the Jumbotron, Spurs fans entered into a fervent rendition of his song. The match became a side-event and Bolton, having not gained a single point in their first nine away games, managed to score twice in two minutes to stun White Hart Lane. Ironically, having eulogised one ex-Spurs player, it was another of the same era, Gudni Bergsson, who scored Bolton's equaliser. Had they held on to win, Spurs would have moved up into second place over Christmas. Bolton's first goal, scored in the 76th minute, ended 602 minutes without conceding a goal – a new club record.

It was a rare moment of incompetence in what had otherwise been a highly efficient season. Over the Christmas period Spurs drew 0-0 at Southampton before finally suffering a defeat, at Blackburn, in the final game of 1995.

Over the festive period the squad was hit by a number of injuries. Anderton had been sidelined since September but Fox, Mabbutt and Howells had also picked up knocks. This necessitated Francis bringing Ilie Dumitrescu and Darren Caskey in from the periphery and both started in midfield for the New Year's Day fixture at home to Manchester United. It was a really makeshift midfield with Sol Campbell selected to sit centrally in front of the back four but yet proved to be part of the perfect start to 1996.

Sheringham and Campbell scored in the first half either side of Andy Cole's equaliser. United's goalkeeper Peter Schmeichel had to be withdrawn at half-time owing to a muscle injury and then Armstrong struck twice without reply in the second half to give Spurs an emphatic 4-1 victory. It was a particularly remarkable result for Gerry Francis who, as QPR manager, had enjoyed the same result against the same opponent on the same day in 1992. It was Spurs' first victory over Manchester United since a Gascoigne-inspired win in April 1990.

Gerry Francis recalls:

> I was obviously delighted with the result and performance – we'd done a lot of work in preparation to try and expose the few weaknesses Man United had, specifically the way they defend crosses. All four goals we scored that night came from crosses. We got the plaudits in the media in the days that followed but that irritated me a little because we'd played equally as well in other games that season and not received the same credit. On the night everything went right for us but you can't score three or four goals every game.

It proved to be Dumitrescu's final appearance in a Spurs shirt. He was sold to West Ham the following month where he made just 13 appearances in two seasons before being sold to Club America in Mexico.

The FA Cup third-round draw, for the fourth successive year, provided Spurs with lower-league opposition. Hereford, famous for an FA Cup upset in 1972 when they beat Newcastle, hosted Spurs at Edgar Street in the first week of January. A full-strength Spurs were given an almighty scare, escaping with a 1-1 draw in the original tie, but comfortably dispatched the fourth-tier side back at White Hart Lane with Sheringham (3) and Armstrong (2) scoring the goals in a 5-1 win.

In the league Spurs won, lost and then drew their next three games and also reached the FA Cup fifth round having beaten second-tier Wolverhampton Wanderers in a replay at Molineux. Featuring on the front page of the programme for the original tie at White Hart Lane was Andy Sinton, who had joined from Sheffield Wednesday for £1.5m. Like Clive Wilson, Sinton had also worked with Francis at QPR. The winger had earned 12 senior England caps earlier in the decade and was capable of playing on either wing, though he was an understated signing when he arrived at White Hart Lane. Just shy of his 30th birthday, you couldn't help feeling that, like Ruel Fox, he would have been a more exciting signing had he joined a few years earlier when approaching his peak.

The fifth round of the FA Cup saw Spurs once again paired with Nottingham Forest. Including the 1991 FA Cup Final the two teams had played each other in cup competition in four of the past six seasons. The original tie was scheduled for The City Ground on Monday night. As fans travelled up the M1 they hit heavy flurries of snow that did not relent as the players warmed up. The game had to be abandoned after 15 minutes, at 0-0, with visibility virtually zero. The rearranged game was played the following midweek and produced a thrilling cup tie. Armstrong scored twice in between two free-kick goals scored by Forest's Ian Woan, one of only two survivors from the 1991 FA Cup Final.

The replay, at White Hart Lane, was played in torrential rain on a heavy pitch and both teams scored in the first half; Bryan Roy gave Forest an early lead but Sheringham equalised against his old side from a free kick curled into the top corner. The next 90 minutes, which included extra time, produced no further goals though Rosenthal had an effort cleared off the line in the dying moments and young striker Steve Slade, making one of just seven first-team appearances, very nearly made himself an instant hero, also coming close to a late winner.

The tie would therefore be decided by a penalty shoot-out. Spurs had won both the two previous penalty shoot-outs that they had been involved in; famously the 1984 UEFA Cup Final which had been won by goalkeeper Tony Parkes's save, and then as recently as 1994 when Peterborough were beaten in the FA Cup fourth round. Just as had been the case with the two previous shoot-outs the kicks were to be taken in front of the home fans at the Paxton Road end.

This should have provided Spurs with an advantage but they were to be thwarted by an inspired Mark Crossley. The Forest goalkeeper had an enviable record facing penalties; he famously saved Gary Lineker's penalty in the 1991 FA Cup Final and was also the only goalkeeper to have saved a Matt Le Tissier spot kick – the Southampton player scored 47 of the 48 spot kicks he took in professional football.

Clive Wilson and Ronny Rosenthal both saw their penalties saved. Although Ian Walker saved Bryan Roy's effort, Forest scored their other three. With the score 3-1 it meant that Sheringham needed to score to keep the shoot-out alive. It was a decent-enough contact on the ball but Crossley read it perfectly and parried the ball away before embarking on a 100-yard sprint to the Forest fans in the South Stand.

The FA Cup exit was a crushing disappointment but it at least spared Spurs the ignominy of having to play bogey team Aston Villa three days later in the quarter-final. Forest were beaten 1-0 with the physical and emotional exertions of the epic three-game fifth-round tie undoubtedly taking its toll.

With ten league games remaining Spurs were well positioned to qualify for the UEFA Cup via their league position. England had been allocated five spots for 1996/97 competitions – the league winners in the Champions League, the FA Cup winners in the European Cup Winners' Cup and then three UEFA Cup places, for the League Cup winners and next two best-placed teams in the league. As Aston Villa, then in fourth, would go on to win the League Cup it meant that fifth place would secure qualification. Following the cup exit Spurs sat in sixth, one point behind Arsenal but with a game in hand – but only six points separated seven teams between Arsenal in fifth and West Ham in 11th. Of Spurs' remaining ten games, four were against teams in that group.

The first of these ended in a 3-2 defeat to reigning league champions Blackburn in which Alan Shearer became the first opposing player to score a hat-trick at White Hart Lane since 1981.

March provided two wins, away at Bolton and at home to Coventry, but defeat at Old Trafford against Manchester United was unfortunate. Spurs should have been awarded a corner but instead the referee awarded a goal kick. Within 15 seconds Eric Cantona scored what proved to be the only goal of the game. Easter weekend saw Spurs lose at Nottingham Forest and draw at home to Middlesbrough. The single point gained was less than all the other teams in the UEFA Cup race.

Spurs remained in sixth two points behind Arsenal, whom Spurs would play next at Highbury. In one of the least remarkable derbies of the decade it felt as though both teams were more concerned with not losing and a goalless draw was played out; of greater significance Darren Anderton returned to action as a second-half substitute, having missed nearly seven months through his troublesome hernia injury. Anderton started the next game, a 1-1 draw at home to Chelsea, and then starred in the 3-1 victory away at Leeds in May, scoring twice.

Going into the final weekend of the season Spurs were one of four teams that could clinch fifth. Sitting one place lower at the start of the day, Spurs needed to better Arsenal's result but could barely have asked for a tougher set of fixtures. Arsenal were at home to already relegated Bolton while Spurs travelled to Newcastle, who still had an outside chance of winning the league. Everton (seventh, at home to Aston

Villa) and Blackburn (eighth, away to Chelsea) sat two points behind Spurs. The final day also provided fascinating plot lines at both ends of the table. Manchester United would become champions, ahead of Newcastle, as long as they avoided defeat at Middlesbrough. At the bottom Manchester City, Southampton, Coventry and Sheffield Wednesday all went into the day knowing they could be relegated.

Spurs' visit to St James' Park was selected for live TV coverage though the focus was almost entirely on the home team. Newcastle had led the Premier League for much of the season and due to the charismatic Kevin Keegan and the swashbuckling style that his team had deployed were most people's 'second team'. Keegan had personally been the subject of Alex Ferguson's psychological warfare as Manchester United gradually ate away at Newcastle's seemingly impregnable lead that was as big as 12 points in January. Keegan finally cracked as United overtook them and in an iconic Premier League moment when interviewed live on Sky stated, 'I would love it if we beat them.'

Spurs weathered the early storm and by the time news had reached the stadium that Manchester United had taken the lead at Middlesbrough, a sense of resignation manifested itself on the pitch. At half-time the game was goalless and with Arsenal, Everton and Blackburn all drawing too, little had changed for Spurs' situation. Ten minutes into the second half the title race was sealed. No sooner had Andy Cole added a second for Manchester United than Jason Dozzell scored a well-executed goal to give Spurs an unlikely lead. It was a fitting end to the season for Dozzell, who had made 28 league appearances and played in every game since the middle of February. The goal was a reminder of his ability at Ipswich that had earned him the move to Spurs; receiving the ball just inside the penalty area Dozzell twisted inside Darren Peacock's attempted challenge and casually curled the ball into the far corner.

With Arsenal and Everton still level Spurs were momentarily up into fifth with less than 30 minutes of the season remaining.

Newcastle were a formidable attacking team – only Manchester United had taken any points from St James' Park all season. Not helped by Sol Campbell having to go off injured midway through the second half, Spurs were on the back foot so it was no surprise when Les Ferdinand equalised in the 71st minute.

By this point Blackburn now occupied fifth place having taken a 3-1 lead at Chelsea. Into the final 15 minutes two significant goals were scored – Everton took a 1-0 lead at home to Villa and then the biggest shock – Bolton went 1-0 ahead at Highbury.

This meant Spurs were now above Arsenal but behind Everton and Blackburn. They needed to find a winner at St James' Park to salvage what at the start of the day seemed a highly unlikely outcome.

Manchester United then took a 3-0 lead at Middlesbrough and this news, which sealed Newcastle's fate, seemed to liberate them. The woodwork and Ian Walker heroically kept Newcastle at bay – Spurs simply couldn't get a touch of the ball let alone try and push for a winner. Meanwhile Arsenal managed to turn around their deficit with late goals from David Platt and Dennis Bergkamp. Spurs held on for a 1-1 draw but it wasn't enough.

The net result was that Spurs ended the season eighth, though they were only two points behind Aston Villa who finished fourth. Spurs' final league position was the lowest spot they had occupied since November and irritatingly Arsenal secured the final UEFA cup spot and finished above Spurs and would continue to do so for the next 22 years.

Daniel Wynne recalls the frustration of those closing minutes of the season:

> Qualifying for Europe via a league place felt like the big achievement we all craved – in the days before the Champions League expanded (only the actual 'champions' qualified in 1996) the 'top six' was something of a holy grail for us. We'd gone close the previous season but this year we'd been in and around

> those UEFA Cup spots all season. We won at Leeds in the midweek which set us up for a position where we could still get in ahead of Arsenal, Everton or Blackburn into fifth on the final day. Despite having the hardest game (away at Newcastle) and Arsenal having the easiest (home to Bolton) we were above them midway through the second half. We played well at Newcastle but they were a great team – having gone 1-0 behind, they battered us until they scored but we still defended resolutely. In other circumstances it would have been a creditable point but all the other results, predictably, went against us. It's the hope that kills you!
>
> Of course, none of us knew at the time that it would be another ten years (2006) until we did eventually finish in a European spot in the league nor that it would be another 21 years until we finished above Arsenal again! This was the closest we were to them for a while.

Spurs' tally was 61 points – one less than the previous season but from four fewer games (the Premier League had been reduced from 22 to 20 teams the previous season). Spurs had largely passed under the radar – a recognition of their consistency but also that they lacked the star appeal and relevance of the previous season. Newcastle had taken over the mantle of the entertainers and Arsenal (with Bergkamp) and Chelsea (Gullit) had more interesting foreign players. Although Spurs had beaten Manchester United on New Year's Day, the chasm between the two clubs on and off the field continued to grow.

Gerry Francis reflected on what is often an underrated season:

> We were very unlucky not to go further in the FA Cup or to get the final UEFA Cup spot. I felt we were a really competitive team that season despite not spending much money, with wins over Arsenal and Manchester United and two good results against

> Newcastle but we were underrated at times especially having lost the quality of players that we did the previous summer. We were in the top three or four throughout the middle of the season and rarely outside the top six. I always think back to those near misses – the penalty shoot-out defeat against Nottingham Forest would have put us through to the FA Cup quarter-final and those two points dropped at home to Bolton in December would have been the difference between finishing level with Villa in fourth or where we did in eighth. Even in that final game at Newcastle we were winning 1-0 when Sol Campbell, who was having a great game against Ferdinand, had to come off injured. Within four minutes Ferdinand scored the equaliser! Small margins.

The numbers support the idea that 95/96 had been even better than the hugely emotional and enjoyable 94/95 season. Even the partnership of Sheringham and Armstrong stood up well against that of Sheringham/Klinsmann; between them they scored 46 goals from 92 combined games. In 1994/95 Klinsmann and Sheringham had scored at an identical rate of 50 goals from 100 games.

As summer approached, attention turned towards Euro '96, which contained plenty of Spurs interest. Calderwood was by now a regular starter for Scotland having only made his debut in 1995. Former Spurs players – Klinsmann and Popescu – had also been selected for Germany and Romania respectively. Most attention was on England, as host nation, in the hope that they could use home advantage to end '30 years of hurt'. Venables would be leading England, though it had already been announced that he would be leaving at the conclusion of the tournament to be replaced by Glenn Hoddle.

Gerry Francis had been a leading contender for the England job and made the final shortlist before telling the FA that he wanted to stay at Spurs.

The England squad Venables selected included four Spurs players – Sheringham, Anderton, Walker and Campbell. The former two were expected to feature prominently with the latter two unlikely to be more than on the periphery.

The periphery felt like an accurate description of where Spurs were headed into the 96/97 season.

1996/97 – FRUSTRATION!

WALKER
CARR CAMPBELL CALDERWOOD WILSON
FOX NIELSEN HOWELLS SINTON
SHERINGHAM IVERSEN

HOW I SAW IT:

Looking back, the summer of 1996 feels like the pinnacle of civilisation with Euro '96 and the golden age of Britpop which I lived through as a 15-year-old. I was completely absorbed by Euro '96 and the heroic progress of the England team supplemented by the ubiquity of 'Three Lions' and its refrain, 'It's Coming Home'. Elsewhere in pop, The Spice Girls' emergence onto the scene captivated my teenage mind and hormones, and images of Emma Bunton replaced those of Teddy Sheringham on my bedroom wall. I found teenage utopia when the Spice Girls took part in a photoshoot wearing the full kit of the team they 'supported' – Emma looked stunning in her Spurs lilywhite!

I gained first-hand experience of Euro'96 and my first taste of a workplace. Dad had signed us both up to volunteer in the Media Centre at Wembley on match days. My main task was to help foreign journalists fax any pre-game updates to their offices around the world. It was really good fun – I exploited the liberties afforded of having accreditation by getting into the stadium bowl and walking around the concourses, making use of the free chocolate-vending machines and hoarding as many match-day programmes as I could before selling them at school.

Following England felt a very similar experience to supporting Spurs. You were always somewhere between abject misery and glorious failure but during Euro '96 in particular I made a huge emotional investment in supporting the England national team. The 4-1 victory over the Netherlands remains the best and most complete performance I've ever seen from any team I've followed. It was bittersweet that the main contributor to this was Terry Venables who, in an alternative universe, might have had Spurs playing like that well into the 90s.

I couldn't wait for the domestic season to start and listened intently to Capital Gold Sport on the opening day of the season as Spurs won 2-0 at Blackburn. Now that I was able to go to home games unaccompanied, I was cross with Dad for booking our family holiday to America for the day after the opening day which meant I wouldn't be able to get to either of the opening home games, against Derby or Everton. In hindsight I should be grateful for having saved £20 I would have spent to watch two tepid draws.

Such was the fervour around Newcastle – who had added Alan Shearer for a world-record fee of £15m to their already bulging array of forwards – Dad requested that he come with me to the home game on 7 September which was hard to argue with as he was paying. It's the last occasion that Dad came with me to a game at the old White Hart Lane, having felt that the baton had well and truly been passed on. For consistency he still insisted on leaving five minutes early to avoid the traffic and then made me run with him all the way along White Hart Lane and up Pretoria Road to the car but, on this occasion, we didn't miss anything as Newcastle casually played out a comfortable 2-1 victory.

Spurs continued to take up more of my focus than my forthcoming GCSE assessments and exams. My mock English literature exam in January provided a result as mediocre as Spurs had produced all season and forced Mum into finding me a private tutor. I did practise my writting skills by preparing a mock press release that I imagined Alan Sugar delivering to the press to announce the surprise triple-signing of Miguel Angel Nadal, Michael Gray and Jamie Redknapp – this highlighted my ability to write fiction I suppose!

My most distressing moment of the season was the north London derby defeat at Highbury in November. I watched most of the game from behind the sofa but it looked as though we were going to get a hard-fought 1-1 draw. Sky Sports, who televised the game, gave armchair fans the opportunity (at a small cost) to dial in with a man-of-the-match nomination. Having taken a straw poll among my fellow Spurs fans watching the game with me I was just dialling to vote for Sol Campbell when Tony Adams and then Dennis Bergkamp scored twice late on. Seeing my cousin Colin, who by now was assistant-first-team physio, jumping for joy immediately behind Arsene Wenger made me question our family plans over Christmas.

Anger built up in me until my friends had all been picked up and then I walked down to Cuffley Station where I just sat on the platform in silence trying to process what had happened. I would have stayed there all night had it not been for the hordes of jubilant Arsenal fans that poured off the next train that arrived from Finsbury Park.

Things got worse within a few days; we lost 6-1 at Bolton in the League Cup. It was a galling evening. I rang my friend Gamey when we went 3-1 down to discuss the perilous situation; our rants were only interrupted by news of three further Bolton goals.

Spurs had gradually eaten away at my optimism and innocence, and I made my debut appearance as a caller on national radio when I called in to Danny Baker and Danny Kelly's Saturday lunchtime show. They were asking for callers who were 'going to a game knowing they were going to lose' – this was ahead of our home game against Chelsea in February and I pointed out that not only were Chelsea our bogey team but that we had Stuart Nethercott marking Gianfranco Zola. We of course lost, 2-1 this time.

Despite the abject mediocrity on the pitch my school friend Chris and I got into a regular routine of going to White Hart Lane. Spurs was my social life. As house parties and gatherings at fields around Potters Bar or Barnet were spoken of among my peers, I was never invited but for me there was no better feeling on a Friday evening sat at home knowing that I was going to be at White Hart Lane the following day.

Chris, who was far more likely to have been at a party or a gathering in a field around Potters Bar or Barnet, would be dropped off at my house; we'd watch the final hour of *Soccer AM* and then be driven to Theobalds Grove station where we'd make the short train ride to White Hart Lane. The journey to and from the games was usually the most enjoyable aspect of the afternoon as we made up names for the regulars we saw on the train.

I always tried to book the same seats – East Upper Block B, which was level with the edge of the penalty area, towards the Paxton Road in the back row. It provided a perfect vantage point and only cost £10 for a junior ticket.

As well as falling into this routine, I also vividly recall deciding on the morning of the game to go with a local friend 'Jarv' to the home match against Sunderland in November. I won't be alone in remembering the time that you didn't need to pre-book tickets with military-like precision and could still go to a Premier League game on a bit of a whim as not many games sold out.

Despite that we somewhat nervously travelled to White Hart Lane several hours before kick-off, anxious that we'd arrive to find out the final few thousand tickets had since been sold. We couldn't get into the member areas with a concession so had to settle for the South Lower and had to pay the full adult price of £17 as soon as turnstiles opened at 1.30. Having spent £7 more than I had anticipated meant I didn't have enough for a programme or any food so it was a rather dull and hungry 90 minutes ahead of kick-off though we were rewarded with an early Andy Sinton goal right in front of us and an eventual 2-0 win.

I spent the final weekend before GCSE exam leave at White Hart Lane to see Spurs stand aside for opponents Coventry to record a vital 2-1 win to avoid relegation. It kind of summed up the season and the state that Spurs were in. I achieved modest GCSE results with some effort that was just enough to comfortably get me into my school's sixth form. Once again, my own fortunes mirrored those of Spurs, who coasted along in mid-table doing the bare minimum to achieve the modest triumph of staying in the Premier League's top half.

SEASON COMMENTARY

Following the last major international tournament in 1994 Spurs had shocked the football world with the signings of Dumitrescu, Klinsmann and latterly Popescu who had all starred for their respective countries. The European Championships of 1996, held conveniently in England, again provided the opportunity for Premier League clubs to delve into the international market for talent.

Until 1996 any club playing in UEFA club competition was restricted to naming a maximum of three foreign players in their match-day squad. England-based clubs had the added complication of not having free pick of homegrown players who were Welsh, Scottish or Irish – these players were classified as 'assimilated' and were restricted to two per match-day squad. The rule had wreaked havoc with Manchester United in the Champions League (rebranded from the old, but simply titled 'European Cup' in 1993); Alex Ferguson had not been able to name a team that included all of Peter Schmeichel (Denmark), Dennis Irwin and Roy Keane (Republic of Ireland), Andrei Kanchelskis (Ukraine) and Eric Cantona (France). He was further limited when trying to include Brian McClair (Scotland), Mark Hughes and Ryan Giggs (both Wales).

The rule had now been lifted and while this did not have an immediate impact for Spurs, who had not qualified for European competition, it meant that the floodgates were well and truly open for foreign-born players to ply their trade anywhere across the continent.

Across London Chelsea continued their foray into the foreign transfer market. With Glenn Hoddle leaving to take the England job, Ruud Gullit was appointed player-manager and he used his reputation and contacts to attract Roberto Di Matteo and Gianluca Vialli – the latter had just won the Champions League, at Juventus – to Stamford Bridge. Vialli was the first high-profile player to join an English club on a

'Bosman' – the other major significant legislative change that had a profound impact on the transfer market.

Jean-Marc Bosman had been a journeyman Belgian footballer who in 1990 hoped to transfer to French club Dunkerque. Under the terms of his contract, which had just expired, Bosman had no freedom to be registered as a Dunkerque player without the consent of his current club, RFC Liege. As an agreed transfer fee could not be reached between the two clubs, Bosman was unable to move to Dunkerque and was not wanted at Liege.

The antiquated transfer system that existed across Europe restricted players' movement and was now successfully challenged in the European Court of Justice, who ruled that players should be free to move when their contracts had expired.

The outcome of this ruling was that any player, at the conclusion of their contract, was quite literally free to join any other club. Agents, aware of their client's market value, could simply request that the redundant transfer fee be paid directly to the player either as a one-off enticement and/or spread across the length of the contract as an inflated salary.

Far from being a 'free' transfer, the biggest summer story was the world-record fee that took Alan Shearer from Blackburn to his native North East to join Newcastle. The £15m Newcastle paid was nearly double the previous record fee between English sides and signalled the intent at St James' Park to go one better than their second-place finish in 1996. A few miles away in the North East Middlesbrough pulled off one of the shocks of the summer by signing Vialli's club and international strike partner Fabrizio Ravanelli for over £8m. The Brazilian midfielder Emerson joined from Porto for £4m to link up with compatriot Juninho, who had emerged as one of the brightest young talents coming out of South America and had moved to Middlesbrough in the previous October. It is hard to imagine a part of England more incongruous with the tropical shores of Brazil than Middlesbrough, yet chairman Steve Gibson had found the funds and been able to sell the charms of Teesside to both.

The Czech Republic were the surprise package of Euro '96 and two of their outstanding performers, Patrik Berger and Karel Poborsky, made their way to Liverpool and Manchester United respectively. Alex Ferguson also signed Jordi Cruyff, son of the Dutch legend Johan, from Barcelona and moved quickly to bring the highly rated young Norwegian striker Ole Gunnar Solskjaer to Old Trafford.

Spurs' biggest financial investment of the summer was real estate. Prior to 1987 Spurs had their own training ground located in Cheshunt, in Hertfordshire. The plot of land was adjacent to a new Tesco supermarket and the price was too good to turn down when an offer came in to develop a new housing estate on the site. Amid Spurs' financial situation in the late 80s the club decided to lease an alternative training ground, eventually settling on the Chase Lodge base in Mill Hill that was owned by Camden Council. This consisted of a Grade II listed 19th-century house – a rabbit warren of corridors and staircases that housed the changing rooms and manager's office – and three full-sized football pitches that were shared by amateur football teams at weekends. Medical facilities were even more rudimentary. Club physio John Sheridan joined the club in 1986 with David Pleat and oversaw the initial transition to Chase Lodge. He described in his 2020 book *The Limping Physio* the lengths that he had to go to make the new facility operational: 'after scouring the adverts in Exchange & Mart, Tottenham bought two old Portakabins directly from a North Sea oil rig.'

Alan Sugar was understandably keen to have a permanent training base and the club purchased a 24-acre plot of land at the bottom of Luxborough Lane in Chigwell, a short drive away from White Hart Lane and in a salubrious part of Essex that was home to many millionaires and footballers. The new training base, named Spurs Lodge, would be able to host the first-team and reserves as well as the burgeoning Centre of Excellence that developed Spurs' celebrated youth teams. It was a significant upgrade in facilities and also ensured that the club now owned their training facilities rather than leasing pitches from the local authority as had been the case in Mill Hill.

By this time in the 90s the more aspirational and progressive clubs were modernising their training facilities to try and match those that were operating across the continent. Mill Hill had never been a permanent Spurs base even though it had been home to the likes of Waddle, Gascoigne, Lineker and Klinsmann.

For Gerry Francis the new training facility was a sign of progress:

> For a start it was our own. The old place in Mill Hill was a shared council facility; we had no privacy there at all and the facilities were ancient. Spurs Lodge was much needed and provided a far more professional setting for both the players and for me and the management team.

David Howells describes the difference:

> The training ground is more significant for players than you might think. We only really travel to the stadium for match days so it's the training ground that we come into most days. I have many fond memories of Mill Hill and we got used to it but the changing facilities were dilapidated and the pitches were basically just public pitches that were used by amateur teams at the weekend. You didn't really know any different at the time but the first-team pitches were right next to the main road so there was no secrecy. We'd regularly look up to see dozens of people yards away from us watching and trying to ask for autographs during the middle of training!
>
> Moving into Spurs Lodge in Chigwell was like stepping into the future. It was secluded and it was branded so it felt like home. The pitches were magnificent, and you instantly felt that you were now in a professional environment. The chairman was rightly extremely proud of the new facility. In hindsight we learned that it perhaps didn't provide

> all the facilities that a modern coach with foreign players needed but these came later. We were all very impressed with Spurs Lodge and it must have helped attract new players to the club.

The opening of Spurs Lodge would be essential to providing a more professional and elite set-up. Speaking at the official opening, conducted by Tony Blair, Alan Sugar described Spurs Lodge as 'a first-class facility with five first-class pitches and a great new changing room and medical facilities'. In the interview, which is featured on the club's official end-of-season review video, Sugar was at pains to point out that the cost of the training facility was a fraction of the cost of an expensive signing but that funds for players were and had always been made available.

Spurs' modest moves into the transfer market initially saw just two incoming players. The Danish midfielder Allan Nielsen joined from Brondby for £1.65m. Describing his new signing in his programme notes for the opening home game of the season, Francis stated: 'He is a player who impressed me last season while playing for Brondby, including a UEFA Cup run that saw the Danish club beat Liverpool … he is a player with lots of experience of European football as well as international football and he will be a great addition to our squad.'

The second signing was also a Scandinavian and saw 19-year-old Norwegian goalkeeper Espen Baardsen follow in the footsteps of Erik Thorstvedt who had retired the previous season. Baardsen would become Ian Walker's understudy as Chris Day also left the club to seek first-team opportunities at Crystal Palace. At least, unlike the previous summer, none of the team's most significant players left the club. The core of the team – Walker, Campbell, Anderton and Sheringham – gave a strong base to build from and Armstrong had proved himself to be capable of scoring 20-plus goals.

All five featured in the opening day of the season victory at Blackburn. Armstrong scored twice but the result was marred by Gary Mabbutt breaking two bones in his leg within the opening 20 minutes. The injury would keep him out for the remainder of the season. In an ominous sign of things to come, Mabbutt's replacement Stuart Nethercott was then forced off through injury midway through the second half and Darren Anderton, starting in central midfield, was also withdrawn through a niggling groin injury that once again played havoc with his season. Anderton played on stoically through the early weeks of the season but eventually underwent surgery again to correct what should have been done properly the previous year.

The injuries mounted up over the coming weeks; Armstrong suffered an ankle injury against Everton but played on, which undoubtedly prolonged the injury in the long term. Sheringham missed virtually the whole of September, which meant a complete lack of senior strikers for the game against Wimbledon at Selhurst Park on 4 September. Ruel Fox and Andy Sinton featured nominally as forwards and Spurs unsurprisingly lost without scoring. The first four games – a win, two draws and a defeat and multiple injuries – set the tone for a very frustrating season.

Free-spending and free-scoring Newcastle were next to arrive in north London. The world's most expensively assembled strike pair of Shearer and Ferdinand were up against a patently injured Chris Armstrong and 18-year-old Rory Allen, making his first start for Spurs. The young striker, who had been part of the 1995 FA Youth Cup team that lost on penalties to Manchester United, had scored goals for the youth and reserve team at the back end of the previous season and had played in the first-team during pre-season but was now in the first-team purely through necessity. Allen enjoyed a dream start, putting Spurs ahead inside 30 minutes with a well-taken half-volley from a Sinton cross. But despite a spirited performance Newcastle were by far the more fluent side and scored either side of half-time through Les Ferdinand to win 2-1.

Anderton, Sheringham and Armstrong did not start another game together until mid-November, by which time Spurs had established a pattern of inconsistent results, keeping them hovering around mid-table. The frustration in the crowd was palpable and the team were booed off following a home defeat by Leicester, newly promoted back to the Premier League. None of Spurs' three best attackers were available, forcing Gerry Francis to deploy Sol Campbell as a centre-forward alongside Rory Allen.

It was a frustrating time for Francis who would particularly be on edge during international breaks:

> To do my best work I needed quality time on the training ground with my whole squad but it seemed I could never get this. We were really unlucky with injuries. Chris Armstrong rolled his ankle in the first week of the season, Gary Mabbutt missed the whole season and Darren had constant problems. International breaks were awful. We had several away with England every time and plenty of others too. It was a nervous time hoping that they'd all come back fit but invariably one would not!

In October Spurs finally beat Aston Villa. The 1-0 victory, courtesy of Allan Nielsen's first goal for the club, was the first in 15 games, a run dating back to autumn 1990. The game is most remembered for an unsavoury incident involving Villa goalkeeper Mark Bosnich. Spurs fans had been baiting him throughout the game in response to the incident in January 1995 when Bosnich had clattered into Klinsmann and knocked the striker unconscious. The German's name was sung throughout in addition to several foul-mouthed rants directed straight at the goalkeeper. Bosnich's response was to turn to the crowd and perform a Nazi salute and walk. The incident was spotted by the linesman but drew a furious reaction from the crowd. Bosnich's actions could have been, and were largely taken, as an anti-Semitic gesture linked to Spurs' historic Jewish connections. He was later spoken to by the Metropolitan Police in response to a number of complaints made by members of the crowd.

Bosnich himself was mortified enough at his behaviour to personally phone in to BBC Radio's national Saturday evening phone-in show *606 t*o apologise saying, 'To be honest I'm a bit distraught … I'd just like to say that it was something done out of ignorance. For me it was a real joke, but it's been taken so much out of proportion and I'm so, so sorry … I thought the crowd were laughing with me. Obviously, I was mistaken. It's been taken out of context and I'm really sorry. I was being taunted all game. I'm so sad.'

Spurs travelled to Stamford Bridge at the end of October just three days after Chelsea had suffered a major tragedy. Their vice-chairman Matthew Harding had been killed in a helicopter crash returning from their midweek League Cup tie at Bolton Wanderers that had stunned all at the club. Harding was a lifelong Chelsea supporter who had invested £26.5m of his own funds into the club in October 1993 to help finance the new North Stand and invest into the playing squad.

Historically Spurs had always been Arsenal's biggest competitor as London's most successful and attractive club. While Arsenal had been built around efficiency to win league titles Spurs had the flamboyance to challenge and win cups. Chelsea and West Ham were some distance behind both in terms of on-field success, supporter base and ability to attract and sign new players.

By 1996 Spurs had finished above Chelsea for the fifth time in seven seasons since they returned to the top division, though they had a frustrating knack of getting results against Spurs. There had not been a Spurs win since the very first encounter of the decade back in February 1990 with six Chelsea wins and eight draws since. Since the Premier League began in 1993 the Stamford Bridge club had finished 11th, 11th, 14th and 11th. As recently as 1991 when Gordon Durie made the move from west to north London, the dynamic had very much been that Spurs were the more aspirational of the two clubs and had been able to attract the better players. While Spurs had signed Klinsmann and Dumitrescu in 1994, Chelsea were gambling on Paul Furlong from Watford and Scott Minto from Charlton.

The dynamic began to shift notably when, in the summer that Klinsmann left Spurs, Chelsea were able to attract Ruud Gullit to west London. Glenn Hoddle has since revealed that when he met with Gullit to discuss the deal he kept him away from their primitive training ground in the shadows of Heathrow Airport and instead took him for a meal on the swanky King's Road in Chelsea. The pattern continued through 1996; not only was Stamford Bridge receiving a major facelift but investment in the playing squad continued. In addition to Gianluca Vialli's salary, a further £7.5m had been spent to bring French international defender Frank Leboeuf and Italian midfielder Roberto Di Matteo to Stamford Bridge. These were the calibre and status of player that traditionally Spurs should have been bringing to London.

Paul Hawksbee describes the dynamic of the rivalry:

> Throughout the back end of the 80s and into the early 90s they were our bogey team – despite having the better players we just couldn't beat them and they absolutely loved it. The phrase 'Three-point Lane' was really grating but we nearly always finished above them. It was still mostly a one-sided rivalry though – when Glenn went there as manager, we'd still give him a great reception but the hostility from them to us was on another level.

Despite previous hostilities, Spurs fans respected the minute's silence before kick-off marking the tragic death of Matthew Harding earlier that week. It made it a highly emotional afternoon at Stamford Bridge and was fitting that Harding's immediate legacy saw Chelsea demonstrate their superiority again with a 3-1 victory.

At the start of November Spurs did enjoy some derby success with a 1-0 home win against West Ham, the only goal coming from Armstrong in what would be his last of the season.

If the dynamic between Spurs and Chelsea was in the process of shifting, the relationship with Spurs' biggest London rivals Arsenal was to undergo an even more profound and painful transformation that was kickstarted in the north London derby at Highbury in November. Despite clinching the final UEFA Cup spot, at Spurs' expense, on the final day of the 1995/96 season, Arsenal's board felt that the team should be aspiring higher than fifth. Since winning the league championship in 1989 and 1991 Arsenal had evolved into a 'cup team' under George Graham. The domestic cup double in 1993 was followed by 1994's European Cup Winners' Cup success. They would have retained the trophy had it not been for Nayim's heroics a year later. However, Arsenal were still renowned as being a team built on efficiency and function rather than flair and flamboyance.

Graham was replaced for non-footballing reasons and his eventual replacement, Bruce Rioch, had established himself as an up-and-coming manager with Bolton Wanderers following a number of high-profile cup victories over Arsenal and Liverpool. Rioch then led Bolton to promotion to the top flight for the first time since 1980, but left to take over at Highbury in summer 1995. His arrival coincided with a cash injection from new club director Danny Fiszman that allowed Arsenal to push through with the record signing of Dennis Bergkamp and also England midfielder David Platt for a combined £12m.

Despite Bergkamp's brilliance in partnership with Ian Wright, and the famously unyielding defensive unit, Arsenal still produced an underwhelming campaign and made no progress in closing the gap between them and Manchester United, but it was still a huge surprise when, on the eve of the new season, Rioch was sacked. Arsenal's vice-chairman David Dein was an Arsenal obsessive and a visionary. There were many parallels between him and Irving Scholar, and Dein appeared to possess all of the former Spurs chairman's best attributes while having the benefit of a more savvy and harmonious board of directors in tow. Dein had scented the winds of change and recognised that there was a competitive advantage to be gained by not only looking to foreign markets for players but also to invest in the largely untapped pool of foreign coaches.

Dein had been a long-time admirer of the Frenchman Arsene Wenger, who had risen to prominence as manager of Monaco. Wenger even had tenuous links with Spurs, having been the manager who signed Glenn Hoddle when he left north London and was also the manager who sold Klinsmann to Alan Sugar. Wenger was reportedly offered to Spurs in 1984 when Keith Burkinshaw left the club!

Although he only won one league title in France, Monaco won the French Cup and reached the UEFA Cup Final and the semi-final of the Champions League. He might have taken over at Bayern Munich but the two clubs could not agree compensation and instead Wenger eventually left Monaco in 1994. Dismayed at the corruption in French football, Wenger chose to make a complete lifestyle change by moving to Japan to manage Nagoya Grampus Eight in the J-League. David Dein had closely followed Wenger's career and agreed a deal to bring him to Arsenal to replace Rioch.

Wenger didn't officially take over until 1 October but had already recommended a couple of French players he wanted to sign, one of whom was Patrick Vieira, a highly promising central midfielder who was struggling to get a look-in at AC Milan. Such was the insularity of English football that Wenger's appointment was met with derision from both the media and even from the Arsenal squad. The *London Evening Standard* led with the back-page headline of 'Arsene Who?' on the day his arrival was announced.

The Frenchman looked and conducted himself in a manner as far from a traditional English football manager as you could imagine. He held a degree in engineering and a Masters in Economics and was able to articulate his thoughts on football and the wider world in a highly erudite manner. Having already signed Vieira, Wenger had begun to scout in untapped markets – specifically France-based players who invariably provided much better value than anything available in England. He introduced revolutionary methods in nutrition and physical preparation which were significantly ahead of any practice already adopted in England.

Although many of his established squad were initially wary of him, he quickly won them round. although his methods were revolutionary, he recognised the great asset he had in his back four and goalkeeper. He had inherited a team that started the season well and a run of four unbeaten games sent Arsenal to the top of the table before suffering his first defeat at Old Trafford.

By the time of the north London derby at Highbury on 24 November, Wenger was already earning plaudits for the way his team were playing. The back four still defended resolutely but with the ball there was now far more emphasis on playing progressively and with creativity and finesse that could be channelled through Bergkamp. However, the teams seemed well matched: Spurs went into the game in their best form of the season having won five of their last six in all competitions and avoided defeat at Highbury in their last four visits.

In a pulsating game Spurs put in a determined and competitive performance. Sheringham narrowly shot wide from 20 yards but it was Arsenal who took the lead. Bergkamp twisted inside the area and made the most of minimal contact from Clive Wilson. Ian Wright converted the penalty. In the second half several heavy fouls went unpunished by referee David Elleray, Armstrong in particular being very fortunate to avoid a second yellow for a nasty challenge on Vieira.

Spurs' equaliser was scored in controversial fashion. Arsenal had kicked the ball out so that a player could receive treatment. Spurs refused to return possession to them and from a resulting attack equalised when Andy Sinton's shot cannoned off the post and onto the back of John Lukic's shoulder and in.

With over half an hour to play either side could have won it; the game ebbed and flowed from end to end. Just when it looked like Spurs would gain a highly credible draw they were undone by Tony Adams. The fact that the defender was inside the Spurs penalty area was early evidence of the way that Wenger wanted his team to attack as a unit; Adams received the ball from a Bergkamp flick and fired a left-footed volley into the far corner with just three minutes remaining. It was hard to take for Spurs but further punishment was to come. In the final moments Wright wriggled away from Clive Wilson and delivered a deep cross to the far post; Bergkamp brought the ball under control in one magnificent action and deftly shot into the far corner with his second. This was not how Arsenal were supposed to play.

The performance might have earned a draw on another day but the nature of defeat seemed symbolic of the direction that both teams were heading in. Whenever Arsenal had dominated in the past Spurs could at least point to the fact that they attempted to play the better football but now they were even losing this quintessential part of the club's DNA to Arsenal.

Having come close to getting a good point at Highbury, Spurs were suddenly in the midst of a crisis within four days when they were humiliated in a crushing 6-1 defeat at second-tier Bolton Wanderers in the League Cup. Spurs had picked their strongest XI with Walker, Campbell, Anderton, Sheringham and Armstrong all in the team. They simply fell apart in the second half. Anderton picked up another injury and would miss the next two months. Unrest about Sugar's investment in the team and Francis's abilities to turn things around on the pitch were palpable on the radio phone-ins and in the media.

The next game was a home league match against Liverpool and it was felt that a win was essential to turn the season around. But Liverpool won 2-0 and although Spurs started the game on the front foot, they regressed into their shell once the visitors scored just before half-time. Liverpool's second goal seemed to sum up the moment perfectly; midway through the second half Steve McManaman got away from his marker and hit a tame low effort from 25 yards; the ball barely had pace to reach the line but ricocheted off a loose piece of turf and deflected over the helpless Ian Walker's shoulder. This was undoubtedly the lowest time in Gerry Francis's two-year period at Spurs.

Francis reflected on those harrowing eight days:

> I remember each of those three games but I'd forgotten they came one after another. We lost a lot of confidence very quickly and could feel the disappointment and frustration of the crowd. Spurs supporters are so passionate and we could feel when

> they were hurt but so were we so it was hard to turn around.
>
> We played very well at Arsenal and were well in the game at 1-1 with the final minute approaching. It was the first time I'd lost a game against Arsenal as Spurs manager in three years! The league cup game at Bolton was a huge disappointment – not just the result but the nature of it and then to compound matters we then faced a very good Liverpool side who could have beaten anyone.

It was almost two years to the day that Alan Sugar had enjoyed his greatest popularity as Spurs chairman after he had successfully fought the FA to get Spurs' points back and reinstated in the FA Cup. By December 1996 he was again subjected to verbal abuse by supporters.

In early December reinforcements did arrive with the long-anticipated signing of 20-year-old Norwegian striker Steffen Iversen, who joined from Rosenborg for £2.6m. This was hailed as something of a mini coup as Iversen, who had risen to prominence as part of Rosenborg's surprise progress through the Champions League group stage, had supposedly been on the radar of Barcelona and Juventus.

Gerry Francis had spent many spare midweeks and weekends tracking the Norwegian:

> Chris Armstrong had been fantastic for me in his first season but the ankle injury he picked up right at the start of 96/97 meant that he was really struggling. Even once he'd come back into the team he was always limping. The best teams always had a variety of top-quality strikers anyway so we needed reinforcements. We'd been aware of Iversen for a while and I was flying around Europe watching him score hat-trick after hat-trick so I definitely wanted him but we weren't alone. I'd often see people from Manchester United at his games so I thought it would be a difficult deal to get over the line. I invested a lot of time with him and his

> parents so I was delighted when we got the deal done. He was very talented and this felt like a big coup for us.

His arrival to bolster the quota of strikers was imperative as Armstrong aggravated his ankle injury again and was ruled out indefinitely. Symbolically Iversen was handed the number 18 shirt that had been vacant since Klinsmann's departure. Iversen made his debut away at Coventry on 7 December in a game that Spurs desperately needed to win to stop the rot. His power and pace provided a new focus for Spurs' attacks and although he didn't get onto the scoresheet, he contributed to a much-needed 2-1 win.

Before the end of the week another transfer was completed. Defender John Scales left Liverpool to join Spurs, having turned down a move to Leeds. Scales was well suited to playing on the right of a central defensive trio – part of a new tactical fad starting to be seen more frequently by the mid-90s.

Gerry Francis had seldom strayed from a back four but now had the defenders available to try something different.

> We desperately needed to strengthen the squad and John was available. He had great experience, was an England international, and was adaptable as he could play as a right-back, centre-back or as part of a back three if we wanted to change the shape. It kind of sums up the season that he came in, played twice and then suffered an injury that kept him out for two months!

Francis was also able to add reinforcements from within in the shape of Irish full-back Stephen Carr who had been with the club since he was 14 years old. Carr had made his senior debut as a 17-year-old under Ossie Ardiles in 1993, filling in for a couple of games, but had since gone back to the youth team where he played in the 1995 FA Youth Cup Final. Carr was recalled to the first-team against Preston North End in the League Cup in late September and was now first-choice right-back.

Two draws followed away at Leeds and at home to Sheffield Wednesday before Iversen opened his Spurs account with two goals against Southampton in a 3-1 victory on Boxing Day. Since that miserable eight-day period, Spurs had seemingly turned their fortunes around with two wins and two draws and now sat just three points behind their next opponents Newcastle who occupied sixth place.

For the final game of 1996 Spurs were given an absolute thrashing. Newcastle scored seven and would have had more but for a string of saves by Ian Walker. Allan Nielsen's 90th-minute consolation at least avoided the ignominy of matching the club's record league defeat recorded in 1978. It was a performance in such stark contrast to the stoical and resolute display at the same ground when Spurs gained a credible 1-1 draw on the final day of the previous season. The way that Spurs capitulated was too similar to the embarrassment suffered at Bolton only 30 days prior and was telling of the mood within the camp.

Teddy Sheringham, who started at St James' Park, described the season as his most miserable in professional football. He even picked up an injury and, although he finished the game, was then out for two months in addition to Armstrong and Anderton, who were no nearer to a return to training. Almost comically, Iversen then developed an injury which meant that Spurs had no fit senior centre-forwards available

It was somewhat of a welcome relief that the scheduled New Year's Day fixture at Leicester was postponed but the FA Cup draw had been unkind, sending Spurs to Manchester United in the third round. Rory Allen returned to the starting XI and was accompanied in attack by his reserve-team strike partner Neale Fenn – another product of Spurs' youth system. Between them they had a combined age of 38 and had only Allen's 11 senior appearances (most from the bench) in experience. With 6,000 travelling fans at Old Trafford, Spurs huffed and puffed but were outclassed and eventually outdone with two second-half goals. Coming only a week after the debacle at St James' Park it was at least a respectable scoreline even if it effectively ended the season within five days of the New Year.

Before the next league game, also against Manchester United, Gerry Francis made yet another defensive reinforcement. The Swiss defender Ramon Vega joined from Cagliari in Italy for £3.75m after some notable performances for his country at Euro '96. Vega had been close to joining Spurs in the summer but at the time preferred a move to Italy.

Having played in Switzerland and briefly in Italy, Vega was shocked to discover how antiquated Spurs, and English football in general, were regarding health and medical science. While Wenger was starting to revolutionise Arsenal, Vega found in Spurs a club still stuck in a previous era. Speaking candidly on *Quickly Kevin* podcast in April 2021 Vega revealed that on his first day at Spurs Lodge, he was stunned to be handed a membership card for the local David Lloyd leisure centre in Chigwell as the training ground hadn't been built with a gym!

Vega also joked about the incredulous attitude towards him from his new team-mates when he was seen eating muesli and fruit before training and games instead of the standard fry-up breakfast. In Vega's opinion it was no surprise that the team's energy levels dipped so dramatically in the second half of games. By 1997 this was still all relative – only Arsenal (Wenger – France) and Chelsea (Gullit – the Netherlands) had managers from overseas.

The only other foreign players among Vega's new team-mates were Scandinavian (Baardsen, Nielsen and Iversen) and Ronny Rosenthal who had been in England since 1990. Vega, who was multi-lingual and spoke workable English, recalls the cultural challenges and in particular the difficulties trying to decipher the colloquial language. He remembered having to ask Ian Walker why everyone was talking about Gerry Francis 'living in Barnet' only to discover that it was in fact cockney rhyming slang discussing the manager's trademark mullet hairstyle!

The Swiss defender made his debut, in a back three, alongside Campbell and Calderwood at home to Manchester United but was guilty of not getting tight enough to Ole Gunnar Solskjaer as United took an early lead. Iversen was at least back and he assisted Rory Allen to score an equaliser just before half-time. Spurs put up a fight but were always second best. David Beckham, who had grown up just miles from White Hart Lane in Walthamstow, was making his breakthrough season at Old Trafford and for England. Having scored the second goal at Old Trafford a week beforehand, Beckham scored his first at White Hart Lane in front of his grandad – a lifelong Spurs fan and season ticket holder.

As Beckham rose to fame that transcended football, it transpired that he had been on trial at Spurs as a teenager and, while always favouring a move to Manchester United whom he supported, was underwhelmed by the interest shown in him by then manager Terry Venables. Beckham has subsequently shared his experience as a highly talented teenager, being invited to meet Venables in his office at the training ground but the manager seemed more concerned by the packet of peanuts he had dropped on the floor! By contrast Alex Ferguson regularly invited Beckham to match days at Old Trafford, even inviting him into the changing rooms before and after games to mix with the first-team players.

Despite another dismal run of just one win in six, by early March there were always enough teams between Spurs and the bottom three to stave off the fear of another relegation battle. One of those teams was West Ham, whom Spurs met in the most entertaining yet frustratingly fruitless game of their season. Upton Park was always a hostile place to go especially for Spurs, and this was under the floodlights on a freezing-cold Monday night in February.

West Ham, then managed by Harry Redknapp, were in the bottom three, having endured an even worse start to 1997 than Spurs. They had lost five of six league games and also been dumped out of the FA Cup in a replay at home to third-tier Wrexham. Redknapp had just bought a twin strike force of John Hartson (Arsenal) and Paul Kitson (Newcastle) to try and keep them up; both started at home for the first time against Spurs with somewhat predictable results.

Both scored in a topsy-turvy encounter that Spurs initially led through Sheringham who returned to the team for the first time since December. Anderton, who had also recently returned, provided the assist for Sheringham and then equalised all within the opening 30 minutes only for West Ham to retake the lead before half-time. David Howells had suffered personal tragedy following the death of his father in the days before the game. Poignantly he scored to make it 3-3 early in the second half but it was to be West Ham's night. Hartson was fouled by Howells and Julian Dicks slammed in the penalty.

In each of the previous six seasons Spurs still had plenty to play for through until at least Easter. In 91, 93 and 95 the FA Cup became the main focus. In 92 the European campaign continued through into March; in 96 the race for the final UEFA Cup spot went down to the final minutes of the season and even 94 provided a relegation battle to retain focus.

In 1997, once Spurs were knocked out of the FA Cup at the first hurdle and mid-table mediocrity was all but guaranteed by March, the final ten games felt like a real endurance test. Anderton and Iversen were both in and out of the side and Sheringham scored only one more goal. With so many changes to the team, mostly enforced through injury, there was little identifiable pattern.

Spurs travelled to Filbert Street in mid-March in a game against Leicester that, like so many of the time, felt so totally irrelevant to anything other than the two-hour slot that it filled for supporters. Yet, watching your team even in the most mediocre of moments could bring joy.

Steffen Chirazi travelled to the match at Leicester and recalls the sheer euphoria of Teddy Sheringham's stoppage-time equaliser that kept Spurs in the top half of the table at Leicester's expense:

> It was one of those nights that for some almost ludicrous reason manages to elevate itself alongside far more illustrious memories over the decades. Filbert Street was an old school dump with charm, the sort which nostalgia greatly enhances. The view was moderate to rubbish, and I remember we were almost in line with the dead ball line, halfway up in the corner of the ground.

> Robbie Savage came in for pelters (and remember, this was before 'that' final). It was a nothing game really, albeit there was a glorious 'who ate all the pies' mid-second-half aimed at one specific fan of the crust, and it did look as though we were schlumping along to a really nondescript and utterly boring 1-0 defeat after Steve Claridge had scored in the 74th minute. Teddy's equaliser was not the best technical goal by any stretch, a scruffy header in the box, I believe from a set piece, but what I remember far more clearly is exploding into throes of joy, the sort associated with winning the cup, and storming towards the pitch to hug the hero of the 90th-minute moment. I was outsprinted by about 500 other maniacs all going absolutely limb-loose caveman, and was personally beaten to the fifth row by my friend, a Luton fan who had come along for the ride and found himself utterly wrapped up in the electricity of this (non) seminal moment in our history. Perhaps it was the stupefying boredom of the 89 minutes which had preceded it, perhaps it was the brutal lack of joyful moments in our season thus far, but here I am, still vividly remember 'that' goal on 'that' night. An absurd 'great' moment.

The only discernible highlight from the final third of the season was Iversen's hat-trick at Sunderland in early March. The 4-0 victory was Spurs' biggest in the league since New Year's Eve 1994 and only the third time they had scored three or more all season. From that point onwards Spurs remained in either ninth or tenth place and the season ended fittingly with a tame defeat at home to Coventry, who secured their survival in the Premier League for another season with a 2-1 victory at Middlesbrough's expense.

It was at least a memorable occasion for two Spurs youngsters – Paul McVeigh scored Spurs' goal in what proved to be his last of three first-team appearances and Jamie Clapham, a left-back, played in his one and only league match for Spurs, having previously played the Intertoto Cup games. Just about the only positives from the season had been the development of Sol Campbell, appointed as captain, and of Steve Carr, who had begun to make the right-back position his own.

In the club's official end-of-season video review Gary Mabbutt stated 'For me personally and for the club this was one of the most frustrating seasons I've experienced here.'

By May, 26 different players had been used though only seven played more than 30 of the 43 matches. Not on one occasion was the same starting XI selected in successive games.

Spurs were a club on the drift. It was galling to see other clubs progressing while Spurs stagnated. Arsenal continued to progress under Wenger, finishing the season third. They were playing winning football that was also achieved through skill and creativity. Chelsea signed the highly gifted forward Gianfranco Zola in November – another player very much in the traditional Spurs mould – and embarked on an FA Cup run that ultimately resulted in their first major trophy since the 70s. Both would be competing in European club competition the following season which would only raise their profile and generate additional revenue.

The feeling of helplessness only intensified when the press reported that Teddy Sheringham had rejected a new contract offer and stated his desire to leave the club. Alan Sugar recounted in *What You See is What You Get* that, following the final game of the season against Coventry, Sheringham requested to meet with him and Francis and demanded to know what plans were in place to improve the squad. The meeting ended in a heated argument that Sugar stormed out of. Sheringham, giving his account in *Teddy,* maintains that he desperately wanted a reason to stay but only if he felt the club was moving forwards. The impasse remained through the coming weeks of the off-season

Sheringham was offered a new three-year deal but turned it down. When Manchester United offered £3.5m for the 31-year-old, Sugar felt it was a good deal for the club and Sheringham promptly joined Alex Ferguson at Old Trafford for the promise of winning silverware for the first time in his professional career. It marked the end of an era. Aside from Klinsmann's all-too-brief stay, Sheringham had been Spurs' talisman and, along with Anderton, bridged the gap from the highly promising team under Venables, via the boom and bust of Ardiles into what all Spurs supporters hoped would be a brighter future.

Sheringham was in all senses a classic Spurs player, oozing class, skill, finesse and vision. He epitomised the famous number 10 shirt and all that it stood for in Spurs' romantic history. He had been allowed to leave due to a perceived lack of ambition and it only intensified the toxicity that was engulfing the club.

Mark Jacob recalls the growing relevance of TAG during this period:

> Sugar patently didn't understand the traditions of the football club and was failing to communicate with the fans. TAG was building momentum; we were essentially just 'two men and a fax machine' but we were receiving positive publicity and backing among an increasing number of supporters. We held a meeting at Rudolph's, the bar on the High Road immediately outside the ground, around this time and it was packed with Spurs fans absolutely appalled at the direction the club was moving in; for two seasons we had been going backwards; we were seeing mediocre players achieving progressively worse results yet the chairman was continuing to act in a brazen manner – he appeared on an ITV show and claimed that if he didn't win the league in the next two seasons he'd let some other 'brain surgeon' have a go instead. It didn't take a brain surgeon to know that we were a million years away from a league title.

1997/98 – GROSS MISJUDGEMENT

WALKER
CARR CAMPBELL VEGA WILSON
FOX NIELSEN BERTI GINOLA
FERDINAND KLINSMANN

HOW I SAW IT:

When Teddy Sheringham was sold to Manchester United a bit of me died inside. Sheringham was my favourite player – his five-year period at White Hart Lane surpassed the amount of time that Gascoigne, Lineker, Waddle and Klinsmann had been Spurs players. Increasingly it felt as though Spurs just weren't Spurs anymore.

I enjoyed a long summer in 1997 once my GCSE exams had concluded, which provided a lot of reflection time to consider Spurs' situation. I purchased *Championship Manager* and spent many hours 'managing' Spurs myself with some modest success. The game was, in 1997, a more simplistic form than the modern version but it did provide an incredible resource to learn about foreign players that might benefit Spurs.

In July I had my first thoughts on Spurs published through a letter to the opinions page on Teletext. Reading it back now, I clearly grasped the stagnation that the club was in and captured the mood of the time; it really did feel as if there was no inspiration in the transfer market and a host of great players were going elsewhere. While the gist of my letter was spot on, I hadn't even mentioned David Ginola as a potential target who, in hindsight, was more of a Spurs player than David Hopkin of Crystal Palace, whom I had suggested Francis should buy.

From August I had a Sunday job working as the switchboard operator at a local independent furniture store in Waltham Cross. This paid £3.85 per hour for a six-hour day that was vital to pay for Spurs tickets now that I was over 16 and so had to pay full adult price. My first game of the season was an early midweek game against Aston Villa and Chris and I sat in the South Stand upper tier for the first time.

The game was a rare highlight in a miserable season, with Les Ferdinand scoring twice. He looked a natural goalscorer and promised to be as effective and prolific as he had been for QPR and Newcastle. I remember on the journey home listening to the other results and hearing how the embryonic league table was shaping up. We were ninth and we all commented that we were 'just one more win away from the top six' – that felt like the ceiling of our optimism yet that elusive 'one more win' was never forthcoming.

Any optimism soon faded through a miserable autumn. I only went to one other home game until December and that was a 0-0 bore draw at home to Wimbledon. I became apathetic listening to us conceding four second-half goals at Anfield in November and it was inevitable that Gerry Francis would leave imminently.

Coming home from school one day I remember being told that Spurs had appointed a new manager that no one had heard of. That was my introduction to Christian Gross's appointment. We initially hoped that we had our equivalent of Arsene Wenger but that hope lasted less than a week …

Chris and I were there for his first home game – a chastening 6-1 defeat by Chelsea in which I left a game early for the first time under my own steam. The result and humiliation really solidified my dislike of Chelsea. The only Spurs joy during that period was learning that Klinsmann was returning – the news broke just before Christmas Day but any good feeling was short-lived as I watched us hammered at Villa on TV on Boxing Day.

Chris and I kept going back for more punishment – due to the North Stand rebuild we mostly watched from the South Upper this season and for four games in a row had the indignity of seeing our opponents score an equaliser down in front of us. I took my frustration out on Ruel Fox – as the full-time whistle sounded in the home draw against Coventry – by shouting as loud as I could 'Fox, you're shit' to which a steward turned around and stared at me – I worried for weeks that I was going to be reported and banned.

If our plight wasn't bad enough, Arsenal won the double and Chelsea won both the League Cup and European Cup Winners' Cup. Our school was full of Arsenal fans but we had one token Chelsea fan. It still grates on me today that he and an Arsenal-supporting friend were joking at how they'd both won a double and that Tottenham couldn't even do a double over Barnsley.

They had a point; we were objectively shit and Arsenal were objectively very good. When they'd been much better than us earlier in the decade, they'd still played a really negative and defensive style of play but now they were playing delightful attacking football that Spurs had traditionally been associated with. It was my lowest point as a Spurs fan.

SEASON COMMENTARY

Teddy Sheringham's protracted transfer to Manchester United took until the end of June to complete and generated a lot of mudslinging in the media between him and Alan Sugar. The net result was that Spurs required a new-look attack. Even with Sheringham, goals had been a problem and Spurs equalled a club-record low of just 19 goals scored at home in the league. Iversen hadn't played since 22 March and Armstrong had made just 12 appearances all season. But before a striker was signed an opportunity arose for Alan Sugar to secure the signature of an iconic player who continues to be eulogised at Spurs today.

David Ginola possessed all the attributes to become a Spurs legend; the Frenchman incorporated all the best of the club's DNA as a mercurial talent oozing flair and elegance. Ginola had a chequered past in his native France and was vilified by his national team manager Gerard Houllier for his role in their failure to qualify for the 1994 World Cup finals. Ginola, playing on the right wing, had the ball in the Bulgarian final third with seconds of the final qualifying game to play. The score was tied at 1-1 and the draw would have been enough to see France qualify from their group at Bulgaria's expense. Instead of keeping the ball by the corner flag, Ginola over-hit a deep cross and within 15 seconds Bulgaria broke and scored to send them through to the World Cup. Houllier branded Ginola 'a criminal'.

Ginola sought refuge away from his native land and joined Kevin Keegan at Newcastle in summer 1995. He was part of the swashbuckling side that could and should have become league champions that season. Ginola thrived on the left wing, supplying crosses for Les Ferdinand and was named in the PFA team of the season. Ginola was disappointed that Newcastle would not allow him to join Barcelona when they wanted to sign him in summer 1996 but remained a hero on Tyneside; he played his part in Newcastle's 5-0 demolition of Manchester United in October, scoring a trademark goal, bending in a powerful curling shot from range. However, when Kevin Keegan surprisingly left the club in January and was replaced by the more conservative Kenny Dalglish, Ginola became a peripheral member of the team and was deemed expendable by the summer.

The deal to bring Ginola to White Hart Lane was completed on Alan Sugar's yacht in Monte Carlo just as the deal to sign Klinsmann had been three years previously. Sugar remembers that with typical flamboyance Ginola arrived in Monte Carlo on a speedboat having received the call while in his native St Tropez.

Gerry Francis was very keen to welcome Ginola to the club and hoped that he would be the spark to reignite the team:

> I was devastated to learn that Teddy was leaving. I was on my honeymoon when the chairman phoned me to tell me! Ginola was obviously not a striker like Teddy was but he was a creator, someone to make something happen out of nothing. We'd seen him first-hand playing against us for Newcastle but I felt he needed to score more goals – he'd only scored seven goals in

> two seasons at Newcastle so I set him a target when he joined. He scored nine goals in his first season and seven the next in addition to winning the Players' Player and Football Writers' Player of the Year.

Another Frenchman who nearly joined Spurs that summer was Monaco's versatile midfield player Emmanuel Petit who instead ended up at Arsenal. Gerry Francis explains how Petit got away:

> I'd put a lot of time into Petit probably for best part of a year. We were very close to agreeing a deal with his club Monaco throughout the early part of 1997 but they kept progressing in the UEFA Cup so didn't want to sell. By the time they got knocked out in the semi-final the transfer window had shut so we had to wait until the summer. Unfortunately, by that time Wenger was established at Arsenal and they'd worked together and were close. We agreed a price with Monaco so he came over. Alan and I met Petit, did the medical, and agreed a deal with him. I was excited to have him and would have played him in midfield even though I'd mostly watched him play in central defence.
>
> Unbeknown to us, when he left in the taxi we'd arranged for him he dropped in to see Wenger and ended up signing for them!

Spurs still needed a striker to directly replace Sheringham and fate would have it that Les Ferdinand, whom Francis had worked with at QPR, became available at Newcastle. The England striker was now 30 but had a proven scoring record having netted over one hundred Premier League goals in five seasons. Ferdinand credited Francis with his initial rise to prominence in West London; prior to Francis's arrival in 1991 Ferdinand had been a raw talent but was told by his new manager that he'd play for England. He achieved this within two years and earned the £6m move to Newcastle in 1995 when he'd been Gerry Francis's first-choice replacement for Klinsmann. Spurs were now getting a player who was two years older and for the same fee.

Newcastle manager Kenny Dalglish was reluctant to sell Ferdinand but had been made aware that he needed to sell assets to be able to bring more players in. With Shearer and Faustino Asprilla also at St James' Park, Ferdinand was deemed surplus. The £6m fee agreed between the clubs towards the end of July was nearly double the amount Spurs had received for Sheringham, who was just eight months older. Ferdinand was a boyhood Spurs fan and turned down advances from Sheffield Wednesday in order to reunite with Francis.

The deal almost fell through at the 11th hour; with Ferdinand having agreed to join Spurs, Alan Shearer broke his ankle in a pre-season game at Everton. Newcastle tried to tempt Ferdinand to renege on the deal agreed with Spurs but he had already made up his mind, though would later reveal that he regretted allowing his pride to influence his decision.

Ferdinand and Ginola first appeared in lilywhite together for the home pre-season testimonial in honour of David Howells who, by 1997, had made over 300 appearances for the club. The opposition, Fiorentina, brought a full-strength team and comfortably beat Spurs 2-0. Howells had briefly taken over as captain the previous season following Mabbutt's injury but had been in and out of the side so Gerry Francis decided to formally offer the captaincy to Sol Campbell who, in Sheringham's absence and with Anderton's perennial injury problems, had established himself as Spurs' most consistent performer and most valuable player. As a graduate of Spurs' youth set-up Campbell, like Howells, knew the club inside out and was instantly relatable to the fans and had signed a new four-year deal that tied him to the club until 2001. However, Campbell, in his authorised biography *Sol Campbell,* was beginning to question the ambition of the club and whether it matched his own.

The opening game of the league season provided for a fascinating narrative as Teddy Sheringham returned to make his Manchester United debut at White Hart Lane. He was booed mercilessly from the moment he stepped off the away team coach and with the game goalless Sheringham had the perfect opportunity to silence his critics when United were awarded a penalty.

He had missed the last five penalties he had taken at White Hart Lane for Spurs dating back to the start of the 94/95 season and including the penalty shoot-out defeat to Nottingham Forest in March 1996. It was a bizarre record as Sheringham was otherwise an accomplished penalty taker and had scored twice for England in high pressure shoot-outs during Euro '96. Sheringham was replacing the huge void created at Old Trafford by the departure of Eric Cantona who had surprisingly announced his retirement from all football aged just 32.

Cantona had been United's talisman and played a leading role in guiding the famed 'Class of 92' through their formative years. Sheringham, keen to take on Cantona's level of responsibility, stepped up to take the penalty in front of the South Stand. His fail-safe technique was to open his body and shoot with his instep to his right but on this occasion he shot the other way, perhaps knowing that Ian Walker, in goal, would know his technique. The ball cannoned off the post and back to Sheringham who illegally touched the ball again to concede an indirect free kick. The joy in the home end didn't last long – United scored twice within two minutes in the final ten minutes to record a comfortable 2-0 win.

Ginola and Ferdinand had both made their competitive debuts and there was also a first start for young midfielder Stephen Clemence, son of former goalkeeper and first-team coach Ray. Clemence started alongside Howells in central midfield and his energy earned him plaudits in what was otherwise a disappointing start to the season for the team. It was the first time Spurs had lost on opening day since 1987.

One defeat became two three days later in a 2-1 loss at West Ham though Ferdinand did open his Spurs account with a second-half consolation. Two successive home wins, against Derby and Aston Villa, provided back-to-back wins for only the second time in the calendar year and pushed Spurs up into ninth ahead of the north London derby at Highbury on the final weekend of August.

Arsenal had invested further in their squad over the summer; in addition to Petit, the highly rated Dutch winger Marc Overmars joined for a fee in excess of £7m. A host of other young players from across the continent also followed, giving the Arsenal squad a real continental flavour. Arsenal named five overseas players in their starting XI while Spurs had just Iversen (Ginola was missing through a minor injury).

Spurs' goal was battered from the opening moments yet somehow survived; Arsenal twice hit the woodwork and Walker was forced into a number of saves. A minute before half-time Justin Edinburgh was sent off having received a second yellow card, meaning Spurs had to play the whole second half with a numerical disadvantage. After the break Spurs defended doggedly but still had to rely on Ian Wright uncharacteristically missing the target from six yards out. The 0-0 draw was as undeserved as it was highly uncomfortable to watch for any of the 3,000 Spurs fans in the Clock End at Highbury yet the point was a flashback to the stoicism and determination of Francis's team circa 1995.

There was little time to reflect on the draw against Arsenal as the following morning the news of Princess Diana's fatal car crash in Paris dominated the attention of the nation. The nation was able to pay its respects during the following week's international break with England defeating Moldova 4-0 at Wembley. Sol Campbell and Ferdinand both started the game. The Princess's tragic death did in time generate a strange Spurs twist as David Ginola later took on Diana's role as a Red Cross envoy to campaign against landmines.

Spurs returned to action buoyed by the draw at Highbury and having now gone three matches unbeaten, with a visit to Filbert Street. Any optimism dissipated following a chastening second half in which Leicester simply overpowered Spurs and recorded a comfortable 3-0 victory.

Alan Sugar revealed that Gerry Francis offered his resignation around this time, feeling that he couldn't take the team any further. Sugar was able to persuade him to continue in the short term but it was clear that the team was not progressing.

The only spark of life in September came from another summer signing, Jose Dominguez, whose diminutive frame and direct dribbling at least gave the crowd something to enjoy in an otherwise forgettable pair of 0-0 draws at home to Wimbledon and Blackburn.

Third-tier Carlisle United gave Spurs a scare in the League Cup second round. The Cumbrian team led 2-1 at half-time at White Hart Lane and well into the second half until Ruel Fox and young striker Paul Mahorn, on his debut, turned the game back in Spurs' favour. The second leg proved to be more comfortable with Ginola scoring his first Spurs goal in a 2-0 victory.

Spurs had to wait until mid-October for their next league win. Darren Anderton had continued to suffer from groin and abdominal injuries throughout summer 1997 and was unable to play any part during pre-season. He began to realise that surgery would again be required but has revealed that Sugar personally called him to ask that he agree to be named as a substitute against Sheffield Wednesday just to try and give the crowd something to feel positive about.

Watching on from the bench, Anderton would have been delighted to see Spurs stroll into a three-goal first-half lead. Dominguez scored his first goal for the club, Armstrong, making a rare start, added a second and then just before half-time Ginola cut in from the right to curl a beauty into the far corner. What should have been a comfortable second half was anything but; Spurs allowed the visitors back into the game with two goals and Anderton came on for the remaining two minutes. Although Spurs held on, it caused Anderton further damage.

The victory provided only very brief respite. Spurs had already been knocked out of the League Cup following a home defeat against Derby and following the win over Wednesday lost three successive games against Southampton, Leeds and a heavy 4-0 defeat at Liverpool.

Gerry Francis again offered his resignation, which this time Sugar reluctantly accepted. The chairman had shown real patience towards his manager and held out hope that he would be able to turn the situation around. By 1997 the great example of patience had been seen at Old Trafford where Manchester United's board had shown tremendous faith in Alex Ferguson during the late 80s when many sections of their fanbase and media wanted him out. Having won the FA Cup in 1990, Ferguson took United to the summit of English football where, in a parallel universe, he might have been looking for a new job before the inception of the Premier League.

Francis's departure was confirmed on 10 November – almost exactly three years to the day since he had taken over at White Hart Lane. His spell as Spurs manager can be neatly split into two even halves – when he arrived during the 94/95 season, he provided the necessary organisation and stability, turning a team full of attacking flair but with no defensive organisation away from a possible relegation battle and into one that very nearly reached the FA Cup Final and qualified for European football through the league. Then, despite losing Klinsmann, Barmby and Popescu, he was able to restructure the team and once again take the team to within inches of the UEFA Cup in 95/96.

From summer 1996, however, fortunes always seemed to be against Francis. Injuries mounted up – he was deprived of Mabbutt, Armstrong and Anderton for much of 96/97 – and then Sheringham left. The whole of that season had been utterly frustrating and seemed to reverse the momentum, leaving manager and club in something of a tailspin. By November 1997 it seemed a parting was right for both.

> I could see as the season progressed that it was time for change – for both me and the club. I discussed this with Alan earlier in the season but he wanted me to stay on so I did until November.
>
> I felt that having been highly competitive in the first two seasons, always in and around the top six, we really needed some silverware or to have qualified for

> Europe to be able to kick on but we were unfortunate – losing that semi-final to Everton, the penalty shoot-out defeat the following year and twice narrowly missing out on UEFA Cup qualification.
>
> Managing Spurs at that time was very hard – it took another 11 years until 2006 for them to improve on the seventh place I achieved in 1995 and it was another 22 years from 1995 until they finished as top London club again under Pochettino in 2017. That gives you an idea of what we were up against. It was a difficult climate.

While narrowly missing out on European football may sound a very modest achievement given the way the club has evolved, it is worth remembering that pre-Francis Spurs had been in a genuine relegation battle and not finished in the top six since the halcyon days of Gascoigne and Lineker. Francis should also be congratulated for the development of Sol Campbell into his role as a central-defensive colossus and club captain and for the integration of Stephen Carr as first choice right-back. As youth team graduates, both would go on to be mainstays of the team until their respective departures. Francis continues:

> I loved my time at Spurs especially the first two seasons and I'm very proud of my achievements – when I took over, we couldn't stop conceding goals but within weeks we'd recorded the club's best ever run of clean sheets until we did it again the next season! We also ended up scoring more goals than the Famous Five team. I could have taken the England job when Terry Venables left in 1996 but turned it down because I was enjoying my time at Spurs and felt that I was better suited to club management.
>
> I've never finished outside the top half of the Premier League and managed to finish as top London club with both QPR and Spurs within three years – no manager has achieved this since. With Spurs, especially in the first two years, I never felt I got

> the recognition I deserved especially as I had so little money to work with when compared to some of our rivals at the time. I just so wish that we could have won some silverware and we should have gone further. I've developed a deep affection for the club and am honoured to have been part of its history.

David Howells was sorry to see Francis leave but recognised that it was time for a change:

> When Gerry arrived, he was great and we looked like a title-winning team as he gave us all the organisation that we had lacked under Ossie. Initially he had the perfect balance of creativity and organisation but as the team evolved and the better players left the balance wasn't right. For the last 18 months or so it was difficult. I don't think Gerry was helped by recruitment and we weren't shopping at the high end of the market anymore while Arsenal, Chelsea and even Middlesbrough were attracting the more exciting players.

Having first rejected Francis's resignation in September, Alan Sugar had begun the process of identifying a replacement. If Manchester United had been the example of patience, then Arsenal were becoming the example of innovation, having appointed a largely unknown foreigner in Wenger who was already having a huge impact across North London.

Sugar had been alerted to a largely unknown Swiss coach, Christian Gross, who had earned plaudits in his native country, having won two league titles with Grasshopper Zurich. Sugar went to Zurich to meet Gross and was impressed enough with the 43-year-old that a deal was agreed there and then.

The media reaction to Gross's appointment was similar to that afforded to Arsene Wenger 14 months previously. Alan Mullery, former Spurs captain and now media pundit, responded 'Christian Who?' when asked on national radio for his opinion. That became the newspaper headline the next morning and in Sugar's opinion permeated down to the players.

Gross was due to be unveiled at a press conference at White Hart Lane alongside his new chairman. Sugar recounts that they were supposed to meet at a hotel and then travel down to the stadium together. Instead, Gross went straight to White Hart Lane with his own PR guru. Even the receptionist hadn't known who he was or why he was there. Gross, sat next to Sugar, opened the press conference by infamously pulling a train ticket out of his pocket and explaining that he had taken the tube from Heathrow Airport as he wanted to know how the fans felt travelling to games. Still holding the London Underground ticket aloft Gross uttered the now infamous words 'I hope that this will be the ticket to my dreams.' Many of the journalists in attendance were thinking 'I hope you've bought a return'!

In *What You See Is What You Get* Sugar describes the press conference as a 'total farce' and that he knew Gross was 'dead meat' from that point forwards. Both Sugar and Gross were ridiculed in the press before the new manager had even met his new team. Speaking on *The Last Word on Spurs* podcast in 2020 Ramon Vega explained that the Swiss culture is to be humble and understated; he believed that Gross had simply been trying to demonstrate that he could just be one of the fans and so was happy travelling on public transport to games.

David Howells hadn't heard of his new manager but could understand the logic behind the appointment:

> I felt we all gave him a chance; I hadn't seen the press conference with the ticket but his immediate first impressions with us were that he was a good coach and had some good ideas. Arsenal were doing well under Wenger and there were lots of players coming across from the continent and they were all bringing new innovations and ideas with them. It made sense for the chairman to go down this route.

Having left Sheffield Wednesday shortly after their defeat at White Hart Lane, David Pleat also came back to Spurs to take on the role of Director of Football. Sugar, by his own admission, lacked football insight and had been keen to bring Pleat back before appointing Gerry Francis. Pleat would join the board of directors in January with a remit to help inform matters on transfers, scouting and contracts.

Still awaiting his work permit, Gross watched on as Chris Hughton, now part of the senior coaching set-up, picked the team for the home game against Crystal Palace on 24 November which resulted in another 1-0 loss. It was a fourth successive defeat and Spurs now sat just one place above the relegation zone and one point off the bottom of the table.

Gross had expected to be joined in London by his trusted fitness coach Fritz Schmid. However, as Switzerland was a non-EU country, he had to fulfil additional criteria to meet UK Home Office work permit requirements to work in England. Schmid's methods were integral to the success Gross had enjoyed in Switzerland, and much of his training revolved around innovative training and nutrition. Crucially Schmid was denied a work permit and so Gross was left to work alone with his new underperforming squad.

The new manager finally settled into work with his new squad and had a vital game away at bottom-placed Everton to prepare for the following weekend. Gross picked a more defensive-looking line-up with a back five and three midfielders with Ginola supporting the frontman Les Ferdinand. Fittingly his compatriot, Vega, was brought back into the starting XI for the first time in a month and he scored the first goal of the new Swiss manager's regime with a close-range header from a corner. Ginola added a second shortly afterwards. It was Spurs' first win in six weeks.

Darren Anderton in *Take Note!* describes Gross as a disciplinarian who focused heavily on players' fitness. Anderton feels that Sugar wanted a manager who would work the players much harder to earn their money. It was no surprise that Gross was instantly unpopular among his squad for introducing Sunday warm-downs, full-day training on Tuesdays and Thursdays and overnight hotel stays before home games. This was all very new in 1997 though far more commonplace in the modern game.

Wenger had quickly won around his players, even those most resistant to change, due to his affable personality, strong command of English and successful results. Gross did not possess the same warmth and his command of English proved a barrier to his communication. Despite the win against Everton, Gross's start at Spurs developed into farce following two horrific results, the first of which, in his first home game, was against Chelsea.

After their FA Cup success in May, Chelsea had continued to spend and assemble an expensive team of talented foreign players including Dutch international goalkeeper Ed de Goey and young Norwegian striker Tore Andre Flo. Chelsea had kicked-on since winning the FA Cup and now looked to be genuine challengers to Manchester United.

They started the day in second place while Spurs started fourth from bottom. Gross still only had limited access to Darren Anderton, who was only available to start as a sub. The first half was an even contest. Flo gave Chelsea a lead, only for Vega, scoring his second goal in as many games, to equalise before the interval. Spurs hadn't beaten Chelsea since the very first encounter of the decade but now had the opportunity to end the hoodoo while also giving Gross the perfect start to his White Hart Lane career.

No Spurs manager since Terry Neill, in 1974, had won their first home game in charge and Gross would suffer the same fate but in humiliating fashion. Any momentum Spurs had built going into half-time was lost within 90 seconds of the restart with Di Matteo putting Chelsea back in front. Spurs fell apart after that and Chelsea scored four more goals at ease to record an emphatic 6-1 victory. It was the first time since 1954 that Spurs had conceded six in a home game and the biggest home defeat since 1979.

The home sections of the stadium were half-empty by the time the game ended, in one of the lowest moments of the decade.

It was an even more bleak experience for Paul Hawksbee, who was now working for Chelsea:

David Howells and Jurgen Klinsmann congratulate Teddy Sheringham after his superlative equaliser at Anfield in March 1995.

Ronny Rosenthal wrote himself in Spurs folklore legend with a hat-trick to beat Southampton at the Dell in the fifth round replay in March 1995.

Chris Armstrong, Teddy Sheringham and Darren Anderton celebrate a goal resulting in victory at Sheffield Wednesday in September 1995. The new strike pair scored 50 goals between them that season.

Tony Blair opens the new Spurs Lodge training facility in Chigwell, Essex flanked by Gerry Francis and Alan Sugar. October 1996.

Christian Gross was the surprising choice to replace Gerry Francis as manager in November 1997. A 6-1 defeat to Chelsea in his first game proved a sign of things to come.

Sugar and Klinsmann buried the hatchet with the striker returning in December 1997 to help fight relegation.

Christian Gross looks on with Spurs a goal behind at relegation rivals Barnsley in April 1998.

Two of the finest players to play for Spurs in the 90s – Ginola congratulates Klinsmann as his four goals ensure Spurs' safety at the end of the 97/98 season.

Les Ferdinand celebrates what proved to be the only goal of the game in Christian Gross's final game in charge away at Everton in August 1998.

George Graham is paraded as new manager alongside club mascot Chirpy in October 1998.

Tempers flare in the league game against Wimbledon in January 1999. The two teams met five times in just over a month.

Ginola in action at Coventry in February 2000.

Allan Nielsen with the man of the match award and Worthington Cup trophy after his winner in the 1999 League Cup Final.

George Graham aka 'The man in the raincoat' received very brief acceptance as Spurs manager having delivered the 1999 Worthington Cup.

Allan Nielsen leads the celebration following his late winner against Leicester in the 1999 League Cup Final. It was a drab and forgettable game but Spurs ended the decade with a trophy and return to European football.

It was hard to see a long-term relationship between Graham and Ginola as evidenced here in this pre-season game at Birmingham in July 2000. Ginola was sold the next month.

Onfield battle between Spurs and Arsenal in the final north London derby of the 90s in November 1999. Spurs went on to win 2-1.

Two late goals knock Spurs out of Europe in Kaiserslautern in November 1999.

Captain Sol Campbell is consoled by George Graham following UEFA Cup elimination against Kaiserslautern in November 1999.

> It's safe to say I got a bit of a ribbing at work on the Monday! We'd played quite well in the first half and were level at half-time but the collapse in the second half was horrific. The sixth goal was just embarrassing in the way that Chelsea were able to walk through us. It's the sort of goal a team concedes in a manager's final days when you know their time is up but this was Christian Gross's first home game in charge!
>
> Clearly this result put Gross 'right behind the eight ball' especially as it was such a crushing defeat against a local rival.
>
> The outcome said so much about the direction both clubs were heading in. Here we were with a tired squad and team made up of some average players who'd been assembled on a budget while Chelsea, through Ruud Gullit, were able to attract some of the biggest names and best prospects from across Europe. Leboeuf, Petrescu, Di Matteo and Zola all started and Vialli was on the bench.

The defeat sent Spurs into the relegation zone. The situation only got worse as Coventry then inflicted a demoralising 4-0 defeat on Spurs at Highfield Road in the next game.

Before the home match against Barnsley, Anderton signed a new contract but promptly tore a groin muscle in training. He was asked by Gross to play in the crucial match and somehow managed to play an hour. Barnsley, newly promoted to the top division, were the perfect tonic for Gross, and Ginola enjoyed his best day in a Spurs shirt yet with two goals in a comfortable 3-0 victory though Spurs remained in the relegation zone.

Just days before Christmas there was further joy for Spurs fans when it was announced that Jurgen Klinsmann had agreed to rejoin the club on a short-term deal until the end of the season.

Sugar and Klinsmann's relationship had thawed since the chairman's incendiary interview in 1995 in which he claimed he 'wouldn't even wash his car' with the striker's shirt, gifted to him during his first spell at the club. Crucially Gross and Klinsmann shared the same agent and it was the manager who initiated contact, citing mutual benefits.

Having won his coveted German league title and then the UEFA Cup with Bayern Munich, Klinsmann had moved on to play for Sampdoria in Italy but had fallen out of favour with a new manager. With the World Cup in summer 1998 just six months away, Klinsmann desperately needed regular game time as much as Spurs desperately needed a saviour to keep them in the Premier League.

Klinsmann, Sugar and Gross staged a joint press conference at White Hart Lane on Christmas Eve, though questions were dominated by the relationship between chairman and striker following the fallout of his departure in 1995.

Klinsmann was not signed in time to play at Aston Villa on Boxing Day but the euphoria of his re-signing had masked just how far Spurs had fallen as they were comprehensively beaten 4-1 at Villa Park. Anderton was again named as a sub despite his severe groin muscle injury. He came on late on, unable to kick the ball with his right foot.

Finally, Anderton did have surgery with a renowned specialist recommended by Klinsmann. He didn't play again until April.

Klinsmann's second debut, a home game against Arsenal, was played amidst a febrile atmosphere at White Hart Lane. Despite the perilous league position (now 19th), the return of Klinsmann buoyed the crowd and the team responded with a spirited performance. Allan Nielsen gave Spurs a first-half lead but Arsenal equalised through a deflected effort in the second half. The point was a welcome relief especially as many fans feared another derby mauling just three weeks after the Chelsea humiliation.

By the time Spurs played their first league game of 1998, Klinsmann had managed to convince former Inter Milan team-mate and Italian international Nicola Berti to join him in north London. The Italian midfielder, now past 30, had been a stellar name in European football having played 39 times for Italy including the 1994 World Cup Final.

Bardi, as a half-Italian Spurs fan, remembers Berti with some affection:

> Nicola Berti was a highly accomplished and decorated footballer; in his prime, during the early 90s he was an aggressive, box-to-box midfielder with supreme energy and technique – he played in the 1994 World Cup Final and had won a Scudetto and two UEFA Cups with Inter Milan. He kind of passed under the radar when he joined Spurs as it was at the same time as Klinsmann returned but he played a crucial role in keeping us up. It wasn't just his goals but his touch of class, especially alongside Klinsmann and Ginola.

Berti became a cult hero though his legacy is the terrace chant that was sung at White Hart Lane and can still be heard occasionally at away games some 25 years later!

The chant goes:

> My name is Nicola Berti,
> I'm aged about 30 and I came from a club in Milan
> – Inter!.
> As I walk down the street,
> All the people I meet
> They shout, 'Oi Gorgeous what's your name?'
> My name is Nicola Berti …

Berti provided much-needed experience and quality in midfield but could do little to prevent Manchester United recording a routine 2-0 victory at Old Trafford on his debut.

Having lost to Chelsea and drawn with Arsenal, there was finally some home derby success as Spurs beat West Ham at White Hart Lane, Klinsmann scoring the only goal of the game. Some two and a half years had passed since his previous appearance in lilywhite and while he still demonstrated a lethal eye for goal, as proved with the goal against West Ham, he was quite clearly not the same explosive striker that he'd shown during his first spell. Spurs lost at Derby at the end of January, meaning they'd spent two full calendar months in the bottom three.

The FA Cup was a short-lived experience. Spurs beat up-and-coming Fulham in the third round (in which young Scottish winger Garry Brady made a very encouraging debut and looked to have scored, only for the goal to be officially awarded as an own goal). Brady's Spurs career and the club's FA Cup run didn't go much further though. Spurs were beaten in a replay at Barnsley in the next round with Klinsmann picking up an injury that kept him out of the team for a month. Brady made ten more appearances, all from the bench.

February proved to be kinder – in the most impressive away victory of the season, Spurs won 3-0 at Blackburn. It ended a run of five straight away defeats. Leading through Nicola Berti's first-half strike, Spurs defended resolutely and scored twice late on the break through Armstrong and Fox. It was only Spurs' second away victory in any competition in nearly a year and came against a team who started the day in third place. This was followed by a 1-1 draw at home to Leicester.

By the end of February Spurs made another signing in the shape of midfielder Moussa Saib, who became the first Algerian to play in the Premier League when he joined for £2.3m. The creative central midfielder had almost joined Arsenal the previous summer but the deal fell through and he signed for Valencia instead. The move didn't work out for him in Spain and he provided another midfield option for Spurs.

Klinsmann returned to the team for a crunch relegation match against Bolton Wanderers at White Hart Lane where he would start alongside Chris Armstrong – the player who had been purchased to replace the German in summer 1995. One goal was enough to settle a nervous encounter and it came from Allan Nielsen on the stroke of half-time, though Baardsen, now enjoying a run of games in goal at Walker's expense, earned plaudits for a fine save in the second half. The victory helped open a gap between the two sides, though it left Spurs perilously close to the relegation zone. This proved to be the only win in a run of six games through early spring.

The home fixture with Liverpool on 14 March provided an entertaining 3-3 draw in which Spurs played well and both Klinsmann and Ginola scored. However, the match also exposed Spurs' defensive and psychological fragilities; they led three times but were pegged back on each occasion. The third equaliser was scored in stoppage time.

Though Ginola and Klinsmann both scored, there were also reported tensions between the two. Klinsmann supposedly insisted that Ginola should play wide to supply him with crosses – as indeed he did for the first goal in this game – but Ginola wanted to play more centrally. It was also speculated that Klinsmann had a clause in his contract stating that he had to start when available.

On the same day as the draw with Liverpool – a result that kept Spurs out of the relegation zone just on goal difference – Arsenal recorded a significant 1-0 win at Old Trafford to move within six points of Manchester United with three games in hand. Arsenal had hit a rich vein of form in 1998 and were now in with a real chance of winning the league. It was such a stark contrast to Spurs' predicament.

Tyrone Foster was concerned but still felt relegation was far-fetched:

> It was a horrible time. Arsenal were now the flair team in north London and they were on this great run of wins that would see them go on to win the league. As a Spurs fan it's common to catastrophise but I always believed we'd be okay. As I've said we've always been a team of individuals and even this team had talents like Klinsmann, Campbell and Ginola who I always felt would get us out of trouble.

With eight games remaining Spurs' safety was far from secure though they had matters within their own hands with games against the majority of fellow strugglers coming up. The first of those was bottom-placed Crystal Palace at Selhurst Park on 28 March. Despite an uneventful first half, Spurs finally let their quality show after the break – goals from Berti, Armstrong and Klinsmann contributed to a 3-1 victory; the result virtually ensured that Crystal Palace would be relegated.

While on-the-field matters were chaotic, White Hart Lane's reconfiguration was complete with the North Stand upper tier opened. It now mirrored the South Stand and was joined to the East and West stands to provide a full wrap-around bowl. Capacity was now above 35,000 for the first time since 1992.

After two frustrating home draws against Everton and Coventry – in which Spurs led in both but conceded late equalisers – and the customary defeat at Chelsea, Spurs headed into another relegation six-pointer at Barnsley who sat just one point behind Spurs. Defeat in South Yorkshire could have had catastrophic consequences but Spurs held their nerve in adverse circumstances. Despite going a goal behind, Spurs dug deep.

Calderwood, playing in midfield, equalised from close range just after half-time but Vega was then sent off midway through the second half.

Spurs not only contained Barnsley but they created the better chances to win the game. The draw, given the circumstances, felt like a good one. Spurs still had matters in their own hands and knew that two wins from the final three games would guarantee survival.

In the final weekend of April Newcastle travelled to White Hart Lane having endured a traumatic season of their own. Having sold Ferdinand and Ginola and then seen Shearer injured for most of the season they had scored just 32 goals – nearly a third of the number they had scored the previous campaign. Earlier in the season Newcastle beat Barcelona in the Champions League group stage but in the league they had struggled, dropping down the table throughout 1998.

For the first time since 1995, Klinsmann and Anderton started a game together and with Ginola and Ferdinand also available to play against their old team, Gross was able to field somewhere near his strongest XI. Spurs started brightly and scored when Ginola crossed for Klinsmann to head them into the lead. Ferdinand added a second late in the second half to give a two-goal cushion and the sense of relief around White Hart Lane was palpable.

Safety would have been secured with the result had it not been for Bolton Wanderers recording a surprise 3-1 victory at Villa Park. Crystal Palace and Barnsley were already down but the final relegation spot was now a battle between Bolton, Everton and Spurs, though Newcastle and Wimbledon weren't yet safe.

Spurs' future hinged on another trip to Selhurst Park to meet Wimbledon on 2 May. The Dons had often upset Spurs and had won the two previous home fixtures between the two sides. but Selhurst, however, became a home from home as Spurs fans were able to purchase tickets in all sides of the ground. It was a beautiful early summer afternoon and Spurs, playing in all white, enjoyed their best day of 1998.

Despite the team going 2-1 behind in the first half, Klinsmann produced his most important Spurs performance, scoring four goals in a 6-2 victory that ranks among the most significant contributions he made across both spells in North London. Ferdinand and Saib were also on the scoresheet. The three points lifted Spurs above Wimbledon on goal difference but survival was mathematically secured the following day when Everton were beaten 4-0 at Highbury – a result that secured Arsenal their first league title under Wenger and the club's first since 1991.

Alan Fisher had seen Spurs relegated in 1977, so is well placed to describe the mood and prevailing memories of that afternoon at Selhurst Park:

> I'm not sure what the other results that day meant but I look back on this game as one of the most significant and terrifying in my Spurs-supporting lifetime as a defeat could have led to relegation. Had we lost we would have gone into the final game of the season needing something to avoid going down and then the nerves can take over. Did I have faith that we could deal with that pressure? Sorry, lads, but no, I didn't.

> We had some very good players – Campbell, Berti, Anderton, Ginola, Ferdinand and of course Klinsmann all played at Wimbledon that afternoon – but we weren't a team with any backbone and were always liable to give away a goal.
>
> I listened to it on the radio, pacing the living-room floor. It still felt like I kicked every ball. Klinsmann rose to the occasion with four goals, the mark of a great striker to finish so well when the stakes were at their highest. But what I remember most are the feelings of fear and dread when we went 2-1 down and the palpable relief at full-time. To be honest, when I saw the highlights, I became irritated with the players, celebrating as if it were a doddle. If it was so straightforward, why didn't you play like this earlier in the season and not put us through months of agony?

By the time Spurs met Southampton on the final day of the season it had been announced that Klinsmann would not stay on for the following season. Sugar had always been quite transparent that the short-term deal was just until the end of the season and the relationship felt primarily transactional. He scored his final Spurs goal in a 1-1 draw that meant Spurs finished the season on a four-game unbeaten run and in 14th place.

The paltry 44 points gained was even less than the previous turgid season and of Spurs' 11 league wins five had come against teams that had sat in either 19th or 20th position. Having spent 16 consecutive weeks from the start of November through until May in 16th or lower and eight weeks in the bottom three it was simply too close for comfort.

Klinsmann's nine goals in 15 appearances ultimately kept Spurs up. The other three strikers – Armstrong, Ferdinand and Iversen – all suffered injury-ravaged campaigns, scoring just ten goals in 53 appearances between them. Anderton, so often the provider, had only been able to start seven games.

The only chinks of light had been the brief moments of magic from Ginola and the steadying maturity of Sol Campbell who, as captain at 23, had been Spurs' most consistent performer of the season. The defender had now cemented his position in the England back-three that would go on to play in the summer's World Cup tournament in France.

The end of the season marked the end of esteemed Spurs careers for both Gary Mabbutt and David Howells, who had been informed that their contracts would not be renewed. Club captain Mabbutt had made just 11 appearances during his final season and had fallen out with Gross. Having not featured since Boxing Day, he was at least afforded a welcome send-off, coming on as a late substitute on the final day.

Mabbutt's legacy continues well into the 21st century. Only Steve Perryman has made more appearances for the club. At 36 Mabbutt retired from professional football and, despite offers to go into management, has remained involved in football through his work as a club ambassador. During the COVID lockdown he made over 2,500 phone calls to elderly or vulnerable Spurs fans. He was awarded an MBE for services to football in 1994.

For Howells it was not a fitting farewell. Having begun the season with a testimonial, he had gradually been ostracised from first-team action and was not even named on the bench for the final game of the season:

> It was a really disappointing end to my Spurs career and the club didn't handle it well. I was initially offered a new contract but Christian Gross wanted to bring his own players in, which I understood, but the contract offer was then withdrawn.

His Spurs career encompassed 356 appearances and 22 goals over a 12-year period in the first team alone. Howells had played under seven managers and starred alongside Glenn Hoddle, Paul Gascoigne, Gary Lineker, Jurgen Klinsmann and David Ginola.

With Arsenal winning the League and FA Cup double in flamboyant style, and Spurs narrowly avoiding relegation with no style, it was hard to remember a less enjoyable moment since relegation in 1977. As the decade approached its final full season, Spurs' position on and off the field had continued to wane. Arsenal and Chelsea had left Spurs behind – even West Ham were better!

1998/99 – SPURS ARE ON THEIR WAY TO WIMBLEDON

WALKER
CARR CAMPBELL YOUNG EDINBURGH
ANDERTON FREUND NIELSEN GINOLA
ARMSTRONG IVERSEN

HOW I SAW IT:

This season was my final year at school with my A levels in History, Government & Politics and Business Studies culminating in exams in the summer. While all my peers pondered over which university they were going to apply for, I had decided higher education wasn't for me and that I was going to get a job when I finished school. My main motivation was that getting a full-time job would enable me to fulfil my lifetime ambition of owning a Spurs season ticket.

It was inevitable that Christian Gross would be sacked and I remember the furore of George Graham's appointment. I don't recall having particularly strong opinions either way – perhaps as an A level History student I understood all too well that there were two sides to the debate and logically I could see that despite being the antithesis of what Spurs were supposed to stand for, he was a manager with a proven track record of improving a team and winning football matches.

My cousin Gary had always spoken very highly of George Graham, having worked with him at Arsenal, so with this in mind I don't recall ever being offended at the time by the style of play. I was used to seeing tepid and mediocre performances from Spurs so it felt like an improvement that Graham was able to instil a collective determination and professionalism that we hadn't seen in a number of years. I saw some exciting games – the 2-2 draw at home to Manchester United, the 4-1 win over Everton between Christmas and New Year and the 5-2 FA Cup win over Watford were all infinitely better than what I'd endured previously.

The League Cup semi-final first leg against Wimbledon felt like a huge game – maybe the biggest and most important I had personally been to at White Hart Lane. Getting tickets seemed like a really big deal and I sat in the back row of the Paxton upper for what turned out to be a mostly forgettable 0-0 draw.

I applied successfully for second-leg tickets at Selhurst Park – the first time I had been to an away game without Dad. The game fell perfectly on a school half-term and I travelled down with my friend Matthew all the way from Cuffley through Central London to Selhurst Park. The atmosphere all the way from Victoria Station to the Arthur Wait Stand was electric. I know there were many George Graham naysayers but the sense of togetherness and anticipation that turned into euphoria when Iversen scored and we subsequently won is something that has stayed with me ever since. Returning home just after midnight with a hoarse voice on a freezing February night was well worth the overall experience.

Being only a club member, I had a very anxious wait to find out whether I'd been successful with my application for League Cup Final tickets. There was no loyalty point system in 1999 so all club members who applied were put into a giant ballot. You were given the price points and just had to state what you'd be prepared to pay up to. In the days before email the quickest way of finding out whether you had been successful was to check whether your bank account had been debited. For several days I went to an ATM to get a balance statement and eventually the Saturday before the final saw that £72, for two tickets, had been debited.

I'd waited eight years to watch Spurs in a cup final at Wembley. Chris and I sat midway back in the lower tier behind the goal that Spurs eventually scored in. Although Dad had also managed to source a ticket, he wasn't sat with me so I didn't hold back on screaming at Robbie Savage for his role in getting Edinburgh sent off. I might even have dropped the 'C Bomb' but I do take credit for starting a rendition of 'Savage, what's the score?' as Leicester collected their runners-up medals. The League Cup may have been ridiculed but it felt like a seminal moment for Spurs. As Chris and I walked back along Wembley Way we talked about the potential European glamour ties that awaited us and it really felt as though we were on the cusp of a much brighter future.

The success felt like a personal one of endurance and perseverance and my hoarse voice was my own proud battle scar. Having endured five years of Arsenal fans gloating, we finally had something to feel proud about.

The euphoria and any sense of north London supremacy lasted just a matter of weeks. We played Arsenal at White Hart Lane in a midweek game in early May in which they desperately needed to win to stay in the title race. They beat us convincingly but I took great offence to Nwankwo Kanu celebrating the decisive third goal in front of us in the north-east corner of the ground. Such was my irritation that I called through to the BBC Radio phone-in special presented by Spurs fan Richard Littlejohn on the way home. I was live on national radio explaining that not only should Kanu be banned for three games but also that Spurs had been the better team and deserved at least a draw. My understanding and analysis of 19th-century European history was fortunately much more attuned than my football analysis as I found out the following day that I had achieved an 'A' grade for that module, which cheered me up.

We had the curious situation of going into the final game of the season at Manchester United with nothing to play for but knew that defeat would ensure that Arsenal didn't win the league. We watched the game at my house with a number of friends including Arsenal fans. I'm afraid to admit that I winced when we took an unlikely lead and then cheered both United's goals. I had to reflect that we had a lot to be thankful to Manchester United for and, as a result, really got behind them for the Champions League Final success against Bayern Munich later that month.

SEASON COMMENTARY

The summer of 1998 produced another iconic World Cup tournament, which was won by the home nation, France. England suffered heartbreaking defeat on penalties again – this time at the hands of Argentina in the second round. Darren Anderton featured in each game for England as a right-wing-back and scored a terrific goal against Colombia during the group stage.

During the tournament, another Spurs player, Sol Campbell, showcased his talent to a global audience playing on the left of a three-man defence for England. Campbell had made his England senior debut immediately before Euro '96 and quickly after, once Hoddle had taken over, began to establish himself as a regular in the starting XI. He even captained the team, aged just 24, in Alan Shearer's absence, in a pre-tournament match against Belgium.

Now established as club captain Campbell had, since his first-team debut, been used all across the pitch by various Spurs managers but he eventually settled into his most natural role as a central defender by 1997. Despite being picked alongside a variety of different central-defensive partners and in both a back three and back four, Campbell had been a rock in the Spurs defence totally no matter the chaos surrounding him. For Spurs, Campbell had demonstrated not just his robust defensive qualities but also the ability to carry the ball forwards from defence. Against Argentina Campbell embarked on such a run, highlighting his unique skill set to an international audience.

Talk of Campbell's future beyond his contract expiry in 2001 continued to rumble on with no clear indication that he was assured the club matched his ambitions; he was reportedly wanted by Manchester United, Liverpool and a number of high-profile clubs on the continent.

Throughout the summer Spurs were heavily linked with a number of prominent players from abroad. In David Pleat Spurs now had a Director of Football to lead scouting and contract negotiation but newspaper speculation could never be taken at face value as agents would often leak misleading information. Among those players linked were the Dutch twins

Ronald and Frank de Boer, their compatriot Patrick Kluivert and Argentine striker Ariel Ortega.

These names were consistent with David Pleat's assertion that the club only wanted to sign the best players, though the rumours did sound fanciful at best and at worst a desperate PR strategy to give an impression of ambition in the transfer market.

The internet was in its embryonic stages but lent itself to primitive message boards and football websites. As a result, the club set up a dedicated phone line that supporters could ring to find out whether the daily rumours had any substance. Pleat usually spoke, invariably just dismissing any rumours that existed.

The only summer transfer expenditure Spurs made was to sign Italian left-back Paolo Tramezzani from Vicenza for £1.5m. Tramezzani, 28 at the time, had started his career at Inter Milan where he had been a team-mate of Nicola Berti. The pair had remained good friends and Berti talked Tramezzani into joining him in North London. He was expected to become Spurs' first-choice left-back ahead of Justin Edinburgh and Allan Nielsen, who had deputised at left-back towards the end of the previous season.

It was patently clear that the team that had narrowly avoided relegation and lost its top goalscorer and two most senior stalwarts needed more reinforcements than Tramezzani. But the only other summer incomer was veteran goalkeeper Hans Segers who was signed on a dual player/goalkeeping coach basis.

Christian Gross began pre-season unusually early and took the squad members not involved in the World Cup for a vigorous workout in the Swiss Alps. Training was geared around physical preparation and included daily uphill bicycle rides in the mountains. Sol Campbell recounts in his authorised biography *Sol Campbell* that he was asked to return, having played in the World Cup, to pre-season quicker than he felt ready. Having fallen out with Mabbutt and Klinsmann the previous season Gross now risked his relationship with his captain.

The opening day of the season sent Spurs back to Selhurst Park to play Wimbledon 105 days since the epic 6-2 victory that guaranteed safety.

There were just three changes to the starting XI from the previous visit to Selhurst Park – Tramezzani made his debut at left-back in place of Nielsen, Calderwood replaced Vega in central defence and Armstrong filled Klinsmann's place in attack.

As the season opened the kits were the same, the weather was equally as hot but the outcome could not have been more different. Wimbledon had had nothing to play for back in May but would undoubtedly have relished the opportunity to avenge that defeat by Spurs and scored twice inside 12 second-half minutes to take a two-goal lead. Fox pulled one back but it was an abject Spurs display capped by a third from the home side in the closing minutes.

It was not just Klinsmann's departure that set apart the two performances. In May Spurs had displayed an inner determination and ultimately their superior quality had shone through but now in August, at a time in the season where expectations should have been high, there had simply been no fight in a meek and defeatist performance that indicated that all was not well.

Both Gross and Sugar came under intense pressure that ramped up to fever pitch for the first home game of the season against Sheffield Wednesday. Although the team started the game on the front foot, the atmosphere inside the stadium turned toxic as the away side scored twice before half-time. An organised protest to wave white handkerchiefs would have been stronger had so many of the original 32,000 fans inside the stadium not left early. Spurs conceded a third in the second half by which time Vega, error-prone in central defence, had been substituted at half-time. The plans Gross had worked on all pre-season had effectively been proved worthless within a game and a half of the new season.

The defeat gave greater prominence to Mark Jacob's TAG movement and he was regularly being invited onto local and national media platforms to share his, and other fans', views of the current predicament:

> The press smelt a story brewing and were salivating over the situation; Gross should have been sacked at the start of the summer; the poor bloke clearly wasn't up to the job and was being left out to dry. TAG was always about supporting the team and I always made sure to emphasise that point – but demand a change in ownership. We needed to make sure our voice was being heard – this was simply not good enough. Arsenal were winning doubles and we had just avoided relegation, yet what happened that summer? Nothing.
>
> Results were getting worse; our signings were a joke and even the share price was falling. On top of that Sugar's conduct was appalling and he kept getting involved in public slanging matches he didn't need to. He even took it out on us – he told an interview that he'd give it another two years … if TAG would let him! It was pure contempt towards the fans and the proud history of the club.
>
> The defeat at Wimbledon was shambolic and it was time for action – I'd watched a lot of Spanish football and suggested that any fans at the ground for the next home game carry out a protest by waving a white handkerchief to show our disapproval. Of course, we went on to lose 3-0 to Sheffield Wednesday which I took no joy from but outside the stadium thousands of fans congregated to tie hankies to the Bill Nicholson gates.

Gross was expected to leave the club immediately but the newspaper headlines were dominated by stories about Sugar's desire to sell up. The club, still listed on the stock exchange, saw its share price continue to drop.

The manager was given a stay of execution that saw him lead the team to Everton – the same venue where he had begun his Spurs career. Gross replaced Walker with Baardsen in goal and also made a change to the formation – Armstrong, a striker, was sacrificed for Calderwood, a defender, to shore the team up. Ferdinand's powerful header gave Spurs an early lead which proved to be the only goal of the game. The decision had already been made, though, and the following weekend, while club football took a break for international fixtures, news was released that Gross had been sacked.

David Howells believed Gross was unfortunate but ultimately always had his cards marked:

> He had some good training methods and, as a foreign coach with a decent reputation, I can understand why the chairman had gone for him in the first place. He was a very nice guy at heart but his personality didn't help. It was almost impossible to fall out with Gary Mabbutt and Jurgen Klinsmann but somehow, he managed to ostracise both of them early on and I don't think he ever recovered from that.

He will be remembered as a joke figure for his time in England from the moment he brandished the train ticket from his top pocket in his unveiling press conference but his reputation elsewhere remained intact. Back in his native Switzerland Gross went on to win four more league titles with Basel and also managed Stuttgart in Germany.

In David Pleat Sugar at least had a credible interim coach to look after team affairs while he considered Gross's replacement. Pleat was assisted by Chris Hughton and the pair oversaw a narrow 2-1 victory against Blackburn at White Hart Lane in mid-September but there was disappointment when visitors Middlesbrough, newly promoted back to the Premier League, won 3-0 live on Sky the following weekend.

Middlesbrough included Paul Gascoigne in their team that day and the game took place almost exactly a decade to the day that Gazza had scored on his home debut for Spurs against Arsenal. Both Spurs and Gascoigne had endured ups and downs since his sale to Lazio in 1992. Gascoigne had completed three seasons in Italy and then joined Glasgow Rangers where he won a Scottish league title in each of his three full seasons at Ibrox. He provided some magic moments in Scotland and also scored a truly memorable goal for England, against Scotland, at Euro '96 but he was never able to recreate the levels he achieved as a Spurs player.

However, Gascoigne's personal demons continued to play havoc – he remained a front-page personality invariably for the wrong reasons throughout the decade. Having missed out on selection for the final England squad for World Cup '98, Gascoigne – by then a Middlesbrough player – trashed manager Glenn Hoddle's hotel room where the bad news had been broken to him. Gascoigne left the camp in tears and would never play for England again.

Back at White Hart Lane he was among friends and despite the fact that his new team dismantled his previous one he received a warm reception in his first competitive appearance against Spurs since he had left.

With Pleat and Hughton continuing to lead the team on a caretaker basis there was mass speculation in the press about who would take over. Joe Kinnear at Wimbledon had been a decorated Spurs player during the 1970s but was perhaps tarnished with the style at Wimbledon that lacked the refinement needed at Spurs. Martin O'Neill of Leicester was another highly respected manager and Sugar recalls that Pleat did mention him in a board meeting but the suggestion went no further.

George Graham, so synonymous with Arsenal's success of the late 80s and early 90s, had suffered an ignominious departure from Highbury in 1995. Graham had been part of Arsenal's double-winning 1971 team as a player and then, as manager from 1986 until his sacking in 1995 he delivered two league titles, the FA Cup, two League Cups and the European Cup Winners' Cup. His languid playing style that earned him the nickname 'Stroller' was incongruous with his disciplinarian style of management initially developed at Millwall where he came to the attention of his former club Arsenal.

He was simply 'Mr Arsenal' but, as was common, had been involved in the minutiae of all club affairs including the details of transfers. Graham had authorised and personally benefitted from a 'bung' – an illegal financial payment – during several transfers involving the Norwegian agent, Rune Hauge. Details of Graham's misdemeanours had originally leaked midway through the 1994/95 season but initially the Arsenal board refused to sack him, drawing an outburst from Sugar, of all people, who labelled them 'gutless'. As further revelations were revealed Graham was eventually fired in February 1995.

Following an FA enquiry, Graham was banned from football for 12 months. In September 1996 he was given a route back into management by Leeds. Graham took over a team in ninth place and finished the season in 11th. The following season saw improvement; Leeds finished fifth and qualified for the UEFA Cup. A move back to north London appealed to Graham; he had commuted from the capital to Yorkshire and had no intention of relocating his fiancée and family to Leeds. Graham remained bitter at his treatment by Arsenal and surely relished the opportunity to get one over on his ex-employers.

Graham's name continued to be discussed in the Spurs boardroom and Sugar revealed that former Spurs and England player Martin Peters, a non-executive director of the club, advised that Graham was the only manager with the credentials required to turn Spurs around. It was a huge dilemma for Sugar – having fought such an anti-corruption campaign against Venables – and lambasted Arsenal for failing to take immediate action against Graham initially, it would be an incredible U-turn to then appoint him as a new manager.

In a twist of fate, Spurs' next league game was the home fixture against Leeds on 26 September. Both sets of fans seemed equally torn on the badly kept secret that Spurs wanted Graham, and that Graham wanted to come to Spurs. From a Leeds perspective there was a feeling that they had provided him with an opportunity to return to football when others wouldn't have touched him. Spurs fans were torn between his track record of success and his association with Arsenal as well as the style of football, which was seen as the antitheses of the Spurs way.

Officially neither club had stated anything publicly but it was widely reported that initial discussions had taken place between both about an official approach and that Graham was keen on the move. Graham, much like his close friend Terry

Venables, had many friends in the press – both were astute at being able to surreptitiously share their innermost thoughts to a national audience. Perhaps Sugar should have been more aware of this fact.

It was easy to forget that there was a game of football due to take place, especially when Leeds chief executive Peter Ridsdale found it necessary to personally address the travelling fans at half-time. Leeds took a 3-1 lead but were pegged back by two late goals by Iversen and then Campbell. The naivety of the defending by both teams would have alarmed Graham, as much as the determination by Spurs to rescue what looked a helpless situation would have offered encouragement. His Arsenal team had been famous for scoring late goals.

Following Leeds subsequent UEFA Cup fixture in Portugal, Ridsdale confirmed that they had accepted a request from Spurs to talk to Graham and later that day on 1 October it was announced that George Graham had been appointed as the new Spurs manager. It was seen as Sugar's last throw of the dice in a desperate attempt to bring success to White Hart Lane.

For Mark Jacob, and his TAG followers, this was the final straw:

> I remember the look on Sugar's face at the press conference – even he couldn't believe what he'd done in appointing the very antithesis to Tottenham Hotspur's proud traditions as the new manager. Graham was already yesterday's man. His Arsenal teams had continued to play archaic football and Leeds were boring and in mid-table. What was worse, though, was that just three years earlier Sugar had been on a public crusade to rid football of sleaze and financial impropriety; he went after the Arsenal board when they didn't initially sack him and now here he is, at White Hart Lane unveiling Graham as his new manager.

Graham, like Venables, was a polished media performer and was confident in front of a camera and knew just how to emphasise particular points and to create and perpetuate a narrative. During his unveiling, when questioned on what Spurs fans would think of a former Arsenal man taking over a club with such a rich history and demand for stylish football, Graham was quick to articulate that he wanted 'winning football' and he was quick to tell his new players in their first meeting that winning was all that matters.

Speaking on Sky Sports' *Hold the Back Page* programme that weekend, esteemed sportswriter Henry Winter summed up the situation: 'Expediency rules in football. And what Tottenham need is a manager like George Graham who will come in and sort out the defence … that defence needs a good two months of George Graham drilling on the training ground. And then I think towards the end of the season, or certainly the season afterwards, they could be pushing for Europe.'

Paul Hawksbee had personal experiences of George Graham so saw the appointment from a slightly different perspective:

> I'd got to know George a bit while he was out of the game and I was editing *Goal* magazine. I'd spend some time with him each month talking to him about all aspects of the game for his column in the magazine and had got to like him on a personal level. He was good company, very interesting and had a great sense of humour. When he went to Leeds, I'd remained in contact with him and he did well there but I know he was very keen to return to London. I suspect he felt he had a point to prove to the directors at Arsenal whom he felt had sacked him very unfairly so that was motivation for him to come to Spurs. It was a job he was very keen on so on a personal level I was pleased for him though there was always a nagging doubt in my mind that ultimately it wouldn't prove a good match because of that Arsenal connection.

Having only arrived at the club on the Thursday Graham watched from the stands as David Pleat picked the team to play at Derby on 3 October. The new manager did address the team in the changing room telling them that he expected to see hard work. He would have been delighted to observe a hard-fought 1-0 victory courtesy of Sol Campbell's second-half header. The '1-0 to the Tottenham' era had begun.

It was not a perfect afternoon though – Sol Campbell was accused of assaulting a Derby steward following a tunnel melee in the aftermath of the match. The allegations were unfounded and eventually dropped but it is implied in his authorised biography *Sol Campbell* that the captain felt the club hadn't supported him sufficiently and this would have significant ramifications for his long-term relationship with the club.

Another international break provided the new manager with two weeks on the training ground with his new team before the next fixture which was away at Leicester in Sky Sports' Monday night fixture. The game had extra significance because Martin O'Neill was wanted by Leeds to fill the vacancy created by Graham's departure. The home supporters at Filbert Street ran a charm offensive with an emotional level of support and appreciation for their manager, which added to the atmosphere and determination of the Leicester players.

Graham made just one change to the team that had won at Derby – Clemence replaced the injured Nielsen in midfield – and stuck to a 4-5-1 with Anderton playing centrally behind Ferdinand. The England pair combined early on to give Spurs a lead but Leicester were able to overpower Spurs – Heskey equalised when he outmuscled Vega, and then Izzet scored a wonderful volley from long range with five minutes remaining. The win and emotion of the night was enough to convince O'Neill to stay at Leicester – Leeds instead turned to Graham's former assistant David O'Leary. The defeat left Spurs in 14th place, just three points behind Arsenal in fifth but only three points above the relegation zone.

Even before Graham's arrival at White Hart Lane had been confirmed, the media speculated about his potential relationship with David Ginola. The new manager was well known for his thorough defensive organisation and his demand for all players to work hard off the ball. Ginola was somewhat typecast owing to his flamboyance and good looks, which saw him become the face, or at least hair, of Vidal Sassoon's shampoo and conditioner products. Ginola has always been quick to defend his supposed lacklustre approach to defensive responsibilities but was aware enough of his reputation to confront Graham early on to ask what role his manager had in mind for him. In *Le Magnifique* Ginola recounts that Graham told him that all players had the opportunity to earn their manager's trust.

Ginola kept his place in Graham's starting XI for the home game against Newcastle on 24 October though the formation reverted to a standard 4-4-2 with Ginola and Anderton wide. Iversen, on as a substitute for Ferdinand, scored twice in a comfortable yet unspectacular 2-0 win to give Graham his first victory as Spurs manager. His reign had begun with a win, a draw and a loss that highlighted Spurs' mid-table credentials.

Throughout November results were equally mixed – defeats at Aston Villa and West Ham, both in the top six places, another no-frills home win – this time against Nottingham Forest – and most notably a goalless draw at Highbury to mark Graham's first return to his old stomping ground as Spurs manager. The draw at Arsenal owed as much to luck as it did to organisation and doggedness. Ginola was left out to accommodate a very specific tactical approach to nullify Arsenal in a 5-3-2 shape.

Graham had set to work on Spurs' defensive frailties; a popular myth existed from his time at Arsenal that he would train the back four with a rope tied between them with the purpose of ensuring that as play developed from one side of the pitch to the other the back four would retain safe distances between them.

While working on the shape of his defensive unit Graham also had to decide on his strongest personnel. Baardsen was his inherited number one but, after a mistake at West Ham, was replaced by Walker, who retained the position for the remainder of the season. Carr and Campbell were mainstays and Edinburgh played at left-back unless injured. It was the second central defensive position that was most changeable; Vega began as Campbell's partner but was replaced by Scales, whom Graham had wanted to sign at Leeds. Neither convinced, so Graham called up 19-year-old youth graduate Luke Young to make his senior debut against West Ham.

In Walker, Carr, Young and Campbell Spurs had virtually a full defence made up of homegrown players. Two other defenders, Ledley King and Alton Thelwell, were also making a good impression in the youth team and reserves.

While league results were mixed in Graham's initial spell, Spurs were able to gain some momentum through the League Cup. They navigated through a two-leg tie against third-tier Brentford before Graham arrived and then won 3-1 at Northampton in the third round. The fourth-round draw sent Spurs to Anfield in mid-November where Spurs faced an out-of-sorts Liverpool undergoing their own managerial uncertainty. Scales, starting in a back three, scored what would be his only Spurs goal, against his old team. Iversen and Nielsen added a second and then third respectively for what proved to be a comfortable 3-1 victory. It was the first time since Spurs had won at Anfield in the FA Cup in 1995 that they had recorded a cup win against any top-flight opponent.

In the first midweek of December Manchester United travelled to White Hart Lane for the quarter-final. Though Alex Ferguson made several changes he still brought a strong team that included Sheringham, Solskjaer and Giggs in attack. It proved to be a great night for Ginola, who delivered two wicked assists for Armstrong and then scored the decisive third himself. United would go on to win a historic treble – only Spurs stopped them winning all four available trophies!

White Hart Lane was slowly becoming a fortress – Liverpool were beaten before Manchester United returned just ten days after the League Cup encounter. Spurs played at great intensity but fell behind to two goals scored at terrific pace on the break. Ginola then managed to tie Gary Neville up in knots and forced him into two yellow card offences before half-time. Despite the two-goal deficit Spurs eventually made the numerical advantage count with two very late goals, both scored by Sol Campbell.

The style of play may not have been pretty but it was becoming effective. Graham had undoubtedly instilled a resoluteness and determination that had been badly missing previously. The customary defeat at Stamford Bridge in the final game before Christmas did not dispel the feeling that momentum was building. On Boxing Day Spurs recorded a 1-1 draw at Coventry and then two days later beat Everton 4-1 at White Hart Lane with Chris Armstrong scoring a hat-trick. The win put them in 12th place but closer to sixth than the relegation zone as the New Year approached.

The year 1999 began with a 5-2 home victory over Watford in the FA Cup third round; Spurs fell behind to a first-minute goal but were 4-2 ahead by half-time in an unusually chaotic and loose performance. The draw for the fourth round paired Spurs with Wimbledon whom they were also due to meet in the two-legged League Cup semi-final. Including the upcoming league match, it meant that Spurs were now scheduled to play Wimbledon four times between 16 January and 16 February.

Two defensive reinforcements were made over the winter period. The long-protracted transfer of Ipswich's Argentine full-back Mauricio Taricco was completed in early December and the German midfielder Steffen Freund arrived from Borussia Dortmund for the modest fee of £750,000. Having been part of the Germany squad that won Euro '96 and then the Borussia Dortmund team that won the 1997 Champions League, Freund felt something of a coup. Freund made his debut in a goalless draw at Sheffield Wednesday – the first of six consecutive draws in the league.

Having played out a goalless draw with Wimbledon in the league, the next meeting came in the FA Cup at Selhurst Park. Predictably this was also a cagey affair that ended in a draw resulting therefore in yet another meeting for the replay. The first leg of the League Cup semi-final at White Hart Lane felt like a really big occasion – a near-capacity crowd watched with great expectation but ultimately observed another tedious 0-0 draw, meaning it was all to play for in the second leg.

However, the next encounter in the sequence was the FA Cup replay, played at White Hart Lane the following midweek. This proved to be the least intense of the now five-game sequence; George Graham rested Ginola but otherwise went with his usual XI while Joe Kinnear picked a clearly under-strength team; only 24,049 attended but saw Spurs get off to a great start when Sinton, in for Ginola, opened the scoring inside three minutes. The game was played at a much lower intensity than the previous three games, which seemed to suit Spurs more than Wimbledon; two further goals by Allan Nielsen in the second half contributed to a 3-0 victory and set up another narrative-fuelled cup tie with George Graham returning to Leeds.

Ahead of the tie at Elland Road Tim Sherwood made his much-anticipated move from Blackburn to Spurs. The deal to bring the 1995 Premier League-winning captain to north London had first been mooted the previous summer; Sherwood was determined to make the move back south and had been so unsettled that he had been left out of the Blackburn team earlier in the season. Sherwood provided leadership qualities and undoubtedly provided greater depth and quality in central midfield.

Both Berti and Saib had left the club, having fallen out with Graham about their rehabilitation from respective injuries; Graham had insisted that any injured players spend the whole day at the training ground to receive treatment and had therefore clashed with Berti, Saib and Tramezzani, who had also wanted to return home to recuperate. None of the three ever played for Spurs again.

Sherwood made his debut at Elland Road for the FA Cup fifth-round tie and made an immediate impact, scoring a deflected goal from range to give Spurs a second-half lead. They were unable to hold onto it, though, and had to settle for a draw, which required a replay at White Hart Lane to add to a chaotic schedule – it meant that by the end of February Spurs had played as many matches in the cups as they had in the league in 1999.

The League Cup semi-final second leg at Selhurst Park took place in mid-February and there was a huge sense of anticipation. Since winning the FA Cup in 1991 Spurs had failed to win any of their next three semi-finals but under George Graham it felt as though the right ingredients were now in place to mentally handle the occasion. Sherwood and Taricco were both cup-tied. Vega, with his height advantage, was preferred to Luke Young but otherwise Spurs were at full strength.

As was the case in the first leg, the game developed a very scrappy pattern from the first whistle; Ginola was effectively double-marked and so Spurs had to rely on attritional tactics but it was a moment of luck and high quality that proved the difference. With six minutes until half-time, a long ball forward was controlled by Ferdinand with his back to goal; he attempted to flick the ball forwards but was tackled by Cunningham who deflected the ball into the path of Iversen, who was standing a yard offside. The Norwegian controlled the ball on his thigh, turned and looped a volley over Neil Sullivan and into the far corner of the net. It was a goal of Hoddle-level technique. The replays showed that Iversen was offside though it was unclear whether Ferdinand or Cunningham had played the ball to him.

A goal ahead in a tie in which away goals were a factor was the perfect situation for George Graham, and Spurs now had the grit and organisation to withstand an avalanche of direct Wimbledon pressure throughout the second half. Young replaced Ginola, so Spurs ended the game with a back five and Ferdinand and Iversen spent more time on the edge of their area than they did at the other end; Spurs survived a late onslaught and again fortune was on their side, just as it had been against them in previous semi-finals, when Robbie Earle's shot skimmed the top of the crossbar in stoppage time.

That was the final action and as the full-time whistle sounded the Spurs fans who seemed to be in the majority at Selhurst Park were as one with George Graham who quickly got himself off the pitch ahead of a mini invasion. It was a typically committed and pragmatic George Graham performance when it was most needed and the biggest vindication yet of his appointment. For the first time in eight years Spurs had a cup final to look forward to and it would be against Leicester, who had beaten Sunderland in the other semi-final.

Had Graham's appointment achieved the impossible by uniting the fans and club behind a team that was actually capable of winning now? Mark Jacob describes in *What's the Story? Boring Glory* – his published diary of the 98/99 season – the euphoria and mixed emotions about the new manager as thousands of Spurs fans travelled home from South London:

> The journey brings back memories of the Wolves semi-final in 1981. The banter, the songs, the jokes, the atmosphere … The songs just kept coming. We sing 'Spurs are on their way to Wembley'. Brilliant, this is what it's all about. And we sing 'Que Sera'. We sing 'It's a grand ol' team' and 'Giorgio Armani's Blue and White Army.' George Graham has got us to Wembley, but we still can't chant his name … Only when the double and European Champions Cup sits proudly at the Lane, and Mr Graham exceeds his achievements at Arsenal, will we really accept this mercenary Gooner.

One of those significant achievements at Highbury was the double domestic cup success in 1993 which Spurs could still emulate. On another electric night under the lights at White Hart Lane, a 2-0 victory over Leeds in the FA Cup replay raised hopes that Graham might be able to deliver another cup double. Anderton and Ginola both scored wonderful goals – as good a pair of goals scored in a game all decade, though it was a great goal that wasn't scored that brought as much media attention.

At the start of the season the very thought of George Graham celebrating a Spurs goal seemed completely preposterous. The image of him cheering, arms aloft in joy, for a goal that didn't even go in has to go down as a cult moment. With the score 0-0 Ginola picked up the ball on the right of the penalty area. Running horizontally across the edge of the box he teased the opponents and supporters by feigning to shoot at each challenge and, having seemingly gone too far wide on the left, struck a shot back across the goalkeeper that hit the inside of the right post, rebounded back along the line and agonisingly back past the other post.

The TV cameras picked up Graham's visceral reactions perfectly as he believed, from his low vantage point in the dugout, that Ginola had just scored one of the goals of the season. The look of disbelief on Graham's face as assistant Chris Hughton told him it hadn't gone in seemed to match that of all the supporters within the ground. For a micro second Graham and the Spurs supporters were all feeling exactly the same emotion.

Now only second-tier Barnsley stood in the way of another semi-final.

The league campaign began to feel like an inconvenience among all the high-octane cup games. Spurs remained in mid-table after the run of six successive draws was broken with a comfortable 3-0 win over Southampton and then followed up with a 2-0 defeat at Leeds, who had seemingly improved since Graham had been replaced by David O'Leary.

The original FA Cup quarter-final tie at Barnsley was postponed on the morning of the game due to snow, so by the time the rearranged game came around in the midweek before the League Cup Final, Spurs already knew that victory at Oakwell would mean a semi-final against Newcastle in April.

This appeared again to be a sign of the luck that George Graham brought with him from Arsenal as Spurs had avoided their North London rivals and Manchester United who had been drawn against each other in the other semi-final. As Sherwood and Taricco were cup-tied for the League Cup both started at Barnsley but otherwise Graham named the same team he would pick at Wembley for the League Cup Final four days later.

Ginola once again stole the show with the only goal of the game and having scored wonder goals in the two previous rounds against Wimbledon and Leeds, it felt that he was trying to outdo himself in each successive round. On this occasion Ginola picked the ball up just inside the Barnsley half on the left touchline before slaloming through four challenges and then slotting into the corner from just inside the penalty area. It was the only goal of the game and Spurs could look forward to a semi-final against Newcastle.

The League Cup, now sponsored by Worthington's Bitter, had been unfairly renamed colloquially as the 'Worthless' Cup owing to the lack of interest that the leading teams, Manchester United, Arsenal and Chelsea, had shown in it since the prominence of the newly expanded Champions League that admitted three English teams to the competition. As Manchester United had done in the quarter-final, it was not uncommon for the biggest clubs who aspired to finish in the top three places to pick significantly weakened teams in the League Cup.

Leicester had exploited that indifference by winning the competition in 1997 and under Martin O'Neill had proved an obdurate and stubborn opponent with a pragmatic approach that served them well. The intangible attributes and qualities of Leicester were now matched by George Graham's Spurs and with both teams going into the game firmly in mid-table it was hard to identify a favourite.

Since returning to the top flight in 1996 Leicester had got the better of Spurs as evidenced by the three wins and two draws in the five league encounters, though in Ginola Spurs had the maverick match-winner.

By March 1999 the iconic Wembley Stadium, scene of so many of Spurs' greatest moments, was only 18 months away from complete knockdown and rebuild. Spurs were back for the first time since the 1993 FA Cup semi-final six years earlier. The condition of the dilapidated stadium seemed totally incongruous with the high-volume music and pyrotechnics that greeted the players as they emerged from the players' tunnel at the east end of the stadium – the far side from the end that Spurs' supporters occupied. Equally as incongruous was the choice of entry music, 'Let me entertain you' by Robbie Williams, which preceded one of the most tedious games of football the stadium had ever witnessed. O'Neill devised an effective plan to mark Ginola out of the game and there was little intent or ability from either side to create any chances.

Little happened in the match until, out of nowhere, an incident between agent provocateur Robbie Savage and Justin Edinburgh, the only survivor from the 1991 FA Cup Final, sparked the final into life. In 91 Spurs had been fortunate that an experienced and likeable referee, Roger Milford, had been overly lenient towards Gascoigne when he could quite justifiably have reduced Spurs to ten men. Against Leicester, Spurs and Edinburgh suffered a reversal of fortunes; the Spurs full-back was scythed down crossing the halfway line but Savage knew what he was doing when reacting and coerced Edinburgh into a flick of his hand towards Savage's face which actually made contact with his long, flowing blond locks. The contact caused the Leicester midfielder to fall to the ground in mock agony. Edinburgh was sent off and Spurs reduced to ten men.

The effect of the incident acted only to galvanise the remaining Spurs players. Nielsen dropped in to cover at left-back with Anderton moving centrally in midfield and Iversen and Ferdinand taking it in turns to cover the right wing. The tempo of the game may have increased but chances were at a premium with both sides cancelling each other out until stoppage time at the end of the 90 minutes.

Sinton replaced Ginola, which allowed Nielsen to move back into central midfield and the Dane was crucially in exactly the right place to react quickest and smartest when Leicester's goalkeeper Kasey Keller parried an Iversen cross shot. Nielsen dived to head the ball home from eight yards out to send the fans behind the goal into wild celebration, matched only by the Spurs team and substitutes who mobbed Nielsen.

It was surely only a coincidence that Ginola, Spurs' talisman in this cup run, had been off the field when Spurs had scored the winning goal – just as Gascoigne, the talisman in 1991, had left the pitch before Spurs went onto win the FA Cup Final?

This was the classic George Graham script and yet another 1-0 victory. As the final whistle sounded, the jubilation from the Spurs end was only broken by jeers and boos for Robbie

Savage who could be seen weeping as he collected his runners-up medal. Finally, the stage was set for Sol Campbell as Spurs captain to walk the famous 39 steps to collect and lift the League Cup trophy.

Bardi remembers:

> It was a horrible game, much like both the semi-final ties. I was elated when Nielsen scored the winner in such dramatic circumstances but it did feel like more of a relief than a celebration. This team of Ginola, Campbell and Anderton finally had something.

Perhaps the player whom a positive result meant the most to was Justin Edinburgh who, having been sent off, was in the changing room feeling disconsolate when he heard the roar of the Spurs crowd cheering the late goal. For most observers Edinburgh had been the unfortunate victim of Robbie Savage's gamesmanship. Even Savage himself, in his 2010 autobiography, admitted that he'd overreacted. Edinburgh heard the roar of goal, having just stepped out of the shower. He later ignored protocol and returned pitch side where he was awarded his winners' medal, thus becoming Spurs' most decorated player of the decade.

It is a good moment to remember Edinburgh, who in total made 266 appearances for the club before leaving in 2000 to join Portsmouth. It means he is the only player to have appeared for Spurs in each calendar year of the decade. Post-retirement Edinburgh went into management but remained an active member of the Spurs Legends set-up and also regularly appeared in the hospitality lounges at both White Hart Lane and the new Tottenham Hotspur Stadium. He tragically died in summer 2019 of a sudden heart attack just months short of his 50th birthday.

The players all enjoyed pitch-side post-game celebrations in the pouring rain while George Graham made his way back across the pitch to the changing rooms at the far side of Wembley; the Spurs fans broke out into a conciliatory rendition of 'The Man in the Raincoat's blue and white army'. They may not have been able to say his name but there was at least a grudging respect and acknowledgement that the former Arsenal man had delivered a trophy to White Hart Lane.

It is notable that in Alan Sugar's autobiography there is little more than a sentence reserved for the 1999 League Cup success that must have brought the chairman as much relief as it did joy. However, he does recount that the following morning Graham called the club's finance director to request an early payment of his agreed bonus for winning a trophy. Sugar then spoke with Graham to tell him in no uncertain terms that the payment would only be made, as per the contract, at the end of the season.

Ginola, reflecting in *Le Magnifique*, speaks of his pride at winning his first trophy in English football and first club honour since winning the French Cup with PSG in 1994. Ginola remembers the lap of honour at Wembley and being able to wave to his family and parents inside Wembley Stadium. Ginola had enjoyed a terrific season even if he had been marked out of both the semi-final and final; his mere presence had been enough to occupy at least one designated marker.

Like Gascoigne in 1991, the Frenchman had become talismanic for Spurs amid the culture war between him and Graham; his biggest achievement had arguably been to make himself undroppable. When he first met Sugar to sign for Spurs in summer 1997, Sugar had told him that he needed Ginola to get Spurs into Europe; the League Cup success meant that he had achieved that promise within two years.

Spurs harboured hopes of returning to Wembley for the FA Cup Final but up against Newcastle in the semi-final at Old Trafford luck once again worked against them. Spurs should have been awarded a penalty early in the second half when Newcastle defender Nikos Dabizas inexplicably flicked an outstretched hand against the ball from an Anderton cross inside the penalty area. Experienced referee Paul Durkin somehow missed it and waved play on.

Had Spurs taken the lead you would have expected Graham's team to have held on in a stoical manner. Instead, the game, another tedious affair devoid of any serious chances, went to extra time where Sol Campbell repeated Dabizas's action but this time Durkin awarded the penalty which Shearer converted.

With Ginola having already left the field in normal time there was no moment of magic for Spurs, who were chasing the game, and Shearer added a second late on. In all likelihood Spurs would have struggled against Manchester United in the final but it felt like another opportunity that had been cruelly taken away.

The league season ended in something of a whimper. After the Wembley success in March Spurs won just two of their final eight games and both of those came against sides who would be relegated, in Charlton and Nottingham Forest. The 1-0 victory at The City Ground proved to be the final encounter of 23 between the two clubs during the 90s of which Spurs had won seven and lost ten.

The rivalry had been an almost purely football one and had produced many absorbing encounters, though you couldn't help conclude that both clubs' prominence in the English game had diminished. It would be another 24 years until Nottingham Forest returned to the top flight to play Spurs in the Premier League again.

It was just as well that Spurs' final four fixtures hadn't come the previous season when they were desperately scrapping for points to stay up as Liverpool, Arsenal, Chelsea and Manchester United lay ahead! On 1 May Spurs took an unlikely 2-0 lead into half-time at Anfield through an own goal and Steffen Iversen but the momentum swung when Maurico Taricco was sent off just before the break. Spurs conceded three second-half goals but the game did see a substitute appearance for Ledley King who would go on to enjoy an esteemed career at Spurs.

At the other end of the spectrum, the Spurs defence included Norwegian Roger Nilsen who had signed from Sheffield United on a short-term contract to mitigate the departure of Colin Calderwood at the end of March. Nilsen made his last of three appearances for Spurs at Anfield.

Spurs remained in mid-table throughout the season but went into the final stretch of the season as kingmakers. Arsenal and Manchester United were by now the two dominant forces in English football and went into the final weeks of the season trading places at the top of the table. Arsenal travelled to White Hart Lane on 5 May needing a win and hoping that Manchester United would drop points in their crucial game away at rivals Liverpool. The timing of the two fixtures, both rescheduled from semi-final weekend, provided a unique opportunity for Sky Sports to televise both games simultaneously.

Arsenal, now two and a half years into the reign of Arsene Wenger, had well and truly stolen Spurs' mantle as the most entertaining team to watch in London and the previous season had supplemented style with substance by winning the League and Cup double. A mixture of pace, power, flair and panache was supplemented by the collective defensive organisation that Graham had initially built with those hours on the training ground with the mythical rope tied between Lee Dixon, Tony Adams, Steve Bould and Nigel Winterburn.

At White Hart Lane Arsenal were simply too good for Spurs all over the pitch with Bergkamp pulling the strings. His inch-perfect weighted passes set up Anelka and then Petit to provide a two-goal lead. Anderton pulled a goal back from a free kick but Spurs were barely able to land a punch before Kanu scored the goal of the night, flicking the ball over Young's head with his back to goal and then firing a volley past Ian Walker. Meanwhile Liverpool had come back from 2-0 down to draw with Manchester United in what felt like a seminal moment of the season's title race. The results provided Arsenal with a three-point lead with just two games to play. In 1971 Arsenal had secured the league title at White Hart Lane with George Graham in their team, now in 1999 they might just have won another title with Graham in the home dugout.

The final home game of the season nearly saw Spurs overcome their Chelsea hoodoo. Despite falling behind to an early goal Iversen, and then Ginola, put Spurs ahead only for Chelsea to equalise. It would be the final meeting between the two teams during the 90s with Spurs' solitary win coming back in February 1990. The wait for a win over Chelsea would only come to an end in 2002 in a thumping 5-1 League Cup victory, though it would take until November 2006 to record a league win.

By the time Spurs travelled to Old Trafford on the final day of the season Arsenal had dropped points at Leeds while Manchester United had picked up enough points to take a slender one-point lead with a superior goal difference. It meant that the only way that Arsenal could win the league would be if Spurs were able to take a point from Old Trafford while Arsenal would need to win their home game against Aston Villa.

With Spurs mired in mid-table there was a unanimous feeling among fans that they would be happy to see Spurs lose just to avoid Arsenal winning the title. The dynamic was reversed at Highbury where Arsenal fans listened in to updates from Old Trafford praying that their rivals could do them a favour; the net result was that Spurs fans were desperate to see their team lose while Arsenal fans were equally desperate for a Spurs win. George Graham joked in the days leading up to the game that Spurs would take the game incredibly seriously and go to Old Trafford looking for a win … but with Jose Dominguez in goal!

Bardi recalls his mixed emotions going into the game:

> When Teddy left us in summer 1997 to join Man United to 'win things' it was amusing that he then went and won nothing the following season, hence the song we all used to sing, 'Oh Teddy, Teddy, went to Man United and he won f*** all'. When we knocked them out the League Cup in the December it felt like we had a genuine curse on him so at the time part of me would have found it hysterical had he continued to win nothing! But there was a balance because it was Teddy or Arsenal for the league title and they'd won the double the previous season.

Old Trafford had been a graveyard for Spurs throughout the decade – they had gone the whole of the 90s without a win there and had only drawn just two of ten games including the semi-final against Newcastle a month previously. They'd only scored four goals during that period and the most recent was in October 1993 so it was a huge shock when Les Ferdinand silenced the whole stadium when he managed to loop a shot over Schmeichel to give Spurs the most unlikely of leads.

Normal service soon resumed and eventually Manchester United regained the flow and rhythm that had seen them brush aside so many opponents all season; Beckham had become a pantomime villain for Spurs fans but you suspected there was always something of a thinly veiled respect attached to it and his popularity in N17 peaked when he lashed a ball past Walker into the Spurs net to equalise just before half-time.

United famously rotated four international quality strikers including Sheringham into two starting positions but, on this occasion, it was Andy Cole, whom Graham had sold to Bristol City while Arsenal manager a decade earlier, who popped up with what proved to be a match- and championship-deciding goal shortly after half-time.

A tired Spurs team that had played 52 games during an epic season appeared to lack the energy, application and possibly motivation before a travelling crowd who were desperate for the home team to maintain their position, to make any sort of concerted effort and add a late sting to the season. The final half an hour played out as a title-winning procession enjoyed by all four corners of Old Trafford.

Bardi continues:

> As soon as the ball hit the net and we went 1-0 ahead effectively handing Arsenal the title I realised where my loyalties lay. Teddy's barren mantlepiece was no longer an issue for me. It was time to grow up. We needed to make sure we did what we invariably always did against Manchester United and cave in to deny Arsenal another league championship. The Teddy situation aside, Manchester United were a team most

> Spurs fans were very affectionate about in the 90s and 00s – perhaps even our second team. I remember going into school (in a part of north London where it was equal Spurs/Arsenal split) the following morning jubilant as if it was us who had won the league.

Spurs ended the season with a trophy in the cabinet, UEFA Cup qualification and another near miss in the FA Cup but this was secured at the expense of league form. Spurs were famed for being a 'cup team' but it still felt as though Graham's style of football was a huge sacrifice. Throughout the season Spurs secured just three more points than they had in the relegation-haunted 97/98 campaign and one more than Francis's final full season in 96/97.

Ginola developed as the leading protagonist of a remarkable season. In the final week of the season, he was awarded both the PFA and Football Writers' Player of the Season awards, putting him in the same bracket as Klinsmann and Lineker to have won both awards as a Spurs player during the 90s. Despite Spurs' mediocre league performance Ginola's accolades proved that the best and most exciting players still had a platform at White Hart Lane.

Paul Hawksbee always felt Ginola would be a classic Spurs player, even before he joined the club:

> The first time I remember seeing Ginola in the flesh was when he played against us for Newcastle in his first season in England. On that day (October 1995) the weather was awful with the rain pouring but he seemed completely undisturbed by the conditions and put on a master show scoring their goal. At one point he'd gone down injured and our fans at the front of The Shelf down by the Park Lane obviously thought he was milking it so were giving him some stick. It always stuck with me the way he responded in kind with a smile on his face and he managed to win them over. That and his abilities on the ball made him perfect for Spurs so I was delighted when he arrived.

He lived up to all the characteristics of a Spurs legend – flair, creativity, a match-winner and joins a pantheon of Spurs entertainers I've been able to enjoy over the years – Alfie Conn, Glenn Hoddle, Waddle, Gascoigne. Like all of them, though for all the brilliance there was a mercurial side to him – he was never consistently brilliant and could be anonymous for large parts of games but in some ways that is what added to the mystique.

He scored three phenomenal goals that season, all of which could have won Goal of the Season – the winner against Manchester United in the League Cup; our second against Leeds with the first-time volley, but it's the one at Barnsley in the FA Cup that stands out the most.

1999/2000 – A THURSDAY IN CHISINAU

WALKER
CARR CAMPBELL PERRY TARICCO
ANDERTON FREUND SHERWOOD GINOLA
ARMSTRONG IVERSEN

HOW I SAW IT:

Summer 1999 was my last one of freedom, after finishing school and while waiting to start full-time employment. Once my exam period ended, I kept myself busy writing and editing our school yearbook and then had my first lads' holiday to Gran Canaria – having spent the last five years complaining that Dad always booked holidays at the start of the football season, I was then outvoted by my friends emphatically and we embarked on a two-week holiday straddling the opening of the new season. I discovered that this wasn't necessarily a bad thing as there was more live football shown on TV abroad than there was in the UK. I was able to watch our first three games of the season in a bar in Playa del Ingles.

I got my first full-time job working for an investment management company in the City of London but felt really lost without my nurturing school environment and friends who all left home to go to various universities around the country. Football was my emotional refuge – I started playing football on a Saturday afternoon for my school's alumni network, Old Owens Football Club, and was nominated to 'manage' the 6th XI. This involved playing anywhere across London and the Home Counties every weekend but I did build some new friendship networks. Due to Spurs' involvement in the UEFA

Cup, most of the home games were played on Sundays, which was perfect for me as it meant I was still able to get to games with my enhanced income from a full-time job.

European football was a new adventure for me; I hadn't gone to any games in the 1992 European Cup Winners' Cup campaign but I recognised the significance of 'Spurs in Europe' so much that I ate into my modest 21 days' annual leave to take mornings off when tickets for our first two home games went on sale. White Hart Lane was midway between home and work in the City so I got the train to Enfield Chase, made the familiar walk through to Enfield Town and then got off at White Hart Lane by 8.30 to make the nervous walk to see where the queue for the ticket office would begin. Expecting to see fans snaked around all four corners of the stadium I approached with trepidation that I would miss out on Spurs' first European game in seven years. It turned out that there were more people waiting outside Jack's Café than the ticket office, so I was among the first to purchase my seats, in the East Lower, to see us play the exotic-sounding Zimbru Chisinau.

Having friends dotted around the country did come with its benefits. Gamey had gone to York and this presented a great opportunity for Matt and me to go to the away game at Leeds in February and then to spend the night on campus with more of our group.

It proved to be a chastening experience – Spurs lost 1-0 in an abject performance that I would have got more annoyed at had I not been petrified of giving away my southern accent among an aggressive mob of Leeds fans. To make matters worse, as we thought we were heading back from Leeds to York, Gamey got himself locked in the train toilet and didn't notice that we were heading the wrong way through the dark February night.

The ticket inspector eventually turfed us off the train in the middle of the dark Yorkshire countryside and by the time a train had come back the other way, taken us back to Leeds and then back out to York the campus bar had shut. Six of us spent the next hours desperately walking around campus seeking alcohol and girls without joy and then had to find somewhere to sleep in a one-bed student apartment. I spent the night unable to sleep on a wooden chair.

Watching Spurs was something of an endurance bar the early-season home wins against Arsenal and Manchester United, where it briefly appeared that George Graham's Midas touch would extend into a second season; but as 1999 gave way to the new millennium it felt very much like old Spurs. In my final year as a teenager, now with a full-time job, Spurs was as important to me as they had been as a nine-year-old still at primary school.

SEASON COMMENTARY

At Arsenal, George Graham had won the 1987 League Cup in his first full season and that proved the catalyst to create a double league-winning side by the start of the 90s. At Highbury, Graham's initial success had earned him the credibility among his board, players and supporters to dispose of Charlie Nicholas, whom Graham believed was too much of a maverick to fit his highly disciplined system.

Over the next two seasons Graham gradually built an Arsenal team in his mould that consisted of highly gifted and hungry young players such as Adams, Michael Thomas, David Rocastle and Paul Merson and he was also backed in the transfer market to sign players like Lee Dixon and Bould (from Stoke), Winterburn (Wimbledon) and Kevin Richardson (Watford), who may not have been the big money and high-profile signings that Liverpool or Manchester United would have thrown money at, but had the characteristics to fit into the system Graham was looking to build.

Fast-forward 12 years across north London and Graham was in a similar position, having won the League Cup with Spurs. Immediately after the season had ended Ginola put pen to paper on a new three-year deal but it was never entirely clear to what extent this was with the blessing of the manager. Unlike at Arsenal, Graham was not solely responsible for contracts and transfers, as Spurs had David Pleat in the role of Director of Football. Pleat's outward message about the club's transfer policy was that they would look to bring in either young British players or would seek value in trying to sign only the best players available from further afield. The dynamic between Graham, Pleat and Sugar never seemed right especially when the manager was consistently telling the media that he required at least six new players to allow the team to kick on.

With Ginola signed on for another three years, attention turned nervously towards the contract situation with Sol Campbell who was now just two years away from the expiration of his current deal. The League Cup success, in which Campbell became the first black captain to lift a major trophy at Wembley, only added to the Spurs captain's ambition to regularly compete for the highest honours.

Unbeknown to most Spurs fans, there was a growing chasm between Campbell and the club. The assault allegation made against Campbell following the altercation with a steward at Derby back in October hadn't gone away, with the player having to provide witness statements both at Tottenham Police Station and then up at Derby. According to Campbell's biography, the club encouraged him to accept the charge and pay a small amount of compensation to avoid the case going to court.

Campbell remained adamant that he was completely innocent and refused to comply, at which point he was written to by the club secretary advising him that the club would no longer act for him in the matter. Campbell then instructed his own solicitor who, having reviewed the evidence, found that the case was weak and that the player had nothing to answer for – it was even discovered that the steward received hospital treatment for his shoulder injury before the alleged incident occurred.

The case was eventually dropped by the CPS on 8 July to Campbell's huge relief. Writing in his authorised biography, Campbell questions whether the club's complete lack of desire to support him properly was in fact just to create leverage over him to sign a new contract? Either way Campbell describes the moment as 'the beginning of the end' for him at Spurs. He felt further alienated when George Graham ordered a rejig of the squad numbers to represent the traditional 1–11; Campbell was made to switch from his favoured number 23 to take the number five vacated by Colin Calderwood, who had left the club during the previous season.

Spurs buffooned their way through the summer transfer period and despite the lure of playing in Europe and for supposedly one of the best coaches in the world, the only signings they were able to make were underwhelming. Dutch winger Willem Korsten, who had achieved moderate success while on loan at Leeds, chose White Hart Lane over Elland Road and signed for £1.5m but the subtext of the deal was very much that George Graham had signed a left-winger to put Ginola under pressure.

Having watched Spurs play Wimbledon six times the previous season, Pleat and Graham had seen defender Chris Perry enough times to evaluate his credentials. Despite his relatively diminutive frame for a central defender, Perry was regarded as one of the most consistent players in the league and perhaps the best English defender yet to be capped at international level. For £4m Perry fulfilled a very pressing need in the team as Vega and Scales were clearly not to Graham's taste although it should be acknowledged that the Swiss had had one of his best performances in the League Cup Final where a last-ditch challenge on the edge of the area had denied Emile Heskey a certain attempt at goal.

On the eve of the season another former Wimbledon player joined Spurs, albeit via Liverpool, when Norwegian winger Oyvind Leonhardsen completed a £3.5m move to White Hart Lane. It was yet another low-key signing and was a reminder of Scholar's protestation all the way back in 1992 when he suggested that Spurs were in danger of morphing into Crystal Park Rangers. That had now been four managers ago yet Spurs still appeared to be shopping in the bargain bucket and hoping to find value rather than pushing the boat out to secure the most talented players as their rivals from across London were doing.

It seemed obvious that Spurs needed a centre-forward. Neither Armstrong, Ferdinand nor Iversen had convinced either through injury, lack of fitness or confidence, or an inability to finish chances which became even more palpable with the quality of deliveries from Ginola and Anderton that were not converted.

Spurs were allegedly given the opportunity to sign Croatian striker Davor Suker – by all accounts a classic Spurs-type player – but the deal stalled with the player joining Arsenal instead. One of the ongoing transfer rumour sagas eventually saw Sunderland forward Michael Bridges elect to be one of six strikers at Leeds rather than join Spurs, where he would almost certainly have been a first-choice starter.

Off the pitch Spurs were able to conclude some new sponsorship deals with Holsten returning to the front of the replica shirts on a three-year deal and kit manufacturers Adidas replacing the much-maligned PONY. The German manufacturers felt more in keeping with a club wanting to rub shoulders with the country's and Europe's elite, and they designed a smart new kit with the trademark three stripes adorning the sleeves. However, Adidas had been so synonymous with Arsenal in the late 80s that it served as just another reminder of Graham's past association.

The new season opened earlier than usual owing to the following summer's European Championships and also the newly expanded Champions League that included Manchester United, Arsenal and Chelsea as England's representatives, which required additional midweek slots to accommodate the two group-stage phases. Spurs' opponents on the opening day were West Ham, whose pre-season had been dominated by their successful foray into the Intertoto Cup. As a result, West Ham, who had already played four competitive games, were sharper than Spurs and won 1-0 through a goal from Frank Lampard – whom Spurs had been closely linked with all summer.

Perry made his debut at Upton Park but his partnership with Campbell lasted just 27 minutes after the captain developed an injury that ruled him out for the next ten weeks. In a surprise team selection Graham had picked Jose Dominguez in attack to partner Iversen though Ferdinand replaced him at half-time.

Two days later, under the lights at White Hart Lane, Spurs overpowered Newcastle to record a high-tempo 3-1 victory and then followed that up in similar style to beat Everton 3-2 with Leonhardsen scoring his first goal for the club.

Two wins, having been behind in each game, and six goals felt more akin to Ardiles than Graham but Spurs then did something they hadn't since 1986 by moving to the top of the league table following a third successive league win, at Sheffield Wednesday on 21 August.

It was somewhat ironic that, having denied Arsenal the league title at the end of the previous season by losing at Manchester United, Spurs' time at the top of the embryonic 1999/2000 league table lasted little more than 24 hours before United recorded a 2-1 victory at Highbury the following day but it did at least provide a glance into an optimal future.

The reality of the situation was that Spurs were still an average team, especially without Campbell, as proven with a home defeat at the hands of Leeds and then a very disappointing draw at newly promoted Bradford City, who equalised in stoppage time after Perry had scored his first Spurs goal.

It seemed once again that if Spurs were to have a successful season, it would happen in the cup competitions and with Spurs in the UEFA Cup it increased the number of opportunities for silverware to three. The geopolitical map of Europe had changed significantly since Spurs' previous campaign in 1991/92 with the horrific civil war in then-Yugoslavia resulting in seven independent nations forming. Czechoslovakia had also split and the former Soviet Union was now made up of 13 different countries, each affiliated to UEFA in their own right.

The Champions League had expanded during the summer and would now consist of two sets of group stages followed by a knockout competition. UEFA had now made the Cup Winners' Cup defunct and increased the number of teams playing in the UEFA Cup – traditionally the second tier for clubs competing in Europe.

More radically, in a concept still going strong in the 2020s, it was decided that teams who dropped out of the Champions League qualifying round would fall into the UEFA Cup first round and, later in the competition, teams that finished in third position in the first group stage would be entered into the fourth knockout round of the UEFA Cup.

Spurs' first European opponents (excluding the infamous Intertoto Cup experience) since Feyenoord were Moldovan champions Zimbru Chisinau. Moldova, landlocked between Romania and Ukraine, was a former Soviet republic that gained its independence formally in 1991 and adopted its national constitution in 1994. As a football nation Moldova first reached the British consciousness when the national team shocked Wales in the qualification stage for Euro '96 – 'Rolled Over in Moldova' ran the headline in 1994. Zimbru Chisinau, from the country's capital city, had played in the Soviet regional league system until independence saw them join the Moldovan Super Liga in 1992, winning seven of the first eight championship titles. They had entered the Champions League on two occasions getting knocked out at the first qualifying stage until the 1999/2000 campaign in which they put ten past St Patrick's Athletic of Ireland and then beat Georgian outfit Dinamo Tbilisi.

At the final qualifying hurdle, they came up against PSV Eindhoven, European champions in 1988, and managed a credible 0-0 draw in Chisinau before going down to a 2-0 defeat back in the Netherlands. While to Spurs and in England they may have been minnows, Zimbru possessed far more recent European experience than Spurs.

The first leg at White Hart Lane captured the imagination largely down to the novelty factor of European football and drew a crowd of 32,660 on a Thursday night – the day allocated to UEFA Cup matches.

Bardi, who had now finished school and was imminently beginning university, attended the game:

> A good friend of mine and I decided late that afternoon that we just had to go to the game. I'd never seen Spurs play in Europe but had heard all the stories of the 'glory nights' under the lights. It was the first time I'd been to a match without an adult and looking back it was quite naïve of us just to turn up.

> The tickets were expensive, but we were just excited to be there for what felt like a very important occasion.

Kick-off was delayed by 15 minutes owing to traffic congestion on the North Circular but anyone missing the start may well have been too late to see Oyvind Leonhardsen put Spurs ahead after just two minutes. He became Spurs' first goalscorer in a European fixture since Gary Lineker in November 1991! Perry and Sherwood added further goals either side of half-time to provide a comprehensive 3-0 victory that also provided the luxury of not conceding an away goal.

Low budget airlines like EasyJet, who sponsored the South Stand at White Hart Lane, and Ryanair had opened up low-cost flights to markets across the newly franchised eastern Europe but there was no way of getting to Chisinau unless you were prepared to make the most rustic of journeys, without using the club's official travel package. The tie was effectively over early in the first leg and those fans who did travel witnessed an excruciatingly tedious 0-0 draw that a £0.99 EasyJet fare wouldn't have made feel any more worthwhile.

League results remained frustratingly inconsistent with another home defeat against Leicester in which Spurs led twice but lost 3-2; a victory over Coventry by the same score followed but Spurs had been pegged back from 3-0 ahead with a young Robbie Keane particularly catching the eye. Spurs had overlooked the teenager in the summer with George Graham not feeling he was yet ready for the top flight. A draw at Wimbledon and a win at Derby cemented Spurs' place towards the bottom of the top half before the visit of Manchester United to White Hart Lane.

Spurs had often put in meek performances against United, not least on the final day of the previous season which in fairness the majority of supporters were happy with. Spurs had been in a stronger position than United as the 90s began and anyone who had witnessed the three wins Spurs recorded against Alex Ferguson's team in the 89/90 season would have been something of a soothsayer if they had envisaged the considerable gulf that had developed throughout the decade. Spurs hadn't finished above United since 1990 and had recorded just two wins out of the last 20 ahead of the final instalment of the fixture of the decade on a torrentially wet Saturday in October 1999.

Alex Ferguson's team, now European and English champions, were seemingly hitting new statistical heights every week and possessed a phenomenal record of having never lost a Premier League game in which they had scored the first goal, so when Ryan Giggs gave the away side a lead midway through the first half at White Hart Lane it was hard to see any way back for Spurs.

However, the crowd, recognising the effort and intensity of the team despite their perilous situation, contributed to febrile cup tie-type atmosphere that was heightened by the pouring rain. George Graham's brand of high-tempo power football caused uncharacteristic hesitation in the United defence and Spurs somewhat forced two goals both from corners. With a lead to hold onto Spurs were able to adopt many of the underhand tactics often deployed by United and more particularly Graham's Arsenal teams which prevented the champions from building any momentum. Freund in particular managed to irritate the ever-morose Roy Keane.

With 20 minutes remaining Steve Carr collected the ball on the halfway line and with space in front of him drove purposefully into the United half; still unchallenged, Carr found himself 25 yards from goal and hit an arrow of a shot that flew into the top corner. Spurs stadium PA announcer Pete Abbott was taken so unaware that he announced the goal had been scored by Ruel Fox!

Pete explains:

> My 'studio' was a fully enclosed box right at the end of the East Stand hospitality boxes and down at the far end from where the goal was scored. It was midway through the second half and I was just making note of an imminent substitution. I remember the ball was played across the halfway line so I took the opportunity to check my notes when all of a sudden

> I heard, through the glass, a huge roar and looked out to see the stadium going wild and the players celebrating down by the far corner flag – it looked to me that Ruel Fox was the focus of their attention and it made sense that he might have scored as last time I'd looked the ball was down the right flank. I announced triumphantly, 'Spurs' third goal scored after 71 minutes by number 18, Ruel Fox.' I was quickly corrected and made the correct announcement!

It was the Irishman's third Spurs goal but the second in a month and brought to the wider audience's attention what a trajectory Carr had been on especially since Graham had taken over.

Next up at White Hart Lane was the visit of Kaiserslautern, of Germany, in the UEFA Cup second-round first leg, watched by another large and expectant crowd. Two-legged ties had become a specialism of George Graham dating back to his Highbury days; Graham guided Arsenal to European Cup Winners' Cup success in 1994 and they had progressed to the fourth round the following season before he was sacked; in the League Cup Spurs had already seen their manager's ability to navigate home and away ties against Wimbledon.

David Ginola had earned a reputation of diving long before he joined Spurs and it had become an increasing source of frustration and astonished amusement that English referees seemed to have made up their mind before he hit the ground, which he frequently did, that he was feigning contact. Ginola, a tall and stocky man, had an unnatural gift for gliding past defenders at pace and this meant that only minimal contact would be enough to knock him over, but despite this he had not earned a penalty in nearly two seasons.

Against Kaiserslautern Ginola again tried his party trick, drawing the German right-back into a challenge and then knocking the ball past him just as contact came in; the Turkish referee, who presumably had not judged the incident on the victim's past indiscretions, immediately pointed to the spot. It was something of a novelty as Spurs had at last been awarded a penalty at White Hart Lane, for the first time since 2 January.

With Anderton, the regular penalty taker, out injured there was something of an inquest among the Spurs players before Steffen Iversen almost reluctantly took the ball. There is no record of the Norwegian ever having taken a penalty in a senior game up until this point but he showed tremendous poise and composure by drilling the ball into the bottom corner. The goal proved to be the decisive one. Ginola, who mesmerised the German defence all night, hit the post in the second half but Spurs took the slender lead back to Germany without conceding an away goal.

Going into the second leg the following midweek George Graham made the fateful decision to leave Ginola out of the team, opting for the more functional Stephen Clemence to play on the left in what was a very clear intention to nullify the home team. No one was more surprised to learn of Ginola's omission that Kaiserslautern manager Otto Rehhagel who had initially set his team up to include a man-marker on Ginola; controversially he was allowed to change his starting XI less than 45 minutes before kick-off.

Graham had a track record of getting these sorts of decisions right but it once again stabbed at the very existence of what Tottenham Hotspur was supposed to be all about. The evening proved to be another of those sliding-doors moments that would have significant consequences for the short- and mid-term future as the plan came within seconds of working perfectly.

Spurs had defended diligently with all the hallmarks of George Graham organisation all night until, with the clock ticking into the second minute of stoppage time, France attacking midfielder Youri Djorkaeff received the ball on the half turn and ran at the Spurs defence; drawing a challenge from Campbell, he flicked the ball into the path of striker Andreas Buck, who slipped a first-time shot past Walker for the equaliser.

From the kick-off Graham wouldn't have had enough time to order Ginola to get warmed up before Clemence gave the ball away and Djorkaeff again drove at the heart of the Spurs defence; again he knocked the ball to the right of the penalty area where Buck again found himself in space. Instead of shooting, Buck drilled the ball across the six-yard box where the unfortunate Carr couldn't sort his feet out quickly enough to avoid the ball bouncing off him into the empty net. It was the German team's majestic French playmaker who had made all the difference while Ginola watched on from the bench behind a disconsolate Graham, who had been so used to seeing his Arsenal teams on the right side of this sort of dramatic late comeback.

Steffan Chirazi had travelled from San Francisco to attend the game with a friend and recalls:

> The game was absolutely dead; I was sat in the home end and after the initial optimism and excitement at kick-off died down it looked like Spurs were going to succeed in boring the tie to death. It may not have been the Spurs that we all grew up and loved but it seemed to be effective. Then with about ten minutes remaining Djorkaeff had a shot from range that crashed off the crossbar and it was as if it had set a firework off in the stadium as suddenly everyone came alive. The Kaiserslautern team awoke from a trance and all of a sudden, our players looked like rabbits caught in the headlights. It seemed inevitable from that moment that we'd concede and go into extra time. Perhaps them scoring again just delayed the inevitable?

The European campaign that had been sold as an opportunity to progress the club's reputation and standing had lasted just two ties. The dramatic circumstances in which Spurs were beaten in Germany were as painful as any European experience since Barcelona had literally kicked Spurs out of the 1982 European Cup Winners' Cup semi-final.

A dejected Spurs team then had three days to get over defeat in Germany before a north London derby at White Hart Lane. Arsenal were already six points ahead of Spurs going into the game and had made a good start to their Champions

League campaign, where they played their home games at Wembley in order to maximise match-day income through the larger attendances that the national stadium could provide; it was further evidence of Arsenal widening the gap on the field and commercially between them and Spurs.

When the two sides had met in May and Arsenal had won more emphatically than the 3-1 scoreline suggested, Wenger's team had had the very tangible motivation of winning the league title as an added incentive. Some six months later Spurs were able to match Arsenal's desire from the kick off and found themselves 2-0 ahead within 20 minutes. Iversen opened the scoring when he caught a sweet half-volley from the edge of the area that seemed to take Seaman by surprise and then Sherwood curled in a low free kick to send White Hart Lane into delirium – Spurs hadn't had a two-goal advantage over Arsenal since John Hendry's brace at Highbury in 1993. Eventually Spurs' adrenalin-fuelled start to the game ran out and for the final hour had to endure wave after wave of Arsenal attacks.

When Vieira glanced in a near-post header just before half-time the anxiety was palpable, especially just three days after conceding twice so late on in Germany. George Graham may have relied on resilience and doggedness but there was a reason why his Arsenal team were frequently labelled 'lucky' and that was the pot that the now Spurs manager dipped into to get his current employers the three points.

When Edinburgh clashed with Ljungberg ten minutes into the second half in front of the Shelf side, an altercation broke out between several players; Ginola, who had been nearest to Ljungberg, went to ground holding his forehead, which appeared to be bleeding. Referee David Elleray arrived at the conclusion that Ljungberg had been responsible and eventually brandished a red card. Only afterwards was it discovered that Ginola had in fact been hit by a coin thrown from the Spurs fans though Ljungberg had still acted aggressively towards Edinburgh. In the cold light of day, you'd usually have expected a yellow card for both players.

Perhaps Graham had played on Arsenal's well-documented disciplinary problems, which had been highlighted since

Wenger had taken over. Spurs now had experienced players in their ranks and Sherwood and Freund knew how to gnarl and antagonise and were able to knock Arsenal off their stride. In a key moment towards the end of the game, Walker made an excellent double save and when Keown recklessly lunged at Dominguez in stoppage time he received a second yellow card meaning Arsenal finished the game with nine men.

It was a statement victory for Graham, perhaps more satisfying for him on a personal level than the League Cup Final victory. For Spurs it was a first win in the north London derby since Wenger had arrived on the scene in 1996. Spurs had managed to ruffle Arsenal who were undoubtedly the technically superior team.

Wins against Manchester United and Arsenal within a fortnight provided a tantalising glimpse of what Spurs were capable of in a one-off game. Cup ties by nature come with jeopardy as was discovered in Germany in between the two rip-roaring White Hart Lane successes against England's best. So far Graham had won more than he had lost but was it sustainable?

Victory over Arsenal was followed up with a 1-0 win at Southampton maintaining Spurs' position in the top six but December, the final month of the decade, was a cruel one.

Defending the League Cup, Spurs had brushed past third-tier Crewe in round three with a 3-1 victory. The next round sent Spurs to play Fulham who, under the ownership of Harrods' boss Mohamed Al-Fayed, had begun to spend their way through the Football League and now sat on the cusp of joining the Premier League.

The home team out-powered Spurs who were second best from the first whistle and became the first lower-league team to knock Spurs out of a cup competition since Notts County had cost Ossie Ardiles his job in 1994.

Alan Sugar described in *What You See Is What You Get* his fury at seeing George Graham, with no apparent visible disappointment at the result, meet up with a *Daily Mail* journalist friend to go for dinner immediately after the game. Sugar was furious to read the newspaper the next morning, which stated that Sugar refused to back his manager with the players he needed and that the chairman was 'miserly'.

Sugar recalls bursting into Graham's coaches' meeting the following morning to confront his manager, who denied any wrong-doing. Sugar, no stranger to a litigation case, demanded that Graham act as a witness in a writ against the newspaper that he eventually won. Sugar now knew that he had a manager he couldn't work with, and the relationship continued to fall apart.

With Spurs knocked out of the League Cup and UEFA Cup, the FA Cup offered the only hope of silverware and progress from the previous season. The Football Association had decided to apply to stage the 2006 World Cup and in a desperate attempt to curry favour with FIFA had pushed hard for Manchester United, as European champions, to participate in the fledgling FIFA Club World Championships tournament that would see representatives of each international confederation meet for an eight-team competition in Japan.

The 2000 tournament was scheduled for January but Manchester United responded that they would only participate if they were allowed to withdraw from the FA Cup for the season in order to avoid a fixture pile-up later in the season. The FA agreed to Manchester United's request, which instantly devalued the supposed 'most famous competition in club football'.

In the same season that the FA allowed Manchester United to withdraw from their competition they also experimented by moving the sacrosanct schedule of the third-round weekend in January to the second weekend of December. Having been knocked out in controversial circumstances by Newcastle in last season's semi-final Spurs were given the opportunity to avenge that defeat with a home tie against the same opponents.

The teams had met twice in the league already with each game won by the home side. In another tight game Iversen headed Spurs ahead in the second half but Gary Speed equalised, which necessitated a replay at St James' Park three days before Christmas. FA Cup success had been the height of Spurs' aspirations for most of the 90s but in the final days of the decade Spurs were knocked out of the competition in humiliating fashion with a dreadful 6-1 defeat reminiscent of the 7-1 humbling at the same ground almost exactly three years earlier. Ginola had drawn Spurs level just before half-time but Newcastle ripped Graham's team apart after the break.

George Graham's credentials as a serial cup winner had been badly damaged during an eight-week period in which Spurs had been knocked out of all three cup competitions. What Spurs had sacrificed in style was supposed to be balanced out by grinding out results specifically in the cup competitions; but with Spurs crashing so alarmingly you couldn't help but wonder what purpose Graham provided unless they could rally in the league and secure a UEFA Cup spot at the end of the season.

A Ginola-inspired 4-0 win over bottom-of-the-table Watford at least provided some festive cheer on Boxing Day and the decade came to an end with an inconsequential 1-1 draw at Villa Park which left Spurs in sixth place.

The new millennium opened with a tense but well-earned 1-0 victory over Liverpool but was followed with a run of five games without a win. As spring developed, Spurs regressed further away from the top six and fell back into mid-table and there was very little to feel positive about. Even a 7-2 victory over Glenn Hoddle's Southampton contained aspects of farce and despite Iversen's hat-trick it was a low-quality match played out between two very average teams.

Ginola continued to be the main source of joy and entertainment but invariably looked on in frustration as centre-forwards failed to convert the many chances he put on a plate for them – Armstrong irked the home fans and responded to his goal against Southampton by cupping his ears. The striker had become the most recent unfortunate recipient of booing and jeering from his own fans.

Paul Hawksbee felt this was symbolic of the crowd's pent-up frustration at the direction the club was going in:

> It was a very unedifying episode – the crowd had been on Armstrong's back for a while but when he

> gave them the stare after scoring you knew his time was up. There was a general feeling of apathy which bordered on anger at the way the club was being run and the way the team was playing. I'd always had concerns about whether George was a good match long-term – his more pragmatic style of play, and the Arsenal connections were less of an issue while things were going well but as the season progressed – knocked out of all the cups before Christmas and meandering in the league – the writing was on the wall. It was an unhappy time despite a 7-2 home win!

The season concluded with three wins from the last five games and Armstrong at least finished in good form with nine goals in 13 games but overall the outlook for the team offered little encouragement for the view that Spurs were in fact any better than their tenth position indicated. Spurs were the definition of mediocrity.

The only enjoyment at the conclusion of the season once again came at the expense of Arsenal when another ex-Spurs man, Gica Popescu, scored the winning penalty kick against them in the UEFA Cup Final for Galatasaray.

The season had seen home wins against Manchester United, Arsenal and Liverpool for the first time in a single season since 1989/90 but West Ham, Leicester and Sunderland all finished higher, which demonstrated the lack of consistency and inability to string together a sequence of victories: exactly the sort of qualities George Graham had been brought in to address.

Off the field Graham continued to tell the media that he needed more players and the relationship between manager and chairman continued to disintegrate. David Pleat at least delivered on his promise to sign and develop talented young players. Ledley King had already made his debut the previous season and Peter Crouch, purchased from QPR's youth set-up, was also getting game time in the reserves alongside John Piercy, who had made a couple of first-team appearances in autumn 1999 and Mark Gower, who had played a couple of League Cup ties while Pleat was in caretaker charge.

The highly rated pair from Peterborough – Simon Davies and Matthew Etherington – chose Spurs above Manchester United in January and both made a handful of first-team appearances towards the end of the season. Defenders Gary Doherty (from Luton) and Anthony Gardner (Port Vale) also made the step up to join Spurs, though the signing of Dave McEwan from non-league Dulwich Hamlet appeared to show how far Spurs had fallen.

Symbolically Spurs ended the 80s with the signing of Gary Lineker from Barcelona and started the 2000s by signing McEwan from Dulwich!

Spurs just weren't shopping in the same stores that Arsenal and Chelsea were and this becomes very apparent when reviewing the three clubs' incoming transfer strategies throughout the decade.

Spurs had, prior to the 90s, been synonymous with high-profile signings dating back to Jimmy Greaves's £99,999 transfer in 1961 through to the stunning arrival of Ardiles and Villa in 1978 and even in 1988 when Spurs had beaten Manchester United and Liverpool to secure the signature of Paul Gascoigne for a then-record £2m fee. Sugar should be congratulated for the audacious transfer of Klinsmann in 1994 but that proved to be the last occasion that Spurs turned heads.

Throughout the 90s it was Manchester United, Liverpool and then Blackburn and Newcastle, both bankrolled by benevolent local owners, who really pushed the boat out to secure the biggest signings. By the middle of the decade Arsenal and Chelsea were bringing talented foreign players to England and even Middlesbrough were getting in on the act.

While Alan Sugar will point out that money was still being spent, it was nothing relative to other transfer fees being paid by Spurs' competitors. The £6m paid for Les Ferdinand in summer 1997 was still significantly less than Arsenal, Manchester United, Liverpool, Chelsea and Newcastle were paying at the time and over a four-year period (96–99) Spurs were just the ninth-highest spenders on transfer fees.

It wasn't just the amounts that Spurs were or weren't prepared to pay but also the markets they were shopping in.

It was Spurs who broke the mould in 1994 with the signings of Klinsmann, Dumitrescu and Popescu, though all three had left the club within 18 months and Sugar clearly felt his fingers had been burned by these 'Carlos Kickaballs' (the term Alan Sugar coined to describe what he considered to be foreign mercenaries). From 1995 onwards Arsenal and Chelsea, both with foreign coaches, stole the march and began to flood their respective squads with players from across the globe. Nationality alone is of course no panacea for building a successful squad and indeed signing any player presents an element of risk – many players on the Arsenal and Chelsea lists were not successful – but it highlights Spurs' reluctance to move with the times and embrace new ideas.

More than technical excellence, it was innovation and new ideas off the field that many of these players brought to their existing clubs.

By the end of the 1999/2000 season, it is difficult to avoid the conclusion that Spurs had lost the prominence that they had enjoyed as the 90s began. Just about every metric that could be applied to on- and off-field performance showed Spurs were a regular mid-table performer.

Of Spurs' biggest assets, Darren Anderton signed a contract extension in March 2000 that would see him continue his service to the club through until 2004. Anderton was undoubtedly one of Spurs' best players of the decade but has unfortunately been stigmatised by his 'sicknote' nickname which fails to reflect that he made 241 appearances in the 90s alone, the sixth-highest of any player. Anderton was often the support act – a supplier to Sheringham and Klinsmann and a less flamboyant but more consistent performer in comparison to David Ginola. Having remained loyal to the club, particularly when Manchester United came calling, Anderton should be remembered as one of the stars of the period.

During summer 2000 George Graham won the cold war with Ginola when the Frenchman was sold to Aston Villa for £3m. It meant that Graham had overseen a triumph of pragmatism over panache. In Ginola's book *Le Magnifique* he revealed that, after Graham took over, Ginola started 79 games but was substituted in 36 of them. The relationship took a significant turn for the worse during an end-of-season home game against Derby in which Graham, suffering from an arthritic condition, left first-team matters to his assistant Stewart Houston. With Spurs 1-0 behind, Ginola was substituted and the Frenchman wasted no time in showering, getting changed and leaving the stadium at the earliest possible moment.

Chris Paouros, who in 2014 co-founded The Proud Lilywhites, an official supporters' club for LGBTQ+ fans, still recalls with some enthusiasm the affection for Ginola and even had a chance meeting with him after this game:

> Ginola was simply magnificent. In what was a pretty miserable period in the club's history he was a rare ray of sunlight with his mercurial skills. He was what Spurs were supposed to be all about; he did things with style, with a flourish, he wanted to beat the other lot, not wait for them to die of boredom … Games would come and go often with very little to get excited about but with Ginola on the pitch there was invariably always a moment of magic. My cousin was in love with him, I mean properly infatuated; so much so that superstition be damned, we changed our season tickets for one match in order to sit on the front row of The Shelf — she wanted to be in touching (or at least hearing) distance of him.
>
> As the season progressed it seemed increasingly obvious that Graham was going to get his way and that it would be David who'd be sacrificed. I remember this game when he was substituted and walked forlornly straight down the tunnel. The game was itself (another) miserable one so we left early and took our usual walk around the stadium through Bruce Castle Park and along Lordship Lane.
>
> Unbeknown to us David had left the stadium early too and to our incredible delight he was sat in traffic

> in his car as we walked past. My cousin plucked up the courage to ask him to wind down his window which unbelievably he did and with the trademark smile lit up the whole world! She then realised that in having asked for an autograph (this was before the time of selfies!) she didn't actually have a pen – the best we could muster was her eyeliner and bless him, he signed her programme with it before eventually driving on once the lights turned green. That moment alone symbolised his time with Spurs – he could turn even the most bleak of moments with the flick of a boot or even swoosh of an eyeliner pencil!

The battle between Graham and Ginola followed a pattern of conflict between leading protagonists at the club throughout the decade – Scholar v Bobroff, Venables v Sugar, Gross v players and now manager v talisman; it felt as if the internal conflict was as much a part of the club's fabric as the lilywhite shirt.

With Ginola gone, attentions turned towards the future of Spurs' other biggest asset – captain Sol Campbell who by now had just one year left on his contract and the club ran the risk of losing the player for nothing. Unbeknown to anyone at the club, whether Campbell could be tempted to stay was already a lost battle.

The growing irrelevance of Spurs as a major force had been one of the growing trends as the 21st century began.

POSTSCRIPT (OCTOBER 2023)

I STARTED writing this for therapeutic purposes while the 2022 Spurs were suffering yet another humbling defeat at Arsenal. That game (October 2022) was the 21st north London derby to have been played at the Emirates since Arsenal moved across N5 from Highbury, which of course was the venue for 11 matches covered within this book; and White Hart Lane also is no more.

It's a reminder of how quickly places and people change in football and this became equally as apparent during my research and writing. Being able to look back at the decade with such distance provided some real context and perspective to see the major events play out.

I hope that I have been able to dress up what is essentially lots of occurrences of blokes in lilywhite (and occasionally yellow, blue or purple) kicking a ball around, invariably unsuccessfully, into a wider narrative that describes the major themes and personalities of the time told through the eyes of supporters and players alike.

One thing that really stood out to me was those personalities that dominate particular times and moments and who, no matter how ubiquitous they seemed, are never any more than passers-by in the greater fabric of our great club. As the 90s began the predominant characters were Irving Scholar (chairman), Terry Venables (manager) and Paul Gascoigne and Gary Lineker (players) but by mid-1993 all had gone. Likewise, as the decade drew to a close Alan Sugar (chairman), George Graham (manager), Sol Campbell (captain) and David Ginola (star player) were, for better or worse, the headline acts and within 18 months of the 2000s had also all moved on.

This book ends at the close of the 1999/2000 season by which point Spurs are sitting perennially in the middle of the Premier League table and the mediocrity of mid-table appeared a permanent state of affairs. Alan Sugar sold a controlling stake in the club to ENIC at the beginning of 2001 after a ten-year period as the club's owner and is undoubtedly the leading protagonist throughout the 90s. I have tried to make sure that this book is not a critique of Sugar's running of the club but you will come to your own conclusions about whether or not he was a saviour – not only rescuing the club from its dire financial situation in 1991 but also in trumping Robert Maxwell.

We saw in the early 2000s the story of Leeds – big ambitious spenders as the 90s ended and seemingly a challenger to Manchester United – who flew too close to the sun and endured nearly two decades out of the top division. Perhaps Sugar should be credited for not following this path. Then there are the improvements to infrastructure. White Hart Lane evolved over time at great cost and the new training facility, not without its flaws, was certainly a huge upgrade on the rented facility in Mill Hill. Sugar was also the chairman who signed Klinsmann and successfully fought the FA.

However, that Sugar's frugality and resistance to adapt to the changing macro environment held the club back at a crucial moment in English football's most revolutionary decade in a generation is a legitimate criticism.

With or without Sugar, the 90s still remains a mystical decade in the club's history and produced some incredible moments – the 1991 FA Cup semi-final win over Arsenal and then subsequent success in the final against Nottingham Forest; winning in the last minute at Anfield in 1995, and the delirium of discovering that Jurgen Klinsmann had signed for the club.

In addition to Klinsmann the names of world-class players from the decade roll off the tongue … Gascoigne, Lineker, Ginola, Sheringham, even Sol Campbell though he forever ruined his legacy when he joined Arsenal in 2001. Then there were the consistent stalwarts – Mabbutt, Howells, Anderton, whose roles as the support cast deserve to be immortalised as much as the cult heroes of Nayim, Rosenthal, Paul Stewart and Allan Nielsen who all played their part.

I have spoken to many people while writing this book – many have provided valuable contributions – but without fail when I mentioned 'Spurs in the 90s' eyes invariably roll. What I have learned, and hopefully conveyed, is that while the 90s was, on the whole, a decade in which Spurs' relevance declined, they also sparked emotions of incredible highs and lows. If you lived through the 90s as a Spurs fan, or whether you've read this without first-hand experience of the period, then consider whether you would wish to go back to 1 January 1990 and relive the decade again … or remain in the present day.

ACKNOWLEDGEMENTS

THIS BOOK was only possible with the help of several people. David Howells and Gerry Francis very kindly gave up their time to share with me the inside track on what it was like to play for and manage Spurs respectively and therefore add some great insights. It was really quite surreal talking directly to both.

It was hugely enjoyable speaking with so many fellow Spurs fans about their own memories of the 90s – many of which have been included within the script. Julie Welch, Alan Fisher, 'Bardi', Paul Coyte, Paul Hawksbee, Tyrone Foster, Paul Malshinger, Mark Jacob, Steffan Chirazi, Chris Slegg, Chris Paouros, Pete Abbott, Mike Leigh and Theo Delaney were all very generous in providing either personal recollections and/or making introductions to others.

Julie Welch, Alan Fisher, Chris Slegg and Mark Jacob – all authors of Tottenham Hotspur books – were also wonderfully helpful in helping me understand some of the processes in writing a book.

Special thanks to Daniel Wynne who did all of the above but also, on request, trawled through his library of Spurs programmes and literature to find often obscure details. He also sense-checked several aspects of the narrative.

Richard Thomas, whom I have known since early childhood, was very helpful in checking my early drafts of the book and with his experience as a writer was able to suggest some improvements to the script.

My immense thanks go to Paul Camillin at Pitch Publishing who has taken a chance on a first-time author and brought this publication to market!

Not least I must recognise my wife Ellie who, once again, has allowed me to pursue a spurs related project/hobby!

BIBLIOGRAPHY

BOOKS:

Anderton, D with Donovan, Mike (2010) *Take Note!* Darren Anderton, the Autobiography with Mike Donovan. Derby. The Derby Books Publishing Company Ltd.

Astaire, Simon (2014) *Sol Campbell: The Authorised Biography*. London. Spellbinding Media.

Cloake, Martin and Fisher, Alan (2016) *A People's History of Tottenham Hotspur.* Worthing. Pitch Publishing.

Francis Gerry and Slegg Chris (2017) *The Team that Dared to Do*. Worthing. Pitch Publishing.

Fynn, Alex and Blair Olivia (2001) *The Great Divide.* London; Carlton Publishing Group.

Ginola, David with Silver, Neil (2000) *Le Magnifique*. London. Harper Collins Publishers.

Jacob, Mark (1999) *What's the Story?* Boring Glory. GB: Queen Anne Press.

Ruddock, Neil (1999) *Hell Razor: The Autobiography of Neil Ruddock*. London. Harper Collins Publishers.

Scholar, Irving (1992) *Behind Closed Doors.* London. Andre Deutsch publishing.

Sheridan, John (2021) *The 'Limping' Physio – a Life in Footbal*l. Worthing. Pitch Publishing.

Sheringham, Teddy (1999) *Teddy: My Autobiography*. London. Warner Books.

Sugar, Alan (2011) *Alan Sugar: What You See Is What You Get*: My Autobiography. London. Macmillan Publishers Limited.

Venables, Terry (2014) *Terry Venables Born to Manage*. London. Simon & Schuster UK Ltd.

Welch, Julie (2015) *The Biography of Tottenham Hotspur* (2015 revised version). Kingston upon Thames. Vision Sports Publishing.

FOOTBALL CLUB PROGRAMMES:

Tottenham Hotspur v Coventry City (19 August 1992)
Tottenham Hotspur v Aston Villa (23 August 1995)
Tottenham Hotspur v Derby County (21 August 1996)
Tottenham Hotspur v Chelsea (24 August 1991)

WEBSITES:

The Athletic
YouTube
Enfa.co.uk
Hotspurhq.com
The42.ie
Superhotspur.com
www.independent.co.uk

PODCASTS:

The Last Word on Spurs – *Ramon Vega – Special* (5 April 2020)
The Last Word on Spurs – *Dean Austin – Special* (19 April 2020)
The Last Word on Spurs – *David Howells – Special* (10 May 2020)
The View from The Lane – *JURGEN KLINSMANN EXCLUSIVE* (25 October 2022)
The Spurs Show – *SPURS SHOW LIVE – Colin Calderwood* (30 Sept 2022 and 7 October 2022)
The Spurs Show – *Spurs Show Live! Micky Hazard Special* (28 October)
Quickly Kevin; will he score? *The 90s Football Show – Ramon Vega* (12 April 2021)
Quickly Kevin; will he score? *The 90s Football Show – Darren Anderton* (25 September 2017)
Alive and Kicking – *My 90s – Tottenham with Theo Delaney* (18 May 2022)
The Game is About Glory – *Spurs in the 90s* (15 November 2021)

APPENDIX A – SEASON RESULTS

1989/90

19 Aug	Division 1	Luton (h)	2-1	Stewart, Allen
22 Aug	Division 1	Everton (a)	1-2	Allen
26 Aug	Division 1	Manchester C (a)	1-1	Gascoigne
9 Sept	Division 1	Aston Villa (a)	0-2	
16 Sept	Division 1	Chelsea (h)	1-4	Gascoigne
20 Sept	League Cup 2	Southend (h)	1-0	Fenwick
23 Sept	Division 1	Norwich (a)	2-2	Gascoigne, Lineker
30 Sept	Division 1	QPR (h)	3-2	Lineker 3
4 Oct	League Cup 2	Southend (a)	2-3	Allen, Nayim
14 Oct	Division 1	Charlton (a)	3-1	Thomas, Lineker, Gascoigne
18 Oct	Division 1	Arsenal (h)	2-1	Samways, Walsh
21 Oct	Division 1	Sheffield Weds (h)	3-0	Lineker 2, Moran
25 Oct	League Cup 3	Manchester Utd (a)	3-0	Lineker, Samways, Nayim
29 Oct	Division 1	Liverpool (a)	0-1	
4 Nov	Division 1	Southampton (a)	1-1	Gascoigne
11 Nov	Division 1	Wimbledon (h)	0-1	
18 Nov	Division 1	Crystal Palace (a)	3-2	Howells, Lineker, Samways
22 Nov	League Cup 4	Tranmere (a)	2-2	Gascoigne, OG
25 Nov	Division 1	Derby (h)	1-2	Stewart
29 Nov	League Cup 4	Tranmere (h)	4-0	Howells, Stewart, Mabbutt, Allen
2 Dec	Division 1	Luton (a)	0-0	
9 Dec	Division 1	Everton (h)	2-1	Lineker, Stewart
16 Dec	Division 1	Manchester Utd (a)	1-0	Lineker
26 Dec	Division 1	Millwall (h)	3-1	Samways, OG, Lineker
30 Dec	Division 1	Nottingham F (h)	2-3	Lineker 2
1 Jan	Division 1	Coventry (a)	0-0	
6 Jan	FA Cup 3	Southampton (h)	1-3	Howells
13 Jan	Division 1	Manchester C (h)	1-1	Howells
17 Jan	League Cup 5	Nottingham F (a)	2-2	Lineker, Sedgley
20 Jan	Division 1	Arsenal (a)	0-1	
24 Jan	League Cup 5	Nottingham F (h)	2-3	Nayim, Walsh
4 Feb	Division 1	Norwich (h)	4-0	Lineker 3, Howells
10 Feb	Division 1	Chelsea (a)	2-1	Howells, Lineker

21 Feb	Division 1	Aston Villa (h)	0-2	
24 Feb	Division 1	Derby (a)	1-2	Moncur
3 Mar	Division 1	Crystal Palace (h)	0-1	
10 Mar	Division 1	Charlton (h)	3-0	J Polston, Lineker, Howells
17 Mar	Division 1	QPR (a)	1-3	Walsh
21 Mar	Division 1	Liverpool (h)	1-0	Stewart
31 Mar	Division 1	Sheffield Weds (a)	4-2	Lineker 2, Stewart, Allen
7 Apr	Division 1	Nottingham F (a)	3-1	Stewart, Allen 2
14 Apr	Division 1	Coventry (h)	3-2	Lineker 2, Stewart
16 Apr	Division 1	Millwall (a)	1-0	Lineker
21 Apr	Division 1	Manchester Utd (h)	2-1	Gascoigne, Lineker
28 Apr	Division 1	Wimbledon (a)	0-1	
5 May	Division 1	Southampton (h)	2-1	Stewart, Allen

FINAL LEAGUE POSITION	3rd (63 points)
PEAK LEAGUE POSITION	3rd (match week 36)
LOW LEAGUE POSITION	19th (match week 6)
FA CUP	3rd round – SOUTHAMPTON
LEAGUE CUP (LITTLEWOODS)	5th round – nottingham forest
EUROPE	Did not participate
MANAGER	TERRY VENABLES
TOP GOALSCORER	GARY LINEKER (26)
MOST APPEARANCES	GARY LINEKER (45)

MACRO FOOTBALL CLIMATE

LEAGUE CHAMPIONS	LIVERPOOL
RUNNERS-UP	ARSENAL
FA CUP	MANCHESTER UTD 1-0 CRYSTAL PALACE (in a replay)
(LITTLEWOODS) LEAGUE CUP	NOTTINGHAM FOREST 1-0 OLDHAM
RELEGATED	SHEFFIELD WEDNESDAY, MILLWALL, CHARLTON
BIGGEST TRANSFER FEE	GARY PALLISTER £2.3m MIDDLESBROUGH to MANCHESTER UTD

1990/91

25 Aug	Division 1	Manchester C (h)	3-1	Lineker 2, Gascoigne
28 Aug	Division 1	Sunderland (a)	0-0	
1 Sept	Division 1	Arsenal (a)	0-0	
8 Sept	Division 1	Derby (h)	3-0	Gascoigne 3
15 Sept	Division 1	Leeds (a)	2-0	Howells, Lineker
22 Sept	Division 1	Crystal Palace (h)	1-1	Gascoigne
26 Sept	League Cup 2	Hartlepool (h)	5-0	Gascoigne 4, Lineker
29 Sept	Division 1	Aston Villa (h)	2-1	Lineker, Allen
6 Oct	Division 1	QPR (a)	0-0	
9 Oct	League Cup 2	Hartlepool (a)	2-1	Stewart 2
20 Oct	Division 1	Sheffield Utd (h)	4-0	Walsh 3, Nayim
27 Oct	Division 1	Nottingham F (a)	2-1	Howells 2
30 Oct	League Cup 3	Bradford (h)	2-1	Gascoigne, Stewart
4 Nov	Division 1	Liverpool (h)	1-3	Lineker
10 Nov	Division 1	Wimbledon (h)	4-2	Stewart, Mabbutt, Walsh, Lineker
18 Nov	Division 1	Everton (a)	1-1	Howells
24 Nov	Division 1	Norwich (h)	2-1	Lineker 2
27 Nov	League Cup 4	Sheffield Utd (a)	2-0	Stewart, Gascoigne
1 Dec	Division 1	Chelsea (a)	2-3	Gascoigne, Lineker
8 Dec	Division 1	Sunderland (h)	3-3	Walsh 2, Lineker
15 Dec	Division 1	Manchester C (a)	1-2	Gascoigne
22 Dec	Division 1	Luton (h)	2-1	Stewart 2
26 Dec	Division 1	Coventry (a)	0-2	
29 Dec	Division 1	Southampton (a)	0-3	
1 Jan	Division 1	Manchester Utd (h)	1-2	Lineker
5 Jan	FA Cup 3	Blackpool (a)	1-0	Stewart
12 Jan	Division 1	Arsenal (h)	0-0	
16 Jan	League Cup 5	Chelsea (a)	0-0	
20 Jan	Division 1	Derby (a)	1-0	Lineker
23 Jan	League Cup 5	Chelsea (h)	0-3	
26 Jan	FA Cup 4	Oxford (h)	4-2	Mabbutt, Lineker, Gascoigne 2
2 Feb	Division 1	Leeds (h)	0-0	
16 Feb	FA Cup 5	Portsmouth (a)	2-1	Gascoigne 2
23 Feb	Division 1	Wimbledon (a)	1-5	Bergsson

2 Mar	Division 1	Chelsea (h)	1-1	Lineker
10 Mar	FA Cup QF	Notts County (h)	2-1	Nayim, Gascoigne
16 Mar	Division 1	Aston Villa (a)	2-3	Samways, Allen
23 Mar	Division 1	QPR (h)	0-0	
30 Mar	Division 1	Coventry (h)	2-2	Nayim 2
1 Apr	Division 1	Luton (a)	0-0	
6 Apr	Division 1	Southampton (h)	2-0	Lineker 2
10 Apr	Division 1	Norwich (a)	1-2	Hendry
14 Apr	FA Cup SF	Arsenal	3-1	Gascoigne, Lineker 2
17 Apr	Division 1	Crystal Palace (a)	0-1	
24 Apr	Division 1	Everton (h)	3-3	Allen, Mabbutt, Nayim
4 May	Division 1	Nottingham F (h)	1-1	Nayim
11 May	Division 1	Liverpool (a)	0-2	
18 May	FA Cup Final	Nottingham F	2-1	Stewart, OG
20 May	Division 1	Manchester Utd (a)	1-1	Hendry

FINAL LEAGUE POSITION	10th (49 points)
PEAK LEAGUE POSITION	2nd (match week 2)
LOW LEAGUE POSITION	11th (match week 37)
FA CUP	Winners
LEAGUE CUP (RUMBELOWS)	5th round
EUROPE	Did not participate
MANAGER	TERRY VENABLES
TOP GOALSCORER	GARY LINEKER (22)
MOST APPEARANCES	PAUL ALLEN (48)

MACRO FOOTBALL CLIMATE

LEAGUE CHAMPIONS	ARSENAL
RUNNERS-UP	LIVERPOOL
FA CUP	SPURS beat NOTTINGHAM FOREST 2-1
LEAGUE (RUMBELOWS) CUP	SHEFFIELD WEDS 1-0 MANCHESTER UTD
RELEGATED	DERBY, LUTON
BIGGEST TRANSFER FEE	DENNIS WISE £1.6m WIMBLEDON to CHELSEA

1991/92

10 Aug	Charity Shield	Arsenal	0-0	
17 Aug	Division 1	Southampton (a)	3-2	Lineker 2, Durie
21 Aug	ECWC Qual	SV Stockerau (a)	1-0	Durie
24 Aug	Division 1	Chelsea (h)	1-3	Lineker
28 Aug	Division 1	Nottingham F (a)	3-1	Lineker, Durie, Bergsson
31 Aug	Division 1	Norwich (a)	1-0	Lineker
4 Sept	ECWC Qual	SV Stockerau (h)	1-0	Mabbutt
7 Sept	Division 1	Aston Villa (a)	0-0	
14 Sept	Division 1	QPR (h)	2-0	Lineker 2
17 Sept	ECWC 1	Hajduk Split (a)	0-1	
21 Sept	Division 1	Wimbledon (a)	5-3	Lineker 4, Samways
25 Sept	League Cup 2	Swansea (a)	0-1	
28 Sept	Division 1	Manchester Utd (h)	1-2	Durie
2 Oct	ECWC 1	Hajduk Split (h)	2-0	Tuttle, Durie
5 Oct	Division 1	Everton (a)	1-3	Lineker
9 Oct	League Cup 2	Swansea (h)	5-1	Allen, Lineker, OG, Stewart, Samways
19 Oct	Division 1	Manchester C (h)	0-1	
23 Oct	ECWC 2	FC Porto (h)	3-1	Lineker 2, Durie
26 Oct	Division 1	West Ham (a)	1-2	Lineker
29 Oct	League Cup 3	Grimsby (a)	3-0	Howells, Lineker, Durie
2 Nov	Division 1	Sheffield Weds (a)	0-0	
7 Nov	ECWC 2	FC Porto (a)	0-0	
16 Nov	Division 1	Luton (h)	4-1	Houghton 2, Lineker 2
23 Nov	Division 1	Sheffield Utd (h)	0-1	
1 Dec	Division 1	Arsenal (a)	0-2	
4 Dec	League Cup 4	Coventry (a)	2-1	Allen, Durie
7 Dec	Division 1	Notts County (h)	2-1	Walsh, Mabbutt
14 Dec	Division 1	Leeds (a)	1-1	Howells
18 Dec	Division 1	Liverpool (h)	1-2	Walsh
22 Dec	Division 1	Crystal Palace (a)	2-1	Walsh, Lineker
26 Dec	Division 1	Nottingham F (h)	1-2	Stewart
28 Dec	Division 1	Norwich (h)	3-0	Allen, Lineker, Nayim
1 Jan	Division 1	Coventry (a)	2-1	Lineker, Stewart
5 Jan	FA Cup 3	Aston Villa (a)	0-0	
8 Jan	League Cup QF	Norwich (h)	2-1	Walsh, Lineker
11 Jan	Division 1	Chelsea (a)	0-2	
14 Jan	FA Cup 3	Aston Villa (h)	0-1	
18 Jan	Division 1	Southampton (h)	1-2	Mabbutt
25 Jan	Division 1	Oldham (h)	0-0	
1 Feb	Division 1	Manchester C (a)	0-1	
9 Feb	League Cup SF	Nottingham F (a)	1-1	Lineker
16 Feb	Division 1	Crystal Palace (h)	0-1	
22 Feb	Division 1	Arsenal (h)	1-1	Stewart

1 Mar	League Cup SF	Nottingham F (a)	1-2	Lineker
4 Mar	ECWC QF	Feyenoord (a)	0-1	
7 Mar	Division 1	Leeds (h)	1-3	Allen
11 Mar	Division 1	Luton (a)	0-0	
14 Mar	Division 1	Sheffield Weds (h)	0-2	
18 Mar	ECWC QF	Feyenoord (h)	0-0	
21 Mar	Division 1	Liverpool (a)	1-2	Stewart
28 Mar	Division 1	Coventry (h)	4-3	Durie 3, Lineker
1 Apr	Division 1	West Ham (h)	3-0	Lineker 3
4 Apr	Division 1	Aston Villa (h)	2-5	Lineker, OG
7 Apr	Division 1	Notts County (a)	2-0	Lineker 2
11 Apr	Division 1	QPR (a)	2-1	Gray, Durie
14 Apr	Division 1	Sheffield Utd (a)	0-2	
18 Apr	Division 1	Wimbledon (h)	3-2	Lineker 2, Hendry
20 Apr	Division 1	Oldham (a)	0-1	
25 Apr	Division 1	Everton (h)	3-3	Allen, Minton, Stewart
2 May	Division 1	Manchester Utd (a)	1-3	Lineker

FINAL LEAGUE POSITION	15th (52 points)
PEAK LEAGUE POSITION	3rd (match week 1)
LOW LEAGUE POSITION	19th (match week 32)
FA CUP	3rd round (Aston Villa – replay)
LEAGUE CUP (RUMBELOWS)	Semi-final (Nottingham Forest)
EUROPE	EUROPEAN CUP WINNERS' CUP – Quarter-final (Feyenoord)
MANAGER	PETER SHREEVE (head coach); TERRY VENABLES (Chief Executive)
TOP GOALSCORER	GARY LINEKER (35)
MOST APPEARANCES	GARY MABBUTT (57)

MACRO FOOTBALL CLIMATE

LEAGUE CHAMPIONS	LEEDS
RUNNERS-UP	MANCHESTER UTD
FA CUP	LIVERPOOL 2-0 SUNDERLAND
LEAGUE CUP (RUMBELOWS)	MANCHESTER UTD 1-0 NOTTINGHAM FOREST
RELEGATED	NOTTS COUNTY, WEST HAM, LUTON
HIGHEST TRANSFER FEE	IAN WRIGHT £2.5m CRYSTAL PALACE – to ARSENAL

1992/93

15 Aug	Premier League	Southampton (a)	0-0	
19 Aug	Premier League	Coventry (h)	0-2	
22 Aug	Premier League	Crystal Palace (h)	2-2	Durie, Sedgley
25 Aug	Premier League	Leeds (a)	0-5	
30 Aug	Premier League	Ipswich (a)	1-1	Cundy
2 Sept	Premier League	Sheffield Utd (h)	2-0	Sheringham, Durie
5 Sept	Premier League	Everton (h)	2-1	Allen, Turner
14 Sept	Premier League	Coventry (a)	0-1	
19 Sept	Premier League	Manchester Utd (h)	1-1	Durie
21 Sept	League Cup 2	Brentford (h)	3-1	Sheringham, Watson, Durie
27 Sept	Premier League	Sheffield Weds (a)	0-2	
3 Oct	Premier League	QPR (a)	1-4	Sheringham
7 Oct	League Cup 2	Brentford (a)	4-2	Sheringham 2, Anderton, Turner
17 Oct	Premier League	Middlesbrough (h)	2-2	Sheringham, Barmby
25 Oct	Premier League	Wimbledon (a)	1-1	Barmby
28 Oct	League Cup 3	Manchester City (a)	1-0	Samways
31 Oct	Premier League	Liverpool (h)	2-0	Ruddock, Nayim
7 Nov	Premier League	Blackburn (a)	2-0	Howells, Sheringham
21 Nov	Premier League	Aston Villa (h)	0-0	
28 Nov	Premier League	Manchester C (a)	1-0	Watson
2 Dec	League Cup 4	Nottingham F (a)	0-2	
5 Dec	Premier League	Chelsea (h)	1-2	Campbell
12 Dec	Premier League	Arsenal (h)	1-0	Allen
19 Dec	Premier League	Oldham (a)	1-2	Sheringham
26 Dec	Premier League	Norwich (a)	0-0	
28 Dec	Premier League	Nottingham F (h)	2-1	Barmby, Mabbutt
2 Jan	FA Cup 3	Marlow (a) – played at White Hart Lane	5-1	Sheringham, Barmby 2, Samways 2
9 Jan	Premier League	Manchester Utd (a)	1-4	Barmby
16 Jan	Premier League	Sheffield Weds (h)	0-2	
24 Jan	FA Cup 4	Norwich (a)	2-0	Sheringham 2
27 Jan	Premier League	Ipswich (h)	0-2	
30 Jan	Premier League	Crystal Palace (a)	3-1	Sheringham 2, Gray
7 Feb	Premier League	Southampton (h)	4-2	Sheringham 2, Anderton, Barmby
10 Feb	Premier League	Everton (a)	2-1	Mabbutt, Allen
14 Feb	FA Cup 5	Wimbledon (h)	3-2	Anderton, Sheringham, Barmby
20 Feb	Premier League	Leeds (h)	4-0	Sheringham 3, Ruddock

27 Feb	Premier League	QPR (h)	3-2	Sheringham 2, Anderton
2 Mar	Premier League	Sheffield Utd (a)	0-6	
7 Mar	FA Cup QF	Manchester C (a)	4-2	Nayim 3, Sedgley
10 Mar	Premier League	Aston Villa (a)	0-0	
20 Mar	Premier League	Chelsea (a)	1-1	Sheringham
24 Mar	Premier League	Manchester C (h)	3-1	Anderton, Nayim, Turner
4 Apr	FA Cup SF	Arsenal	0-1	
9 Apr	Premier League	Norwich (h)	5-1	Ruddock, Sheringham 2, Barmby, Nayim
12 Apr	Premier League	Nottingham F (a)	1-2	Sedgley
17 Apr	Premier League	Oldham (h)	4-1	Sheringham 2, Anderton, Turner
20 Apr	Premier League	Middlesbrough (a)	0-3	
1 May	Premier League	Wimbledon (h)	1-1	Anderton
5 May	Premier League	Blackburn (h)	1-2	Anderton
8 May	Premier League	Liverpool (a)	2-6	Sheringham, Sedgley
11 May	Premier League	Arsenal (a)	3-1	Sheringham, Hendry 2

FINAL LEAGUE POSITION	8th (59 points)
PEAK LEAGUE POSITION	5th (match week 35)
LOW LEAGUE POSITION	21st (match week 5)
FA CUP	Semi-final (Arsenal)
LEAGUE CUP (COCA-COLA)	4th round (Nottingham Forest)
EUROPE	Did not participate
MANAGER	RAY CLEMENCE AND DOUG LIVERMORE (FIRST-TEAM COACHES) / TERRY VENABLES (CHIEF EXECUTIVE)
TOP GOALSCORER	TEDDY SHERINGHAM (28)
MOST APPEARANCES	PAUL ALLEN, TEDDY SHERINGHAM, NEIL RUDDOCK (47)

MACRO FOOTBALL CLIMATE

LEAGUE CHAMPIONS (PREMIER LEAGUE)	MANCHESTER UTD
RUNNERS-UP	ASTON VILLA
FA CUP	ARSENAL 2-1 SHEFFIELD WEDS (REPLAY)
LEAGUE CUP (COCA-COLA)	ARSENAL 2-1 SHEFFIELD WEDS (AET)
RELEGATED	NOTTINGHAM FOREST, MIDDLESBROUGH, CRYSTAL PALACE
RECORD TRANSFER FEE PAID	ALAN SHEARER £3.3m SOUTHAMPTON to BLACKBURN

1993/94

14 Aug	Premier League	Newcastle (a)	1-0	Sheringham
16 Aug	Premier League	Arsenal (h)	0-1	
21 Aug	Premier League	Manchester C (h)	1-0	Sedgley
25 Aug	Premier League	Liverpool (a)	2-1	Sheringham 2
28 Aug	Premier League	Aston Villa (a)	0-1	
1 Sept	Premier League	Chelsea (h)	1-1	Sheringham
11 Sept	Premier League	Sheffield Utd (a)	2-2	Sheringham 2
18 Sept	Premier League	Oldham (h)	5-0	Sedgley 2, Sheringham, Durie, Dozzell
22 Sept	League Cup 2	Burnley (a)	0-0	
26 Sept	Premier League	Ipswich (a)	2-2	Sheringham, Dozzell
3 Oct	Premier League	Everton (h)	3-2	Sheringham, Anderton, Caskey
6 Oct	League Cup 2	Burnley (h)	3-1	Sheringham 2, Howells
16 Oct	Premier League	Manchester Utd (a)	1-2	Caskey
23 Oct	Premier League	Swindon (h)	1-1	Dozzell
27 Oct	League Cup 3	Derby (a)	1-0	Barmby
30 Oct	Premier League	Blackburn (a)	0-1	
6 Nov	Premier League	Southampton (a)	0-1	
20 Nov	Premier League	Leeds (h)	1-1	Anderton
24 Nov	Premier League	Wimbledon (h)	1-1	Barmby
27 Nov	Premier League	QPR (a)	1-1	Anderton
1 Dec	League Cup 4	Blackburn (h)	1-0	Campbell
4 Dec	Premier League	Newcastle (h)	1-2	Barmby
6 Dec	Premier League	Arsenal (a)	1-1	Anderton
11 Dec	Premier League	Manchester C (a)	2-0	Dozzell 2
18 Dec	Premier League	Liverpool (h)	3-3	Samways, Hazard, Caskey
27 Dec	Premier League	Norwich (h)	1-3	Barmby
28 Dec	Premier League	West Ham (a)	3-1	Dozzell, Hazard, Anderton
1 Jan	Premier League	Coventry (h)	1-2	Caskey
3 Jan	Premier League	Sheffield Weds (a)	0-1	
8 Jan	FA Cup 3	Peterborough (a)	1-1	Dozzell
12 Jan	League Cup 5	Aston Villa (h)	1-2	Caskey
15 Jan	Premier League	Manchester Utd (h)	0-1	
19 Jan	FA Cup 3R	Peterborough (h)	1-1 (5-4p)	Barmby

22 Jan	Premier League	Swindon (a)	1-2	Barmby
29 Jan	FA Cup 4	Ipswich (a)	0-3	
5 Feb	Premier League	Sheffield Wednesday (h)	1-3	Rosenthal
12 Feb	Premier League	Blackburn (h)	0-2	
27 Feb	Premier League	Chelsea (a)	3-4	Dozzell, Sedgley, Gray
2 Mar	Premier League	Aston Villa (h)	1-1	Rosenthal
5 Mar	Premier League	Sheffield Utd (h)	2-2	Scott, Dozzell
19 Mar	Premier League	Ipswich (h)	1-1	Barmby
26 Mar	Premier League	Everton (a)	1-0	Sedgley
2 Apr	Premier League	Norwich (a)	2-1	Sheringham, OG
4 Apr	Premier League	West Ham (h)	1-4	Sheringham
9 Apr	Premier League	Coventry (a)	0-1	
17 Apr	Premier League	Leeds (a)	0-2	
23 Apr	Premier League	Southampton (h)	3-0	Sedgley, Samways, Anderton
30 Apr	Premier League	Wimbledon (a)	1-2	Sheringham
5 May	Premier League	Oldham (a)	2-0	Samways, Howells
7 May	Premier League	QPR (h)	1-2	Sheringham

FINAL LEAGUE POSITION	15th (45 points)
PEAK LEAGUE POSITION	5th (match week 6)
LOW LEAGUE POSITION	18th (match week 36)
FA CUP	4th round (Ipswich)
LEAGUE CUP (COCA-COLA)	Quarter-final (Aston Villa)
EUROPE	Did not participate
MANAGER	OSSIE ARDILES
TOP GOALSCORER	TEDDY SHERINGHAM (15)
MOST APPEARANCES	STEVE SEDGLEY (50)

MACRO FOOTBALL CLIMATE:

LEAGUE CHAMPIONS	MANCHESTER UTD
RUNNERS-UP	BLACKBURN
FA CUP	MANCHESTER UTD 4-0 CHELSEA
LEAGUE CUP (COCA-COLA)	ASTON VILLA 3-1 MANCHESTER UTD
RELEGATED	SWINDON, OLDHAM, SHEFFIELD UNITED
RECORD TRANSFER FEE PAID	ROY KEANE £3.75m NOTTINGHAM FOREST to MANCHESTER UTD

1994/95

20 Aug	Premier League	Sheffield Weds (a)	4-3	Sheringham, Anderton, Barmby, Klinsmann
24 Aug	Premier League	Everton (h)	2-1	Klinsmann 2
27 Aug	Premier League	Manchester Utd (h)	0-1	
30 Aug	Premier League	Ipswich (a)	3-1	Klinsmann 2, Dumitrescu
12 Sept	Premier League	Southampton (h)	1-2	Klinsmann
17 Sept	Premier League	Leicester (a)	1-3	Klinsmann
21 Sept	League Cup 2	Watford (a)	6-3	Anderton, Klinsmann 3, Sheringham, Dumitrescu
24 Sept	Premier League	Nottingham F (h)	1-4	Dumitrescu
1 Oct	Premier League	Wimbledon (a)	2-1	Sheringham, Popescu
4 Oct	League Cup 2	Watford (h)	2-3	Barmby, Klinsmann
8 Oct	Premier League	QPR (h)	1-1	Barmby
15 Oct	Premier League	Leeds (a)	1-1	Sheringham
22 Oct	Premier League	Manchester C (a)	2-5	Dumitrescu 2
26 Oct	League Cup 3	Notts County (a)	0-3	
29 Oct	Premier League	West Ham (h)	3-1	Klinsmann, Sheringham, Barmby
5 Nov	Premier League	Blackburn (a)	0-2	
19 Nov	Premier League	Aston Villa (h)	3-4	Sheringham, Klinsmann, OG
23 Nov	Premier League	Chelsea (h)	0-0	
26 Nov	Premier League	Liverpool (a)	1-1	OG
3 Dec	Premier League	Newcastle (h)	4-2	Sheringham 3, Popescu
10 Dec	Premier League	Sheffield Weds (h)	3-1	Barmby, Klinsmann, Calderwood
17 Dec	Premier League	Everton (a)	0-0	
26 Dec	Premier League	Norwich (a)	2-0	Barmby, Sheringham
27 Dec	Premier League	Crystal Palace (h)	0-0	
31 Dec	Premier League	Coventry (a)	4-0	OG, Barmby, Anderton, Sheringham
2 Jan	Premier League	Arsenal (h)	1-0	Popescu
7 Jan	FA Cup 3	Altrincham (h)	3-0	Sheringham, Rosenthal, Nethercott
14 Jan	Premier League	West Ham (a)	2-1	Sheringham, Klinsmann
25 Jan	Premier League	Aston Villa (a)	0-1	
29 Jan	FA Cup 4	Sunderland (a)	4-1	Klinsmann 2, Sheringham, OG
5 Feb	Premier League	Blackburn (h)	3-1	Klinsmann, Anderton, Barmby
11 Feb	Premier League	Chelsea (a)	1-1	Sheringham
18 Feb	FA Cup 5	Southampton (h)	1-1	Klinsmann

25 Feb	Premier League	Wimbledon (h)	1-2	Klinsmann
1 Mar	FA Cup 5R	Southampton (a)	6-2	Rosenthal 3, Sheringham, Barmby, Anderton
4 Mar	Premier League	Nottingham F (a)	2-2	Sheringham, Calderwood
8 Mar	Premier League	Ipswich (h)	3-0	Klinsmann, Barmby, OG
11 Mar	FA Cup QF	Liverpool (a)	2-1	Sheringham, Klinsmann
15 Mar	Premier League	Manchester Utd (a)	0-0	
18 Mar	Premier League	Leicester (h)	1-0	Klinsmann
22 Mar	Premier League	Liverpool (h)	0-0	
2 Apr	Premier League	Southampton (a)	3-4	Sheringham 2, Klinsmann
9 Apr	FA Cup SF	Everton	1-4	Klinsmann
11 Apr	Premier League	Manchester C (h)	2-1	Howells, Klinsmann
14 Apr	Premier League	Crystal Palace (a)	1-1	Klinsmann
17 Apr	Premier League	Norwich (h)	1-0	Sheringham
29 Apr	Premier League	Arsenal (a)	1-1	Klinsmann
3 May	Premier League	Newcastle (a)	3-3	Barmby, Klinsmann, Anderton
6 May	Premier League	QPR (a)	1-2	Sheringham
9 May	Premier League	Coventry (h)	1-3	Anderton
14 May	Premier League	Leeds (h)	1-1	Sheringham

FINAL LEAGUE POSITION	7th (62 points)
PEAK LEAGUE POSITION	2nd (match week 2)
LOW LEAGUE POSITION	15th (match week 14)
FA CUP	Semi-final (Everton)
LEAGUE CUP (RUMBELOWS)	3rd round (Notts County)
EUROPE	Did not participate
MANAGER	OSSIE ARDILES (until 31 October); Steve Perryman – caretaker; Gerry Francis (14th November–)
TOP GOALSCORER	JURGEN KLINSMANN (29)
MOST APPEARANCES	TEDDY SHERINGHAM (50)

MACRO FOOTBALL CLIMATE

LEAGUE CHAMPIONS	BLACKBURN
RUNNERS-UP	MANCHESTER UTD
FA CUP	EVERTON 1-0 MANCHESTER UTD
LEAGUE CUP	LIVERPOOL 2-1 BOLTON
RELEGATED	NORWICH, IPSWICH, LEICESTER, CRYSTAL PALACE
HIGHEST TRANSFER FEE PAID	ANDY COLE £7m NEWCASTLE to MANCHESTER UTD

1995/96

25 Jun	Intertoto Cup	Luzern (h)	0-2	
1 July	Intertoto Cup	NK Rudar (a)	2-1	Sampson, Hendry
16 Jul	Intertoto Cup	Osters IF (h)	1-2	McMahon
23 Jul	Intertoto Cup	Cologne (a)	0-8	
19 Aug	Premier League	Manchester C (a)	1-1	Sheringham
23 Aug	Premier League	Aston Villa (h)	0-1	
26 Aug	Premier League	Liverpool (h)	1-3	OG
30 Aug	Premier League	West Ham (a)	1-1	Rosenthal
9 Sept	Premier League	Leeds (h)	2-1	Howells, Sheringham
16 Sept	Premier League	Sheffield Weds (a)	3-1	OG, Sheringham 2
20 Sept	League Cup 2	Chester (h)	4-0	Armstrong 2, Sheringham, Rosenthal
25 Sept	Premier League	QPR (a)	3-2	Sheringham 2, Dozzell
30 Sept	Premier League	Wimbledon (h)	3-0	Sheringham 2, OG
4 Oct	League Cup 2	Chester (a)	3-1	Sheringham 2, Howells
14 Oct	Premier League	Nottingham F (h)	0-1	
22 Oct	Premier League	Everton (a)	1-1	Armstrong
25 Oct	League Cup 3	Coventry (a)	2-3	Armstrong, OG
29 Oct	Premier League	Newcastle (h)	1-1	Armstrong
4 Nov	Premier League	Coventry (a)	3-2	Fox, Sheringham, Howells
18 Nov	Premier League	Arsenal (h)	2-1	Sheringham, Armstrong
21 Nov	Premier League	Middlesbrough (a)	1-0	Armstrong
25 Nov	Premier League	Chelsea (a)	0-0	
2 Dec	Premier League	Everton (h)	0-0	
9 Dec	Premier League	QPR (h)	1-0	Sheringham
16 Dec	Premier League	Wimbledon (a)	1-0	Fox
23 Dec	Premier League	Bolton (h)	2-2	Sheringham, Armstrong
26 Dec	Premier League	Southampton (a)	0-0	
30 Dec	Premier League	Blackburn (a)	1-2	Sheringham
1 Jan	Premier League	Manchester Utd (h)	4-1	Sheringham, Campbell, Armstrong 2
6 Jan	FA Cup 3	Hereford (a)	1-1	Rosenthal
13 Jan	Premier League	Manchester C (h)	1-0	Armstrong
17 Jan	FA Cup 3R	Hereford (h)	5-1	Sheringham 3, Armstrong 2
21 Jan	Premier League	Aston Villa (a)	1-2	Fox
27 Jan	FA Cup 4	Wolves (h)	1-1	Wilson
3 Feb	Premier League	Liverpool (a)	0-0	

7 Feb	FA Cup 4R	Wolves (a)	2-0	Rosenthal, Sheringham
12 Feb	Premier League	West Ham (h)	0-1	
19 Feb	FA Cup 5	Nottingham F (a)	a-a	
24 Feb	Premier League	Sheffield Weds (h)	1-0	Armstrong
28 Feb	FA Cup 5	Nottingham F (a)	2-2	Armstrong 2
2 Mar	Premier League	Southampton (h)	1-0	Dozzell
9 Mar	FA Cup 5R	Nottingham F (h)	1-1 1-3p	Sheringham
16 Mar	Premier League	Blackburn (h)	2-3	Sheringham, Armstrong
20 Mar	Premier League	Bolton (a)	3-2	Howells, Fox, Armstrong
24 Mar	Premier League	Manchester Utd (a)	0-1	
30 Mar	Premier League	Coventry (h)	3-1	Sheringham, Fox 2
6 Apr	Premier League	Nottingham F (a)	1-2	Armstrong
8 Apr	Premier League	Middlesbrough (h)	1-1	Armstrong
15 Apr	Premier League	Arsenal (a)	0-0	
27 Apr	Premier League	Chelsea (h)	1-1	Armstrong
2 May	Premier League	Leeds (a)	3-1	Armstrong, Anderton 2
5 May	Premier League	Newcastle (a)	1-1	Dozzell

FINAL LEAGUE POSITION	8th (61 points)
PEAK LEAGUE POSITION	3rd (match week 18)
LOW LEAGUE POSITION	19th (match week 3)
FA CUP	5th round (Nottingham Forest)
LEAGUE CUP (COCA-COLA)	3rd round (Coventry)
EUROPE	INTERTOTO CUP
MANAGER	GERRY FRANCIS
TOP GOALSCORER	TEDDY SHERINGHAM (24)
MOST APPEARANCES	TEDDY SHERINGHAM and IAN WALKER (47)

MACRO FOOTBALL CLIMATE

LEAGUE CHAMPIONS	MANCHESTER UTD
RUNNERS-UP	NEWCASTLE
FA CUP	MANCHESTER UTD 1-0 LIVERPOOL
LEAGUE CUP	ASTON VILLA 3-1 LEEDS
RELEGATED	BOLTON, QPR, MANCHESTER C
RECORD TRANSFER FEE PAID	STAN COLLYMORE £8.5m NOTTINGHAM FOREST to LIVERPOOL

1996/97

17 Aug	Premier League	Blackburn (a)	2-0	Armstrong
21 Aug	Premier League	Derby (h)	1-1	Sheringham
24 Aug	Premier League	Everton (h)	0-0	
4 Sept	Premier League	Wimbledon (a)	0-1	
7 Sept	Premier League	Newcastle (h)	1-2	R Allen
14 Sept	Premier League	Southampton (a)	1-0	Armstrong
17 Sept	League Cup 2	Preston (a)	1-1	Anderton
22 Sept	Premier League	Leicester (h)	1-2	Wilson
25 Sept	League Cup 2	Preston (h)	3-0	Anderton, R Allen 2
29 Sept	Premier League	Manchester Utd (a)	0-2	
12 Oct	Premier League	Aston Villa (h)	1-0	Nielsen
19 Oct	Premier League	Middlesbrough (a)	3-0	Sheringham 2, Fox
23 Oct	League Cup 3	Sunderland (h)	2-1	Armstrong, Campbell
26 Oct	Premier League	Chelsea (a)	1-3	Armstrong
2 Nov	Premier League	West Ham (h)	1-0	Armstrong
16 Nov	Premier League	Sunderland (h)	2-0	Sinton, Sheringham
24 Nov	Premier League	Arsenal (a)	1-3	Sinton
27 Nov	League Cup 4	Bolton (a)	1-6	Sheringham
2 Dec	Premier League	Liverpool (h)	0-2	
7 Dec	Premier League	Coventry (a)	2-1	Sheringham, Sinton
14 Dec	Premier League	Leeds (a)	0-0	
21 Dec	Premier League	Sheffield Weds (h)	1-1	Nielsen
26 Dec	Premier League	Southampton (h)	3-1	Iversen 2, Nielsen
28 Dec	Premier League	Newcastle (a)	1-7	Nielsen
5 Jan	FA Cup 3	Manchester Utd (a)	0-2	
12 Jan	Premier League	Manchester Utd (h)	1-2	R Allen
19 Jan	Premier League	Nottingham F (a)	1-2	Sinton
29 Jan	Premier League	Blackburn (h)	2-1	Iversen, Sinton
1 Feb	Premier League	Chelsea (h)	1-2	Howells
15 Feb	Premier League	Arsenal (h)	0-0	

24 Feb	Premier League	West Ham (a)	3-4	Sheringham, Anderton, Howells
1 Mar	Premier League	Nottingham F (h)	0-1	
4 Mar	Premier League	Sunderland (a)	4-0	Iversen 3, Nielsen
15 Mar	Premier League	Leeds (h)	1-0	Anderton
19 Mar	Premier League	Leicester (a)	1-1	Sheringham
22 Mar	Premier League	Derby (a)	2-4	Dozzell, Rosenthal
5 Apr	Premier League	Wimbledon (h)	1-0	Dozzell
9 Apr	Premier League	Sheffield Weds (a)	1-2	Nielsen
12 Apr	Premier League	Everton (a)	0-1	
19 Apr	Premier League	Aston Villa (a)	1-1	Vega
24 Apr	Premier League	Middlesbrough (h)	1-0	Sinton
3 May	Premier League	Liverpool (a)	1-2	Anderton
11 May	Premier League	Coventry (h)	1-2	McVeigh

FINAL LEAGUE POSITION	10th (46 points)
PEAK LEAGUE POSITION	5th (match week 1)
LOW LEAGUE POSITION	14th (match week 10)
FA CUP	3rd round (Manchester Utd)
LEAGUE CUP (COCA-COLA)	4th round (Bolton)
EUROPE	Did not participate
MANAGER	GERRY FRANCIS
TOP GOALSCORER	TEDDY SHERINGHAM (8)
MOST APPEARANCES	SOL CAMPBELL (43)

MACRO-FOOTBALL CLIMATE

LEAGUE CHAMPIONS (PREMIER LEAGUE)	MANCHESTER UTD
RUNNERS-UP	NEWCASTLE
FA CUP	CHELSEA BEAT MIDDLESBROUGH 2-0
LEAGUE CUP	LEICESTER BEAT MIDDLESBROUGH IN REPLAY 1-0
RELEGATED	SUNDERLAND, NOTTINGHAM FOREST, MIDDLESBROUGH
BIGGEST TRANSFER	ALAN SHEARER £15m – BLACKBURN to NEWCASTLE

1997/98

10 Aug	Premier League	Manchester Utd (h)	0-2	
13 Aug	Premier League	West Ham (a)	1-2	Ferdinand
23 Aug	Premier League	Derby (h)	1-0	Calderwood
27 Aug	Premier League	Aston Villa (h)	3-2	Ferdinand 2, Fox
30 Aug	Premier League	Arsenal (a)	0-0	
13 Sept	Premier League	Leicester (a)	0-3	
17 Sept	League Cup 2	Carlisle (h)	3-2	Fenn, Fox, Mahorn
20 Sept	Premier League	Blackburn (h)	0-0	
27 Sept	Premier League	Wimbledon (h)	0-0	
30 Sept	League Cup 2	Carlisle (a)	2-0	Ginola, Armstrong
4 Oct	Premier League	Newcastle (a)	0-1	
15 Oct	League Cup 3	Derby (h)	1-2	Ginola
19 Oct	Premier League	Sheffield Weds (h)	3-2	Armstrong, Dominguez, Ginola
25 Oct	Premier League	Southampton (a)	2-3	Dominguez, Ginola
1 Nov	Premier League	Leeds (h)	0-1	
8 Nov	Premier League	Liverpool (a)	0-4	
24 Nov	Premier League	Crystal Palace (h)	0-1	
29 Nov	Premier League	Everton (a)	2-0	Vega, Ginola
6 Dec	Premier League	Chelsea (h)	1-6	Vega
13 Dec	Premier League	Coventry (a)	0-4	
20 Dec	Premier League	Barnsley (h)	3-0	Nielsen, Ginola 2
26 Dec	Premier League	Aston Villa (a)	1-4	Calderwood
28 Dec	Premier League	Arsenal (h)	1-1	Nielsen
5 Jan	FA Cup 3	Fulham (h)	3-1	Clemence, Calderwood, OG
10 Jan	Premier League	Manchester Utd (a)	0-2	
17 Jan	Premier League	West Ham (h)	1-0	Klinsmann
24 Jan	FA Cup 4	Barnsley (h)	1-1	Campbell
31 Jan	Premier League	Derby (a)	1-2	Fox
4 Feb	FA Cup 4R	Barnsley (a)	1-3	Ginola
7 Feb	Premier League	Blackburn (a)	3-0	Berti, Armstrong, Fox
14 Feb	Premier League	Leicester (h)	1-1	Calderwood
21 Feb	Premier League	Sheffield Weds (a)	0-1	
1 Mar	Premier League	Bolton (h)	1-0	Nielsen

4 Mar	Premier League	Leeds (a)	0-1	
14 Mar	Premier League	Liverpool (h)	3-3	Klinsmann, Ginola, Vega
28 Mar	Premier League	Crystal Palace (a)	3-1	Berti, Armstrong, Klinsmann
4 Apr	Premier League	Everton (h)	1-1	Armstrong
11 Apr	Premier League	Chelsea (a)	0-2	
13 Apr	Premier League	Coventry (h)	1-1	Berti
18 Apr	Premier League	Barnsley (a)	1-1	Calderwood
25 Apr	Premier League	Newcastle (h)	2-0	Klinsmann, Ferdinand
2 May	Premier League	Wimbledon (a)	6-2	Ferdinand, Klinsmann 4, Saib
10 May	Premier League	Southampton (h)	1-1	Klinsmann

FINAL LEAGUE POSITION	14th (44 points)
PEAK LEAGUE POSITION	7th (match week 5)
LOW LEAGUE POSITION	19th (match week 21)
FA CUP	4th round (Barnsley)
LEAGUE CUP (WORTHINGTON CUP)	3rd round (Derby)
EUROPE	Did not participate
MANAGER	GERRY FRANCIS (until 11 November) CHRISTIAN GROSS (from November)
TOP GOALSCORER	JURGEN KLINSMANN AND DAVID GINOLA (9)
MOST APPEARANCES	STEPHEN CARR (43)

MACRO-FOOTBALL CLIMATE

LEAGUE CHAMPIONS (PREMIER LEAGUE)	ARSENAL
RUNNERS-UP	MANCHESTER UTD
FA CUP	ARSENAL 2-0 NEWCASTLE
LEAGUE CUP	CHELSEA 1-0 MIDDLESBROUGH
RELEGATED	BARNSLEY, BOLTON, CRYSTAL PALACE
BIGGEST TRANSFER	GRAEME LE SAUX £7.5m BLACKBURN to CHELSEA

1998/99

15 Aug	Premier League	Wimbledon (a)	1-3	Fox
22 Aug	Premier League	Sheffield Weds (h)	0-3	
29 Aug	Premier League	Everton (a)	1-0	Ferdinand
9 Sept	Premier League	Blackburn (h)	2-1	Ferdinand. Nielsen
13 Sept	Premier League	Middlesbrough (h)	0-3	
15 Sept	League Cup 2	Brentford (a)	3-2	Carr, Dominguez, Vega
19 Sept	Premier League	Southampton (a)	1-1	Fox
23 Sept	League Cup 2	Brentford (h)	3-2	Nielsen, Campbell, Armstrong
26 Sept	Premier League	Leeds (h)	3-3	Vega. Iversen, Campbell
3 Oct	Premier League	Derby (a)	1-0	Campbell
19 Oct	Premier League	Leicester (a)	1-2	Ferdinand
24 Oct	Premier League	Newcastle (h)	2-0	Iversen 2
27 Oct	League Cup 3	Northampton (a)	3-1	Armstrong 2, Campbell
2 Nov	Premier League	Charlton (h)	2-2	Nielsen, Armstrong
7 Nov	Premier League	Aston Villa (a)	2-3	Anderton, Vega
10 Nov	League Cup 4	Liverpool (a)	3-1	Iversen, Scales, Nielsen
14 Nov	Premier League	Arsenal (a)	0-0	
21 Nov	Premier League	Nottingham F (h)	2-0	Armstrong, Nielsen
28 Nov	Premier League	West Ham (a)	1-2	Armstrong
2 Dec	League Cup QF	Manchester Utd (h)	3-1	Armstrong 2, Ginola
5 Dec	Premier League	Liverpool (h)	2-1	Fox, OG
12 Dec	Premier League	Manchester Utd (h)	2-2	Campbell 2
19 Dec	Premier League	Chelsea (a)	0-2	
26 Dec	Premier League	Coventry (a)	1-1	Campbell
28 Dec	Premier League	Everton (h)	4-1	Ferdinand, Armstrong 3
2 Jan	FA Cup 3	Watford (h)	5-2	Iversen 2, Anderton, Nielsen, Fox
9 Jan	Premier League	Sheffield Weds (a)	0-0	
16 Jan	Premier League	Wimbledon (h)	0-0	
23 Jan	FA Cup 4	Wimbledon (a)	1-1	Ginola
27 Jan	League Cup SF1	Wimbledon (h)	0-0	
30 Jan	Premier League	Blackburn (a)	1-1	Iversen
2 Feb	FA Cup 4R	Wimbledon (h)	3-0	Sinton, Nielsen 2
6 Feb	Premier League	Coventry (h)	0-0	
13 Feb	FA Cup 5	Leeds (a)	1-1	Sherwood
16 Feb	League Cup SF2	Wimbledon (a)	1-0	Iversen
20 Feb	Premier League	Middlesbrough (a)	0-0	

24 Feb	FA Cup 5R	Leeds (h)	2-0	Anderton, Ginola
27 Feb	Premier League	Derby (h)	1-1	Sherwood
2 Mar	Premier League	Southampton (h)	3-0	Armstrong, Iversen, Dominguez
10 Mar	Premier League	Leeds (a)	0-2	
13 Mar	Premier League	Aston Villa (h)	1-0	Sherwood
21 Mar	League Cup Final	Leicester	1-0	Nielsen
3 Apr	Premier League	Leicester (h)	0-2	
5 Apr	Premier League	Newcastle (a)	1-1	Anderton
11 Apr	FA Cup SF	Newcastle	0-2	
17 Apr	Premier League	Nottingham F (a)	1-0	Iversen
20 Apr	Premier League	Charlton (a)	4-1	Iversen, Campbell, Dominguez, Ginola
24 Apr	Premier League	West Ham (h)	1-2	Ginola
1 May	Premier League	Liverpool (a)	2-3	OG, Iversen
5 May	Premier League	Arsenal (h)	1-3	Anderton
10 May	Premier League	Chelsea (h)	2-2	Iversen, Ginola
16 May	Premier League	Manchester Utd (a)	1-2	Ferdinand

FINAL LEAGUE POSITION	11th (47 points)
PEAK LEAGUE POSITION	8th (match week 10)
LOW LEAGUE POSITION	20th (match week 1)
FA CUP	Semi-final (Newcastle)
LEAGUE CUP (WORTHINGTON CUP)	Winners
EUROPE	Did not participate
MANAGER	CHRISTIAN GROSS (until August); DAVID PLEAT (caretaker Sept); GEORGE GRAHAM (Oct–)
TOP GOALSCORER	STEFFEN IVERSEN (13)
MOST APPEARANCES	SOL CAMPBELL and STEPHEN CARR (52)

MACRO FOOTBALL CLIMATE

LEAGUE CHAMPIONS (PREMIER LEAGUE)	MANCHESTER UTD
RUNNERS-UP	ARSENAL
FA CUP	MANCHESTER UTD 2-0 NEWCASTLE
LEAGUE CUP	SPURS 1-0 LEICESTER
RELEGATED	NOTTINGHAM FOREST, BLACKBURN, CHARLTON
BIGGEST TRANSFER	DWIGHT YORKE £10.5m ASTON VILLA to MANCHESTER UTD

1999/2000

7 Aug	Premier League	West Ham (a)	0-1	
9 Aug	Premier League	Newcastle (h)	3-1	Iversen, Ferdinand, Sherwood
14 Aug	Premier League	Everton (h)	3-2	Sherwood, Leonhardsen, Iversen
21 Aug	Premier League	Sheffield Weds (a)	2-1	Ferdinand, Leonhardsen
28 Aug	Premier League	Leeds (h)	1-2	Sherwood
12 Sept	Premier League	Bradford (a)	1-1	Perry
16 Sept	UEFA Cup 1	Zimbru Chisinau (h)	3-0	Leonhardsen, Perry, Sherwood
19 Sept	Premier League	Coventry (h)	3-2	Iversen, Armstrong, Leonhardsen
26 Sept	Premier League	Wimbledon (a)	1-1	Carr
30 Sept	UEFA Cup 1	Zimbru Chisinau (a)	0-0	
3 Oct	Premier League	Leicester (h)	2-3	Iversen 2
13 Oct	League Cup 3	Crewe (h)	3-1	Leonhardsen, Ginola, Sherwood
16 Oct	Premier League	Derby (a)	1-0	Armstrong
23 Oct	Premier League	Manchester Utd (h)	3-1	Iversen, OG, Carr
28 Oct	UEFA Cup 2	Kaiserslautern (h)	1-0	Iversen
31 Oct	Premier League	Sunderland (a)	1-2	Iversen
4 Nov	UEFA Cup 2	Kaiserslautern (a)	0-2	
7 Nov	Premier League	Arsenal (h)	2-1	Iversen, Sherwood
20 Nov	Premier League	Southampton (a)	1-0	Leonhardsen
28 Nov	Premier League	Newcastle (a)	1-2	Armstrong
1 Dec	League Cup 4	Fulham (a)	1-3	Iversen
6 Dec	Premier League	West Ham (h)	0-0	
12 Dec	FA Cup 3	Newcastle (h)	1-1	Iversen
18 Dec	Premier League	Middlesbrough (a)	1-2	Vega
22 Dec	FA Cup 3R	Newcastle (a)	1-6	Ginola
26 Dec	Premier League	Watford (h)	4-0	Ginola, Iversen, Sherwood 2
29 Dec	Premier League	Aston Villa (a)	1-1	Sherwood
3 Jan	Premier League	Liverpool (h)	1-0	Armstrong
12 Jan	Premier League	Chelsea (a)	0-1	
15 Jan	Premier League	Everton (a)	2-2	Armstrong, Ginola
22 Jan	Premier League	Sheffield Weds (h)	0-2	
5 Feb	Premier League	Chelsea (h)	0-1	

12 Feb	Premier League	Leeds (a)	0-1	
26 Feb	Premier League	Coventry (a)	1-0	Armstrong
4 Mar	Premier League	Bradford (h)	1-1	Iversen
11 Mar	Premier League	Southampton (h)	7-2	OG, Anderton, Armstrong 2, Iversen 3
19 Mar	Premier League	Arsenal (a)	1-2	Armstrong
25 Mar	Premier League	Watford (a)	1-1	Armstrong
3 Apr	Premier League	Middlesbrough (h)	2-3	Armstrong, Ginola
9 Apr	Premier League	Liverpool (a)	0-2	
15 Apr	Premier League	Aston Villa (h)	2-4	Iversen, Armstrong
22 Apr	Premier League	Wimbledon (h)	2-0	Armstrong, Anderton
29 Apr	Premier League	Derby (h)	1-1	Clemence
6 May	Premier League	Manchester Utd (a)	1-3	Armstrong
14 May	Premier League	Sunderland (h)	3-1	Anderton, Sherwood, Carr

FINAL LEAGUE POSITION	10th (53 points)
PEAK LEAGUE POSITION	1st (match week 4)
LOW LEAGUE POSITION	12th (match week 33)
FA CUP	3rd round (Newcastle)
LEAGUE CUP (WORTHINGTON CUP)	4th round (Fulham)
EUROPE	UEFA CUP 2nd round (Kaiserslautern)
MANAGER	GEORGE GRAHAM
TOP GOALSCORER	STEFFEN IVERSEN (17)
MOST APPEARANCES	IAN WALKER (46)

MACRO FOOTBALL CLIMATE

LEAGUE CHAMPIONS (PREMIER LEAGUE)	MANCHESTER UTD
RUNNERS-UP	ARSENAL
FA CUP	CHELSEA 1-0 ASTON VILLA
LEAGUE CUP	LEICESTER 2-1 TRANMERE
RELEGATED	SHEFFIELD WEDS, WIMBLEDON, WATFORD
BIGGEST TRANSFER	EMILE HESKEY – £11m LEICESTER to LIVERPOOL

APPENDIX B

A season-by-season breakdown of the signings from overseas made by Spurs, Arsenal and Chelsea.

	SPURS	**ARSENAL**	**CHELSEA**
1989/90	Nayim (Spanish)		Erland Johnson (Norwegian)
1990/91		Anders Limpar (Swedish)	
1991/92		Pal Lydersen (Norwegian)	
1992/93		John Jensen (Danish)	Dmitri Kharine (Russian)
1993/94			Jacob Kjeldberg (Danish)
1994/95	Jurgen Klinsmann (German) Ilie Dumitrescu (Romanian) Gica Popescu (Romanian)	Stefan Schwarz (Swedish) Glenn Helder (Dutch)	
1995/96		Dennis Bergkamp (Dutch)	Ruud Gullit (Dutch)
1996/97	Steffen Iversen (Norwegian) Allan Nielsen (Danish) Ramon Vega (Swiss)	Patrick Vieira (French) Remi Garde (French) Nicolas Anelka (French)	Gianfranco Zola (Italian) Roberto Di Matteo (Italian) Frank Leboeuf (French) Gianluca Vialli (Italian) Frode Grodas (Norwegian)
1997/98	Jose Dominguez (Portuguese) Moussa Saib (Algerian) Jurgen Klinsmann (German) Nicola Berti (Italian)	Marc Overmars (Dutch) Gilles Grimandi (French) Emmanuel Petit (French) Luis Boa Morte (Portuguese) Alex Manninger (Austrian) Alberto Mendez (German) Christophe Wreh (Liberian)	Celestine Babayaro (Nigerian) Ed de Goey (Dutch) Tore Andre Flo (Norwegian) Gus Poyet (Uruguayan) Bernard Lambourde (French)

1998/99	Paolo Tramezzani (Italian)	Nwankwo Kanu (Nigerian) Freddie Ljungberg (Swedish) Kaba Diawara (French) Nelson Vivas (Argentinian) David Grondin (French)	Pierluigi Casiraghi (Italian) Marcel Desailly (French) Albert Ferrer (Spanish) Bjarne Goldbaek (Danish) Mikael Forssell (Icelandic)
1999/2000	Willem Korsten (Dutch)	Thierry Henry (French) Davor Suker (Croatian) Oleg Luzhny (Ukrainian) Stefan Malz (German) Silvinho (Brazilian)	Gabrielle Ambrosetti (Italian) Didier Deschamps (French) Jess Hogh (Danish) George Weah (Liberian) Mario Melchiot (Dutch) Carlo Cudicini (Italian)